UNCOMMON CATS

Drawing by — Louise E. Jefferson

UNCOMMON CATS

The Who's Who of Cats

Author & Editor -   John R. Guevin

Drawings by ~   Louise E. Jefferson

First Edition

Biographical Publishing Company
Prospect, Connecticut

UNCOMMON CATS

The Who's Who of Cats

Published by:

Biographical Publishing Company
35 Clark Hill Road
Prospect, CT 06712-1011

Publisher's Cataloging in Publication Data
Guevin, John R., 1943 -
Uncommon Cats: The Who's Who of Cats / by John R. Guevin.
1st ed.
Bibliography: p.
Includes index.
1. Cats - Anecdotes. I. Title.
2. Cats - Behavior.
3. Cats - Pictorial Work.
4. Cats - Directory.
SF445.G939   636.8   CIP 93-090382
ISBN 0-9637240-4-5: $23.95 Hardcover

Table of Contents

Uncommon Cats
is dedicated to
ordinary cats
and their extraordinary talents.

ACKNOWLEDGMENTS

The author would like to thank the following for their uncommon assistance in helping to compile this work. Without their contribution the value of *Uncommon Cats* would be greatly diminished.

Cat Fancy
CATS Magazine
Cat World International
I Love Cats
Cat Fancier's Almanac
Design Seven
The Florida Times-Union
Save Our Cats & Kittens
Spay U.S.A.
The 468 contributing authors
The 673 uncommon cats whose stories were told

PICTURE CREDITS

Except where noted, photographs were provided by the contributing authors for their own stories. The author of *Uncommon Cats* is grateful for these offering as well as to those with credit given by their work. Some of the original photographs were edited and converted into graphic images by Biographical Publishing Co. The publisher regrets that all photographs submitted could not be used because of limited available space.

Chapter One

Categories

J ust what is an uncommon cat anyway? Is it some award winning, purebred feline? Or will a simple, common everyday house or alley cat qualify. Is it something the cat <u>does</u> that sets it apart? Like tricks or performing some sort of heroic gesture. Maybe it's an unusual personality or characteristic. Perhaps the kitten just looks a little funny. You know . . . a strange looking tail, or markings in the shape of some geographic area, or a weight that makes Garfield look skinny.

Uncommon cats are all of these, or none of these. They are, in fact, self-defined. They are what they are. Those humans allowed to share time and space with such creatures recognize this uniqueness and now wish to share it with fellow cat lovers – and maybe convince one or two cat-skeptics that cats really are special.

But let's start at the beginning. Why another book about cats? Aren't there plenty already? Perhaps, but not one like this. *Uncommon Cats* is dedicated to ordinary cats and their extraordinary talents. This is the premise, but the cats (as told through their human friends) have really decided what this book is all about.

Here's how it all started . . .

Articles in leading cat magazines and newspapers offered an opportunity for uncommon cats to put their best paw forward and let their meows be heard. They were invited to participate in the creation of a new book. Cat lovers from all over the U.S., plus some from Canada and other countries, received a questionnaire. Information about physical and personality traits was sought. Then the key question: *"Why is your cat special?"*

This book is a composite of their responses.

A few rules of order were suggested:

    1. A limit of one (or at most two) cats per author.

    2. Limit the "why special" story to 100 words or less.

Many found these rules a bit tough to follow. They agonized over how they would select one or two from so many uncommon cats they knew. Others just couldn't contain their thoughts in 100 words. As a result, some of the longer stories were featured in special narrative chapters keyed to certain cat categories.

The completed questionnaires began pouring into the author's Prospect Connecticut mailbox. The family cat Princess joined in the sorting of the mail. She seemed to sense (smell?) which letters came from homes with cats. Using her paws she extracted them from a pile of mail placed on the carpet, pushing them around into smaller piles. Whether or not she was critically accepting or rejecting these selections is uncertain. She didn't bother with bills or assorted junk mail. Just the cat stuff. After a week or two she stopped this activity, either from boredom or a sense that her mission was over.

In reading the letters, patterns began to emerge . . .

1. The episodes describing each kitty seemed to fall into distinct categories. Some were about fantastic tricks. Other discussed obsession with feline fetishes. Many described how their cat survived a fate of almost certain death . . . and so on. Thus the chapters of *Uncommon Cats* began to evolve.

2. At the same time these kitties are really quite complex. Each displays a wide range of personality traits. The chapter categories highlight a particular episode in the cat's life. There is no attempt to stereotype the whole furry feline into one neat little box. Cats resist such over-simplifications. Marie Ballweg, a contributing author, has a view worth pondering.

THE MYSTERY OF LIFE - THE LITTLE THINGS

He laid down his book - called
THE MEANING OF LIFE,
And watched his cat
who seemed to be smiling.

"Such peace of mind you seem to have
oh, child of ancient lands:
I'm sure that you must surely know
much of philosophy."

Nonchalantly her pink tongue
mingled with soft fur,
And the quiet moment stood still
as she gazed straight at me.

"Study if you will your many books
of great men - learn their ways.
But watch me move and play
and love the little things of life."

© *Marie Ballweg, Staten Island, NY*

The spirit and style of the writing is diverse. The stories range from humorous to serious and from heartwarming to simply amazing. Each has its own character. Some are poems. Others cast the kitty as narrator. Many authors used this opportunity to memorialize a favorite pet that graced their life.

4. Another pattern links all felines in a common bond. Key words keep popping-up. Companionship – love. Smart – intelligent. Compassionate – understanding. Intuitive – mood-reading. These words, almost universally expressed, reflect the very close relationship between cat and human.

5. In filling out the questionnaire, some bristled at the word cat *owner*. A few even transposed the term to suggest that the cat was the owner. As a result of such input, the terminology was revised. You will now read about the humans privileged to live with an uncommon cat and not its owner!

6. Most respondents are female. This concurred with marketing data put forth by cat-related publications. Their data indicates that up to 90% of those keenly interested in cats – are women. But then a curious phenomenon developed. While most initial inquiries were from women, it was often the man of the household who wrote or contributed to the story. Perhaps the female had to test the water to make sure it was safe for the male. (After all, men are supposed to like dogs not cats.) He was then free to share feelings about their dear kitten. Can we conclude that perhaps more men are really involved in the life of the family cat than previously supposed? The following poem suggests a clue.

BE READY TO SMILE

Generally speaking cats abound.
Sizes, shapes and hues are found
to satisfy almost everyone.

Cat owners are accused of cutesy names,
and keeping cat photos in golden frames.
Perhaps it's true.

Yet, I'm sure all will agree
that a burly old man of the sea
may become a boy again

as he finds a lost kitten at his door.
For soon he is stroking a tiny paw
and even an upraised chin.

Let's realize cat owners must possess
that trait that gives life a special zest.
They must always be ready to smile.

© *Marie Ballweg, Staten Island, NY*

7. It is obvious that these stories are written from the heart. The authors feel deeply about their cats and aren't afraid to show it. These are real stories about real cats as told by real people. You can't make up stuff like this!

8. Some final thoughts emerge to explain why the cat has replaced the dog as the number one pet in the United States – the "Pet of the Nineties". A cat can stay at home for extended periods of time during the day without attention. This conforms to the modern lifestyle of today's highly mobile family. Cats don't bark nor do they bite the mail carrier . . . although they may occasionally hiss. They are energy efficient (small eaters?) and like modern appliances, they are self-cleaning. What more could you ask?

The Star

Now that these issues are put to rest, let's move on to the real stars – the 673 cats described by 468 families in the following chapters of *Uncommon Cats*. You will be sure to find more than one episode that reminds you of your furry friend. With your favorite feline curled up at your feet or in your lap, read and enjoy.

KEY FOR THE WHO'S WHO CHAPTERS

Information in chapters 10-19 is provided in the following format:

[CITY]   [ZIP CODE]
[Human companion's name]
[Address]
[Cat's name]
[Sex at birth], [Age in years unless otherwise noted], [Color(s)]
[Breed]
[Personality - short description]
[Narrative: "Why this cat is special."]
[Second cat's name]
[Sex at birth], [Age in years unless otherwise noted], [Color(s)]
[Breed]
[Personality - short description]
[Narrative: "Why this cat is special."]

Note: entries may include one or two cats. Some information was omitted at the request of the submitting authors.

Chapter Two

The Good Samaritans

Wwe all remember the biblical story of the Good Samaritan – the one who helped a stranger in time of need. A most unlikely candidate for the role. Others passed by the stranger. The Good Samaritan simply saw someone who needed help. He did not question why he should do this. Nor did he hesitate to act – not even for a moment. He just did what had to be done.

Many uncommon cats show signs of similar behavior. Some help their human friends. Others aid animals. And what is their motivation? Are cats really capable of altruistic behavior and not just self-centered? The owners submitting the following stories no doubt believe they are.

OUR REMARKABLE SHAMAN

Shaman is a black and white long haired male cat. Shaman, in Native American Indian language means "Medicine Man". Our Shaman has lived up to this description countless times.

My wife, Tracie and I met Shaman, when he was six weeks old, in July 1992 at a local pet store. We had enjoyed "window shopping" at pet stores for cats for many years, yet didn't find one that really sparked out interest until we met Shaman. As soon as I made eye contact with him I knew he was special. He looked at me with his bright yellow eyes and said "Hi!" with a little kitten MEOW. I picked him up and held him in my hands while he dug his kitten claws into my shirt and MEOWing to let me know he was not sure of what was happening. I talked to him and petted his small fragile body for only a few minutes when I looked down to see Shaman asleep on my chest looking safe and content. I knew then he was on his way to a new home.

Shaman has developed into a bright, affectionate and playful cat who continually amazes Tracie and me. Shaman arrived home from the pet store and popped out of his carrying box like a kid let out for recess. He trod around and inspected his new surrounding while allowing Tracie and me to stroke him as he passed by us. While I was napping on the couch, a couple of hours later, Shaman joined me, snuggling up under my chin and resting his little body against my neck. I believe it was his way of saying thanks for bringing him home.

Over the next few months he has continued to amaze us with his special gifts. He has learned to sit, lay down, sit-up on his back legs and now he is working on shaking paws all by voice and hand commands.

Shaman enjoys a drink.

What are his other special gifts? Tracie and I often find ourselves negotiating for the bathroom sink with Shaman. He enjoys drinking cold water direct from the faucet. The only problem here is he hasn't learned to turn the water off after himself . . . yet! Shaman is very quick to offer comfort and support. After a long day at work he will curl up with Tracie or me. He typically positions himself on his back and cradles himself in an arm so his soft furry belly is exposed for a series of soft caresses. It's very therapeutic for us . . . and undoubtedly for him as well . . . he purrs long and hard all the while.

Without question the most profound example of Shaman's sensitivity and ability to comfort, happened when I was stricken with a case of cardiac arrest. I was home in bed late one night when the episode took place. Medical help was summoned and while they administered to me, Shaman lay just in reach so I could stroke his soft fur. He also entertained the medics with playful swipes at the monitor tape as it came out of their machine. I was admitted to the hospital and Tracie stayed with me until the worst was over. The first night she made it home, after taking a shower and standing at the bathroom counter, Shaman jumped on the counter and proceeded to stand on his hind legs and placed his front paws around Tracie's chest on either side of her neck. He was letting her know he was there for her while I was in the hospital.

Shaman has been with us for only seven months now and has offered a lifetime of special gifts. Everyday Tracie and I tell him thanks and that we love him and everyday Shaman shares another special gift different than before.

Chris Costenbader, Kent, WA

REGAN'S GREATEST ACCOMPLISHMENT

(A Unique Cat Story)

It isn't everyday that a cat helps to save the life of it's companion cat. Therefore, I would like to share this story with you.

I am the owner of both cats. Francis is an 11-year-old red-mixed-breed neutered male. Regan is an 8-year-old blue-point Himalayan spayed female. As you can see, the cats are as different as night and day - yet they are the best of friends.

My seven acres of land is a real paradise for a cat. There is a small barn with bales of straw for a cool cat nap and a slit rail fence which is just great for a cat to use as a nail sharpener. The lawn is dotted with a variety of trees for climbing and, best of all, there is a garden of tall catnip plants. It is not unusual to see one or more neighboring cats over for a visit.

The rescue took place on a warm Sunday morning in late summer 1983. We've been experiencing months of hot dry weather without any relief in sight. Francis loved to go outside in the early morning for a few hours of exercise and mouse hunting (his favorite sport) before the heat of the day came upon us.

I was in the front of the house getting ready for church, when Regan, who seldom meows and almost never runs, came running to me, meowed, turned, and ran to the back of the house. I followed her with out hesitation, realizing something had to be very wrong.

Regan to the rescue

When Regan ran into the patio, jumped on her perch, and looking out the window, my first thought was of Francis. I looked outside and stared in shock at the sight of a raccoon, ready to attack, only a few feet from a terrified Francis. My cat seemed frozen to the spot which was good. Raccoons have been known to kill a cat, and if Francis moved . . . well, I don't want to think about it.

Another bit of luck was the fact that this took place quite close to the patio door. Apparently the raccoon had come in search of water from the cats' water bowl at the back of the house.

If only I could get the raccoon's attention away from my cat for at least a few seconds. There was a blanket on the couch; I picked it up with my heart pounding, opened the door and threw the blanket in the direction of and hopefully over the raccoon. I then grabbed Francis and leaped back into the doorway. In my haste, I fell on the floor of the patio with Francis in my arms. Regan joined us then, jumping from her perch, and if ever there was a happy trio, it was the three of us. When I looked for the raccoon there was no sign of him - the plan had worked - he had been scared away.

Yes, I did get to church that Sunday and I thanked God for all blessings. I said an extra prayer for my two cats that have brought so much joy into my life.

My thoughts went to Regan and all her accomplishments. Her success as a show cat is evident with the 500 final wins (rosettes and trophies) displayed in my family room. Regan holds 5 Grand Championship titles as well as International Grand Champion in the United States and Canada. Regan's picture has been on 4 cat calendars, she road her own float in a parade, has taken part in the opening day ceremonies of the fair, visited nursing homes, and Regan has been a favorite added attraction at various exhibits and special events. Regan also represented New York State in a cat beauty pageant.

In all our travels, Regan was always the "real pro" and our travels have taken us to 68 cities in 20 states plus Canada. She has always made me proud. However, never have I been more proud of her than I was that warm Sunday morning in late summer 1983 - Regan's greatest accomplishment.

Elizabeth Noce, Henrietta, NY

KITTY GIRL IS A LIFESAVER

My uncommon cat was a friendly stray shadowed by a tiny kitten - starving and frozen but so wild I couldn't get near. I assumed it was hers. One day the kitten disappeared. I kept asking the female, "Where's the kitten?" - and as if understanding - she led me for about 1/4 mile where I found the kitten.

The story took place during an extremely cold winter. It was so cold any can food I put out froze solid within minutes and the kitten could not seem to eat dry food. Because of this it became so weak it could not walk from the place where I found it. If the female had not led me to the kitten when she did, it certainly would have died within a few hours.

I truly believe "Kitty Girl" understood the kitten's plight. The day the kitten disappeared the female appeared very distressed and made deliberate attempts to get my attention to the fact that there was something wrong. When the kitten didn't come with her to eat I became worried and that is when she led me to where it was hiding.

I subsequently found wonderful homes for both. The couple who took the female (a minister and his wife) felt she was very special because of her actions. A vet later verified it could not have been her kitten. Her deliberate actions saved the kittens life!

Kris Conklin, Hurleyville, NY

You will find these fascinating stories about other Good Samaritan cats in the Who's Who chapters 10-19.

Raised other kittens, *Sweets, Phoenix, AZ*

Hearing-aid cat, *Cleo, Phoenix, AZ*

"Hug-a-pet", *Flash, Cupertino, CA*

Helped with therapy, *Chelsea, Menlo Park, CA*

Protects house, *Smokey, Wethersfield, CT*

Comforted after surgery, *Sarah, Daytona Beach, FL*

Saved from wasp sting, *Oliver, Jacksonville, FL*

Stayed by sick daughter, *Bernie, Naples, FL*

Helped through stressful times, *Miss Kitty, Evansville, IN*

Caretaker & survivor, *Baby Girl, New Cambria, KS*

Comforted after operations, *Billy, Lanham, MD*

Founders of feral organization, *Adam & Morgan, Mount Rainier, MD*

Devoted to mother cat to death, *Nathan, Potomac, MD*

Saved puppies' lives, *Miss Kitty, Bessemer City, NC*

Guardian Angel to deformed cat, *Rascal, Basking Ridge, NJ*

Visits nursing homes, *Spunky, Bridgewater, NJ*

Pet therapy, *Starman, Pitman, NJ*

Helps deaf person, *Nikki, Brooklyn, NY*

Defends family against other tom cat, *Shadow, Central Islip, NY*

Helps with nursing home therapy, *M.Y.O., North Tonawanda, NY*

Goodwill ambassador, *Teddy Blue II, Springfield, OR*

Saved life - from smoke, *Abbygail, Morrisville, PA*

Helps out at health care center, *Cookie, East Providence, RI*

Saved house & lives from fire, *Tippy, Phelps, WI*

Warned of intruder, *Aspen, Parkersburg, WV*

Chapter Three

Against All Odds

D o cats really have nine lives? Many contributors to *Uncommon Cats* revealed stories that support this notion. What is there about cats that makes them resistant at times to fates of almost certain doom? We never hear about dogs having nine lives – not even two or three. Just cats. Maybe it's their mystic persona that makes them seem to transcend the ordinary world about them.

Whatever the reasons, the following tales will help to keep these beliefs alive.

A GYPSY'S LIFE

Enraged, my friend and her new husband scooped up the tiny tiger tossed from someone's car onto a busy corner. As intrepid a traveler as they, Gypsy camped in Bar Harbor, was smuggled to Georgia by train. Five years, two kids, and a "no pets" apartment later, I adopted Gypsy "temporarily"; in days, he was sleeping on Dad's head in bed, crying at the bathroom door if we took too long, surveying his new countrified territory, bringing live (greatly alarmed) bullfrogs up from the pond at night.

Fierce with invaders, he was gentle with us and his two older "siblings". Locked-up against his will during a flood and two hurricanes, he vaulted quickly outside to circle the area in shocked reconnaissance afterward. A rag doll before the term was ever heard, he was more "cat" (as I've read somewhere, maybe in Herriot's books) than any cat who has ever owned me.

Fevers and weight loss sent us to the vet in late winter 1991 with a diagnosis of active kidney failure; I learned to do subcutaneous fluid therapy, unappreciated but endured. Gypsy's blood tests, said the doctors, were incompatible with life, but Gypsy didn't know this -- only that warm weather was approaching and the world loved him madly.

That fall, though, his eyes told me to stop the IV's -- to let him go unfettered, unhindered as long as he could. The night before he died, he ate well, cuddled on my chest, was fawned over by my small nephew, and then let out into the balmy October evening. He wasn't there for breakfast; we found him mid-morning, curled peacefully under a tree. His death was startling in its beauty . . . of course, it got us thinking too bad we all couldn't go like that, and then dissolving into fits of anything but irreverrent laughter at the idea of driving along a road and seeing people who'd died peacefully and quietly curled up in their yards, waiting to be discovered.

When the vet stopped into my office a week or so later on an entirely different matter, however, and I told him the story, he smiled. "Knowing Gypsy," he said, "I wouldn't have expected anything less."

Laurie I Blair, Chester, CT

"TRAPPER" JOHN, MD

Memorial day 1983, "Trapper" came home. This poor abandon, abused, unwanted cat had experienced a lot in his life before I became his caregiver.

Trapper was found in a leg hold trap in February 1983, he was taken to the local veterinarian where ¾ of his left front foot was amputated. At the local animal shelter he was placed with the other cats. Being semi-feral he was hard to medicate. Most of the time, he was sick, due to stress. Several weeks later, a volunteer at the shelter was able to tranquilize Trapper and take him to our veterinarian. The cat could not retract his claws on the right front foot, and was in a lot of pain. Surgery was done to alleviate this condition. This left him with ¾ of one front foot and one-third of the other intact.

I was able to pick him up and hold him like a baby, needless to say I fell in love with him. After he recovered from surgery I was to take him home. With four other cats at home, I had him leukemia tested. What a jolt; after all this poor animal had been through, he also tested leukemia positive.

The time had come for me to make a decision; could I keep him in my bedroom for whatever length of time he had to live; would that be fair to a cat that was semi-wild? This was his only chance to know love and have any life at all.

A screen door was put on my bedroom door - this allowed him to be part of the household - to get to know the noises of his home. For 20 minutes each day, (besides sleeping time) I sat on the floor and talked to him, several months past, then one day he came over to me on his own and allowed me the privilege of petting him. Each day it became easier to have more physical contact with him, till one day he came up on my lap - what a terrific feeling that was.

Trapper has been my roommate for nine years, he is a lover. When he curls up under my chin and puts his stubby paw on my cheek to go to sleep, it's worth all the time and effort I put into his rehabilitation.

Trapper earns a nap.

He has had wonderful years of life that he wouldn't have, had I not the courage to put him in a room and give him the life that the good Lord has allotted. He was about 5 or 6 years of age when he come to share his life with us; at 15 or 16 years of age he has come a long way from his desolate beginning.

There are so many cats in need of homes, most shelter can not keep FELUKE positive cats. There are some that do, one that comes to mind is a very special shelter, Friends of Cats located in San Diego, California. They have a special area for their leukemia cats. No one is allowed to visit with these wonderful cats unless you wish to adopt one. They screen potential owners carefully. I am very happy to know that there are others who feel that these cats need love too. This is no kill shelter, unless adopted, a leukemia positive cat lives out it's life there. A FELUKE cat is the same as a handicapped animal - they need <u>love</u> and have so much <u>love</u> to give - in return they ask very little.

A leukemia positive test doesn't mean the cat has leukemia or any FeLV related disease. It's just infected with the virus. Twenty percent of leukemia positive cats are alive after three years. Many live out their lives with out getting sick.

The other animals know that he is in the room and he know that they are in the house, I share my home time by sleeping with Trapper and the oldest dog Whiskers, the rest of my time I am with the others and it has worked all these years. "Where there is a will there is a way."

I am so grateful that God brought Trapper John, MD to me, and I had the courage to take him. He is one great companion.

Trapper died of natural causes in my arms at 11:58, December 26, 1992. He will always hold a special place in my heart be missed very much.

Marlene Pedder, Eastlake, OH

FROM RAGS TO RICHES

My home is Friars Point, Mississippi - a very small town located on the Mississippi River. On an April day in 1991, I was informed by my boss that a deserted house on Moon Lake, twelve miles away, appeared to have a yard full of starving cats.

Well, within minutes, with my 10 lb. bag of Purina Cat Chow and a case of canned food, I took out on my first trip to the lake that has continued to the present on a daily basis.

When I reached the house, all I saw were faces peering at me from any hiding place possible. These kitties were so wild, none came within touching distance. I placed the food for them then retreated a reasonable distance. Starving little bodies came running from all directions. I was absolutely flabbergasted to see these starving little creatures fighting amongst themselves for the food. I backed away with horror as sixty-five little bodies were eating like they had never seen a decent meal.

I heard something behind me and came face to face with a beautiful gray bag of bones who was christened Muffins. As the weeks passed with my daily trips to the lake, Muffins would be in my lap as soon as I opened my car door with his sweet little hugs and purrs. Muffins refused to be one of the gang. He was absolutely terrified of the other kitties. He was strictly a loner unless I was with him. He would wait in a gentlemanly fashion for me to feed the other kitties, then we would sit alone together while he had his meal.

Muffins came into my life at a time when I needed his steady, devoted love. We spent hours together filled with comfort and companionship. I was going through emotional problems that just went away when that little doll was with me. There is no way to explain the bond between us. I have twenty other kitties that are all special and loving but this little doll was so intoned to my feelings that it was almost uncanny.

A year and a half went by and our friendship just blossomed.   The bond that Muffins and I had was extraordinary. He had gotten fat and fine and his little purrs were like a motorboat.   Our time together was so important -   so strong and rewarding.

Muffins in riches.

On a Saturday morning in October of 1992, I reached the lake to find no Muffins running to greet me. I fed all the other kitties and began my panic stricken search. After a good thirty minutes I heard a pitiful meow behind me, and turned to find Muffins staggering toward me. Both his back legs were broken in several places and the skin of one had ripped to the bone.

I grabbed Muffins, my wild little doll, who knew no other human but me, and rushed him to the vet 30 miles away.   This sweet, loving little creature was an absolute mountain lion at the vets.   His back legs were broken in five places, he received 20 stitches, several ribs were broken and he had an upper respiratory infection. The vet could not believe little Muffins was able to come to me in the condition that he was in. I was absolutely beside myself with worry. Here this little doll who had given me so much strength and love was going through the terror that he was.

After six days of unending prayers and treatment, my little mountain lion, Muffins, was released to me cast, stitches, and all. I was in a state of panic. What was I going to do with my beautiful Muffins? I had twenty cats at home, sharing a house with my parents and it was impossible to take Muffins back to where he came from.

Temporarily, Muffins came to stay at my office.   The wild kitty whom the vet couldn't handle, became my pampered little lap cat who never met a stranger. He radiated love and devotion - thankfulness and contentment.

I was absolutely beside myself trying to figure out Muffins fate. For the last four years I had been corresponding with Sandy at a lifetime residence for homeless kitties in Wisconsin.   Sandy and I had developed a long distance friendship. I knew it was a long shot in the dark but I called Sandy and asked her to take Muffins into her home for me, which she readily agreed to do. There was no way to thank her and to ever repay her doing this for little Muffins.

With a thousand borrowed dollars to pay Muffin's vet, our plane tickets and expenses, Muffins and I set out for the airport on a Friday night. I had bought an airline approved carrier because I refused to let Muffins out of my sight. How was this wild little cat with all his casts and stitches going to make this long journey?

A three hour drive to the airport, Memphis to Minneapolis on a plane, 2 nights in a hotel, and a five hour car ride to central Wisconsin which ended on Sunday afternoon. With God's help, and my sweet, well-behaved little Muffins, all was well. It is as if Muffins knew all along how I was trying to help him. His trust and devotion were unending. I felt like he and I were joined at the hip.

When we finally arrived, Muffins and I were greeted with open arms by Sandy and Marge. I felt like our long journey had ended at home. We were shown to Muffin's special little adjustment room complete with toys, cat trees, beds and a gourmet meal.

I had been in tears since I made the decision to take Muffins to Wisconsin. How could I ever part with my special companion who had been by my side when I needed him so. After meeting Sandy and seeing her fat and fine 52 kitties, I knew that God had answered my prayers.

Muffins had gone from rags to riches. His life would be filled with love and care. If I loved him in the way that he had always loved me, I knew I could say goodbye with a smile and a special prayer for God's help in leading me and my special little ray of sunshine to Sandy's home.

Norma Marinelli, Friars Point, MS

TIGER

Tiger had three strikes against him from the first day my husband brought him home from his customer's house. He was only about seven weeks old. That first night, we left him alone on an enclosed porch while we went out to dinner. When we returned the poor little guy was in agony. He had climbed a five-foot shelf, knocked over a can of lye and being a curious little kitten had tried to eat it. We immediately took him to an animal clinic where they advised us to put him out of his misery. I just couldn't. We bought a doll-sized nursing bottle and warmed up some milk, added a drop of whiskey. This knocked him out, he slept for hours. In the morning, even with just half a tongue, he was able to eat.

As he grew up he was very playful and invented games for all of us to play with him. Imagine two adults running up an down a hallway and having a cat leaping out of a closet, growling like a tiger (well, almost). While cooking our evening meal, he would wrap himself around my neck and watch my every move. It's a wonder we did not acquire a few hairballs! When my husband arrived home from work, he would be greeted by this furry creature who climbed his pants legs, ending up around his neck, purring like a threshing machine.

One evening I was, along while my husband was bowling with the company team, the doorknob rattled, scaring me out of my wits. I grabbed a butcher knife from the kitchen and asked, "Whose there?" "Meow," came the answer. He knew what doorknobs were for.

We decided to move back to California. We just put Tiger and his litter box in the car - no carrying case. The litter box was changed daily by digging up dirt along the highway. This was in 1951 before interstates. Tiger adapted well to travel. He curled up on the ledge of the back window most of the time. We would sneak him into motel rooms. He seemed to enjoy this great adventure.

We stopped in Tacoma, Washington to visit my parents, intending to leave Tiger there until we found an apartment or house in San Francisco and return to pick him up.

He adjusted well to living with my parents. My father was a bus driver who worked the late shift, arriving home at 2:30 A.M. Imagine his surprise one morning when who should greet him at the bus stop but little ol' Tiger. He had to walk two and a half blocks from the house to the bus stop, crossing an intersection. How did he know the schedule and where Dad got off the bus? He did this every night (or rather morning).

My mother was alone one day and the doorbell rang. Upon answering it, in walked Tiger, murmuring his thanks to her for opening and letting him in. He had figured out that pushing that little bell would somehow make the door open. My brother hid in the shrubbery one day and took pictures of this act. Tiger jumped on the railing, pushed the bell, and jumped down waiting for the door to open. (Who said cats don't think?)

Unfortunately, we never did return to pick him up, because so many apartments forbade their tenants to have pets and also a year and a day after arriving in San Francisco, we had a baby boy.

Poor little Tiger met his demise while on his way to meet my Dad. He apparently was on his way to meet him when he was hit by a car. Daddy picked up his poor little broken body and carried him home. Next morning, he and Mom buried him the flower garden in the back yard, planting a tiger lily to mark his grave.

Carol E. Sawtell, Silver Spring, MD

CHRISTMAS MIRACLE KITTY

"She's the sweetest kitten, she'll sit on your lap for hours," I said. I was proud of my choice from the many homeless kittens at the local shelter.

"No wonder she sits for so long," my veterinarian said as she finished her exam. "She's a very sick kitty. I suggest you take her back to the shelter and get another healthy cat."

In unison my two children, Erin and Patrick shouted, "No!"

"Can't you give us some medicine for her and let us try to make her well?" I asked, hoping to erase the look of pain from my offsprings' faces.

"I really don't think it will do much good," said the vet, "but I'll give her a shot of antibiotics and some pills you will need to give her; and, oh yes, keep her as warm as possible. Put a heating pad on low under some towels in a warm place and keep track of her temperature for the next forty-eight hours. Call me in two days if the fever isn't gone and I'll put her down for you."

Our hearts were heavy on the ride home even though Christmas was only a week away. I wanted to say something cheerful to lighten up the mood, but there was a lump in my throat that was too big to swallow.

We did as the doctor said and made a warm bed in the pantry with lots of blankets and the heating pad on low and took turns sitting on the floor stroking her soft black fur. A loud rumble could be heard every time we called her name, but Bernie seemed too weak to want to walk around.

The next two days were a rush of Christmas preparations, doses of medicine and temperature readings. We took turns holding her in our laps every evening trying to "love" her into getting better; but three days later when her fever was higher than ever, I called the vet. "Bring her in to me," she said, "and go take the kids to the shelter and get another kitty."

"I will tomorrow," I promised. "She seems so weak, I'm not sure she'll make it through the night anyway."

After dinner I reminded the children they had a "Happy Birthday Jesus Party" to attend at our friend Chris' house. Erin did not want to go, she wanted to spend every minute with Bernie. Patrick, on the other hand, seemed anxious to get going.

"He's handling this well," I thought. "It's better to keep your mind off things," I assured Erin, and drove them to the party.

After some last minute Christmas shopping I arrived at the party to pick up the children. My friend greeted me at the door with her sympathies. "Patrick told me about Bernie. I'm really sorry she's not any better. Patrick asked me if it would be all right if we asked everyone to pray for his kitty so I hope you don't mind, but we sat down and did just that."

"Of course I don't mind, I assured her, "every little bit helps, even if it just gave Patrick some comfort."

As we arrived home we almost hated going into the house, afraid what we might find. Erin was the first to the pantry, but Bernie wasn't there We called to her and out she came from the living room. "Meow," she greeted us, standing on somewhat shaky legs - but standing.

I picked her up and held her close. "She doesn't feel warm. Patrick get me the thermometer."

I took her temperature and held my breath. It was normal! We cried and held her and stroked her fur as she settled down on my lap. Patrick couldn't stop touching her and Erin was having trouble holding back tears.

"Is she going to be all right, Mom?," she asked.

"I think so honey, I think the worst is over," I answered.

I waited until morning to take her temperature once more before calling the vet and telling her the good news.

Patrick learned the power of prayer that Christmas, Erin learned not to give up hope, and I will always remember Bernie walking in from the living room to greet us - our very special little Christmas miracle.

June Stubbe, Naples, FL

CLANCY'S STORY

At age 7 weeks Clancy was given to a retarded senior citizen who kept him in her tiny, windowless bathroom. When he shredded toilet tissue, she dumped him in the lobby and the management of the high rise put him out on the street - at the same corner where Greyhound buses entered and left the terminal. Fortunately the kitten found his way up the alley to a house being renovated. Where the workmen fed him, and let him stay inside (it was December). When he got in the electricians' way, they lowered the kitten over our garden wall.

We have a multi-cat household and took in the 5-month old kitten that could only hop. It took two weeks for him to learn how to walk. "Clancy" is the perfect name for this "carrot-top" cat with a bit of temper. His favorite sport was jumping to the top of any door and perching there until someone passes and he can reach down and grasp some hair.

Clancy the carrot-top

At age 1 year, Clancy survived a 106 degree fever of a week's duration and tested positive for FIP, but he's hale and hearty now and still has his "Irish" temper. When he wants to be petted, Clancy gently taps once on an arm or leg. Ignored, he pokes twice, with more force. Any of my cats that is sick or in distress of any kind is sure to get its ears and head gently washed by Clancy. Normally, at least 6 of my 14 cats vie for space on my bed on cold winter nights. However, when I have bronchitis and prolonged coughing spells, the cats sleep elsewhere. Yet Clancy can always be found, sitting on his haunches besides my bed, paws on the box spring, with chin pressed against the mattress.

Alma Homrighausen, Baltimore, MD

LIFE ON A STRING

In the morning, he sits in front of the bed and cries until I get up. He is very stubborn and does not give up until I give in.

A friend left a message on my answering machine: "I am on my way to Hong Kong and left a cat at the Bergen County Animal Shelter, please fetch him and take care of him.", he said. He forgot to mention the cat's colors or more importantly his name.

I arrived at the Animal Shelter in the latter part of the afternoon, spoke to the animal caretaker regarding the cat which was brought in about two days ago. According to the caretaker, there was no record of the non-described cat. The caretaker persuaded me to look at the cats, hoping I was able to recognize my friend's cat. There were quite a few dozen, however one was sitting up and reminded me of an Egyptian Sphinx, a sort of mystique surrounded him and right there the decision was made to take it home. (It turned out to be the wrong cat.)

Like an Egyptian Sphinx?

All the documents were filled out and the cat was vaccinated. The shelter's veterinarian gave Stringfellow (I named him because wherever I was, he followed me, in other words, if I had a string and since he was a fellow, that's how he received the name Stringfellow) a clean bill of health. He was a very mischievous cat, after a few days, suddenly he became seriously ill. I went to a private veterinarian and he gave Stringfellow intravenous and a couple of other injections. The infections stemmed from the two days that Stringfellow spent in the Bergen County Animal Shelter.

The doctor did not give me any hope that Stringfellow would survive this upper respiratory virus. I had to feed him with my index finger every five minutes and had to use a dropper filled with water - Stringfellow was already dehydrated. On the way to the door, he must have seen in my eyes that it was a distressful message. The doctor stopped me and said: "With lots of loving and caring, there might be a slim chance for him to survive."

Personally, I never owned a indoor cat and did not know what to do when we came home, so I wrapped a blanket around him and spoke softly to Stringfellow, "Please do not leave me and when you are better, you may do anything you want in this house - every antique chair is yours to sleep in."

When we returned to the veterinarian's office, they were amazed that Stringfellow survived and gained weight.

Stringfellow is now a most happy, mischievous, spoiled cat that runs the house. Although, it was the wrong cat that was fetched, it made me happy that Stringfellow is part of my family.

Lotte De Roy Van Zuydewijn, Ridgefield Park, NJ

THE ONE AND ONLY SCOOTER

Very docile, loveable, wants in when he's out; out when he's in. Scooter came to us 8 years ago. I noticed a furry yellow creature hanging upside down in a thorny crabapple tree. I told him to "get down before you get hurt" and he's been here ever since. Two years later he was losing hair and weight - diagnosis: "a cold & coccidia." He tested positive for leukemia and we decided to euthanize. Even though it was to be done at another vet, I called my vet to say it had been done. Next day no Scooter. When he came home he showed no signs of ever being sick.

Later he got oil in his hair from the dirt road we live on, ingested it and almost died. As a result he has a heart condition.

He always had abscesses from fights even though he has been altered; he's one of the 10% that still sprays after altering. He loses consciousness out of fright when put in a cat carrier. He just recovered from a scratched cornea that almost left him blind. The vet is still recovering from treating a "deceased" cat. (I forgot to let him know he made it.)

Now he has a puffy cheek from an infected tooth and enlarged Kidneys due to the leukemia. I'd love to keep him inside year round but when spring is here he sprays and wants out. He's like a wet noodle when picked up; loves to be brushed with the dog's curry comb and always washes his hands in the water bowl before he eats. I dearly love him and dread the day his ninth life is up. He's the best - there will never be another Scooter.

Sheila Cotter Rogers, Arden, NC

The list of uncommon cats with multiple lives goes on and on . . .

Found inside a shoe box in dumpster, *Champion, Windsor, Ontario*
The Scooterman, *Scooter, Orange, CA*
Thrown from car, *Tiny, Redlands, CA*
Lived through all sorts of calamities, *Wyatt, San Diego, CA*
Saved from coyote, *Callie, San Diego, CA*
Only 1¾ oz. at birth, *Amber, Southport, CT*
Another abandoned in a dumpster, *Angel, Miami, FL*
Survived car engine start up, *Sylvester, Mims, FL*
Seven lives left, *Rusty, Clinton, IA*
Survived major medical problems, *Noel, Sleepy Hollow, IL*
Life on 3-legs, *Todd Mikel Freshour, La Porte, IN*
Deformed paws, *Rugums, Alvaton, KY*
Survived many injuries, *Mathew, Princeton, KY*
Two down - seven to go, *Janet, Natchitoches, LA*
Has FID disease, *Sebastian, Buzzards Bay, MA*
Head caught in recliner, *Oscar, Dunkirk, MD*
Seventeen years on three legs, *Stubby, Kansas City, MO*
Survived fire, *Bernie, St Louis, MO*
Blind cat leads happy life, *Bud, Newton, NJ*
Found with mangled eye, *Grumpy, Las Vegas, NV*
Survived palsy & FUS, *Junior, Las Vegas, NV*
Falls five floors, *Maxine, New York, NY*
Faced grizzly & coyote - and still alive, *Keetah, Scappoose, OR*
Mr. Nine-lives, *Ivan, Kennett Square, PA*
Still another in a dumpster, *Thingy, Old Forge, PA*
Walked 20 miles to return, *Scruffy, Upper Darby, PA*
Survived early injuries, *Boots, Pearsall, TX*
Lost tail, Tommy, *Douglas, WY*

Chapter Four

The Tricksters

E veryone knows that cats can't do tricks. Wrong! This is only a myth spread by those who haven't seen what fantastic feats felines can fathom. I have a theory. All cats can do a whole bag of tricks. Some of them just don't feel compelled to flaunt their talents. Non-cat pet owners may find this hard to believe but they should be sufficiently amazed by the uncommon cats in this books.

Most impressive is the number of cats who are self-taught. With little or no training from their human friends, these kitties put on quite a show. After all, have you ever heard of a cat obedience school? Simply not needed. Cats know what to do.

RUDY

My 15 pound Maine Coon is certainly "uncommon" - at least as far as performing tricks is concerned. Everyone that sees Rudy do his tricks is VERY impressed. Most people tell me I should contact David Letterman or send a video of Rudy to one of the TV video show programs.

As RI advisor for Friends of Animals, I've met many who have devoted their lives to animals. One person starting an emergency animal veterinary fund wanted to use him as a spokescat.

Ever since Rudy was 1-1/2 years old, he's known how to:

1) Stay.	6) Beg.
2) Sit.	7) Beg way up [with paws higher up].
3) Give paw.	8) Come.
4) Give the other paw.	9) Jump up and down [where he's told to jump].
5) Lie down.	10) Speak.

He learned all these tricks amazingly quickly - in a period of a few weeks - practicing three times a day for about five to ten minutes each. He does them all willingly if he knows he'll be rewarded eventually.

In addition, when he wants to go outside, if he sees me not reacting to him sitting by the door, and I ask him from across the room if he wants to go outside, he'll answer me by reaching up and tapping on the door knob with his paw. Once I wasn't aware he was at the door and started to go upstairs. He came running after me and batted my shoe. When I looked down at him to find out what he wanted, he looked at me in the eye and then started to run towards the door looking back to make sure I was following.

Rudy – a Maine Coon with a bag full of tricks.

Another extraordinary trait Rudy has is his desire to participate when I exercise. Usually while I'm lying on the floor doing leg lifts, Rudy will lie down next to me and reach his paw up as I lift my leg.

Emily Harding, Newport, RI

YOU CAN TEACH A YOUNG CAT PLENTY

The saying goes that you can't teach an old dog new tricks, but our cat Camille is living proof that you can teach a young cat plenty.

Camille is our two year old black cat who loves to play. Her favorite toy was always a string on a yardstick. Even when she was a young kitten, she would drag it anywhere we were when she wanted to romp. It was many a night when we were sleeping and we'd hear the clump, clump, clump of Camille trying to drag something three times her size up a flight of stairs.

Last fall, Camille's "mom" Joni took a college psychology course. The course was about learning, and as a final project Joni had to try to teach someone a skill. We'd always remarked how smart we thought Camille was, so naturally Joni thought of her first. The skill Joni decided on was to see if Camille was able to jump through a hoop. Not only did Camille learn in no time at all, but Joni was eventually able to raise the hoop three times! Towards the end, Camille was jumping through a hoop that was over eight inches off of the ground. Joni got an "A" on the project and Camille got a lot of Bonkers.

Camille jumps through hoops

We've put the hoop back in the garage now (she likes to play fetch more than perform circus skills). But hoop or not, Camille will always rate an "A+" with us.

Joni Gaines & Mike Zito, Stratford, CT

It was a challenge to highlight the cat tricksters. There are so many worthy applicants. It seemed that almost <u>every</u> cat could fetch something! At the risk of slighting many – here are some with really interesting talents.

Begs at 5:00 A.M. to play fetch, *Romyo, Belmont Shore, CA*

Does tricks & trains other cat, *Nicky Arnstein, Los Angeles, CA*

Fetches, *Ashley, Oelwein, IA*

Catches sponge balls, *Oscar, Arlington Heights, IL*

Fetches aluminum balls, *Chessie, De Kalb, IL*

Retriever "dog", *Blue, Niles, IL*

Plays fetch like dog, *Binky, Clarksville, IN*

"Air Kitty", *Shadow, Indianapolis, IN*

Plays catch with ball, *Shadow, Hays, KS*

Tight rope walker, *Kato, Boston, MA*

Begs like a dog, *Tigger, Cockeysville, MD*

Sits like a frog, *Willie, Grand Rapids, MI*

Sings do re me "do", *Chloe, Greensboro, NC*

Another that fetches like a dog, *Whiskers, Selma, NC*

Soccer player, *Maximillian, Hillsdale, NJ*

Does somersaults, *Pooki, Albuquerque, NM*

Tricks without food rewards, *Angel, Brooklyn, NY*

Stands like dog, *Miss Katter Katty Carney, Springwater, NY*

Plays electric keyboard, *Mystery, Akron, OH*

Jumps eight feet high, *Mistey, Jackson, OH*

Kisses on command, *Bear Jorgenson, Lakewood, OH*

Eight different tricks, *Missy, Newark, OH*

Catches ball mid-air, *Molly, Warren, OH*

Husband needed cat to do dog tricks, *Charlie, Mt Top, PA*

Opens closet doors, *Punkin, Pittsburgh, PA*

Leaps five feet in the air, *Sheba, Saint Marys, PA*

Backflips, *Socks, Herndon, VA*

Fetches and hides, *Samuel P. Katz, Richmond, VA*

drawing by ~ Louise E. Jefferson

A PAIR OF TRICKSTERS ON THEIR PEDESTALS

adapted from a drawing by ~
Louise E. Jefferson

Chapter Five

Working Cats

T hey work hard for the money! Well, maybe not money. More like attention, love, and an occasional favorite treat. Like their cat cousins, the "Good Samaritans", working felines seem driven to help others. Their jobs span a wide range of activities. Some are exciting. Others rewarding. Or really unusual. In many cases these kitten occupations are an extension of their human companion's trade. They add their own personality to the task and compliment their non-feline partners.

Cats are terrific workers. They seldom, if ever, complain. Pay is never an issue. Admittedly fringe benefits <u>are</u> a big issue. Cats do insist on frequent and long rest periods during the working day.

ABBY – ACADEMY AWARD WINNER

Abby - a star is born.   Photo by: Adam Gordon

Abby, a ruddy Abyssinian, comes from a long line of champions. She starred in a public service announcement promoting an exhibit "Man and Animals," at the University Museum of Archaeology & Anthropology at the University of Pennsylvania, which exhibit was on display from October 1984 to June 1985.

The PSA was produced by Videosmith, Inc. and was on TV for eight months. It won two Emmy Awards from the Philadelphia Chapter of National Academy of Television Arts & Sciences, one for "Outstanding PSA" and the other for "Outstanding Individual Achievement in Lighting".

In the Video, Abby, then just a kitten, was featured walking through the museum by moonlight, looking at the artifacts, including a statue of an Egyptian predecessor. The lighting award was won because the moonlight effect was so well simulated.

Abby needed only eight hours of coaching to walk through the museum correctly. Her trainer dangled feathers and toys to successfully direct her movements. Abby cooperated and a kitten star was born. Abby was born June 15, 1984 and is registered with Cat Fanciers Association, Inc. as "Jill of Iron Hill". Her breeder is Mary McCormack, Doylestown, PA.

R Marvel, Philadelphia, PA

LUCKY BANDIT RUBS DADDY THE RIGHT WAY

Lucky Bandit, the youngest in our 5-cat household, had escaped death narrowly, as my husband found him next to his dead brother, who had been stepped on in a factory yard.

Needless to say, L.B. had to be very creative in establishing himself amongst the "older" felines, who immediately began actively protecting "their" important person (me). Bandit had little chance to break the hierarchy. But clever as he is, he soon found a way to compete with the others for my attention.

Noticing that on weekends I would always massage Daddy's shoulders and back, he began kneading my husband's back, purring loudly to keep the others at bay. As he did "his job" on a regular basis, he of course received "goodies" both verbally and snackwise for earning his "keep". Now the others watch respectfully, every Saturday and Sunday as Lucky Bandit jumps up on my husband's back, following the most familiar call: "Bandit, it's time to do your job."

He has even earned the respect of our 15-year old senior feline (a Georgia Belle) named Mohrchen, as she accepts Lucky Bandit's antics and lets him play with her bushy tail. His name came about - "Lucky" because he was rescued - "Bandit" because he has a pirate's mask and always steals the food from his mates; a residual behavior, perhaps stemming from his early past, where he had to scratch for every morsel of food just to survive.

Giselle White, Huntington Beach, CA

THE CAT THERAPIST

I recently found myself recovering from major neck surgery and continuing to have much pain in my neck, shoulders, arm and hands for months after the operation. Unfortunately, during this same time my 14 year old female tortoise shell cat, Rangi, died from a brain tumor. Following a very painful period of grieving, I knew I needed another cat in my life. So I purchased my first pedigree - a six month old female British Shorthair, blue (solid bluish-gray color) with bronze colored eyes - named "Chelsea". When she first arrived in my home she woke me up every morning at 3:00 A.M. For the first few days I thought she was doing this because she was hungry, but her favorite food was available to her on a continuous basis. Then I realized she just wanted my undivided attention and knew this was the only time of day she could get it.

So, we played "ball", wherein I threw a ball with string attached across the floor and slowly dragged it toward me while she showed off her stalking, pouncing, attacking and other hunting skills. As soon as I stopped playing ball, she became very vocal and extremely displeased with my lack of enthusiasm. Because she was so stubborn and persistent (characteristics she has in common with her owner), I would continue to throw the ball. This activity lasted for more than 30 minutes every day and, in the process, the muscles of my shoulder and arms increased in strength and flexibility. I became able, for the first time in over a year, to move my upper body without experiencing pain.

A month after her arrival, I began aquatherapy in a warm water pool. Due to my daily early morning workouts with Chelsea, I was able to begin to swim in just two weeks! During the past three months I have increased my stamina to swimming laps for 30 minutes per day and in the process I have lost 20 pounds! My new kitty came into my life at the perfect moment to benefit me both physically and emotionally.

Barbara, Menlo Park, CA

The Working Cat

Drawing by: Louise E. Jefferson

Still more workaholic cats:

Award winner, *Sidney, Winnipeg, Manitoba Canada*

Convent & school cat, *Honey Bun, Mobile, AL*

"Little mother", *Mercedes, Mesa, AZ*

Rock climbers, *Calico Doe & Ricky, Bear Valley, CA*

Works at a boat shop, *Sox, Lodi, CA*

"Editor", *Abby-gal, Ojai, CA*

Guard cats, *Ginger & Candy, Sierra Madre, CA*

Predicts earthquakes, *Muffin, Venice, CA*

Law office cat, *Blackie, Miss Julie, Torrington, CT*

Weather-cat predicted tornado, *Mittens, Waterbury, CT*

Gives neck massages daily, *Hoby, Lakeland, FL*

Rated dates & picked husband, *Bosco, Sunrise, FL*

Acrylic painting artist, *Casper, Fort Wayne, IN*

Pet-of-the-Year, *Cameron II, Overland Park, KS*

Nurse-cat; watch-cat, *Clancy & Scary, Baltimore, MD*

Official greeter, *Bupka, New Brunswick, NJ*

"PR" cat for old town shops, *Scruffy, Albuquerque, NM*

Calendar & magazine cat, *Scarlet, Pomona, NY*

Critiques piano students, *Maxmilian Maximus, Spencerport, NY*

Award winning model, *Bucky, Toledo, OH*

Chapter Six

Feline Fetishes

C ats are really no different than humans in many respects. We all have our little fetishes. You know – those little idiosyncrasies that others may consider a bit odd. They are not odd to us, of course. In fact they are quite normal. Probably something we've always done. We can't understand why everyone doesn't do things just the way we do. But then there are those other fetishes, the ones we don't have and wouldn't dream of having. These should certainly be considered peculiar.

Well then, if we are to be considered open minded . . . doesn't everyone think they're open minded? . . . then we should allow our cats and kittens the privilege of one small fetish. After all, cats are individuals. And this tiny quirk will make them stand out from the crowd – make them special.

Of course there are a few known cases where felines have had more than one (lots in fact) of these fetishes. Should this be allowed? Then there is the issue of involvement. It's one thing to dabble in a fetish or two, but what about obsessive-compulsive behavior? I mean some of these habits are really carried to an extreme. It has been said, "He who is without a fetish should be the first to cast a net over these cats with capers." Any takers?

THINGS THAT GO CRUNCH IN THE NIGHT!

Humans are known to have many bad habits! They Drink, Smoke, Swear, and even Bite their Nails! But, have you ever encountered a CAT who bites his nails? No? I had never heard of this "habit" either, until one eventful night, as I lay in bed drifting off into dreamland, when, what to my wondering ears did I hear, but a very loud crunching right in my ear! What could that possibly be I wondered, never suspecting the truth! I slowly reached for the flashlight next to my bed, in order to shed some light upon this mysterious sound! I was not prepared for what I saw! There sat Navarré, my Havana Brown, carefully and methodically giving himself a manicure . . . or, should I say, a CATACURE!

Unfortunately (for me) he has neither the desire nor the inclination, or even the

Navarré with a catacure fetish.

consideration to clean up his nail clippings after he has finished his Catacure! He also has never considered grooming the nails of the other two cats with whom he reluctantly shares food and sleeping quarters!

Considering all that I do for him, Don't you think that I deserve more than a bed of nails to sleep upon? Perhaps, in his wee little cat mind, he believes that I used to be an Indian Fakir in another lifetime, who slept on a bed of nails! Now, in this lifetime, he is trying in his own loving way, to provide the same creature comfort for me!

How do I tell him that "That was then, This is now!"

Lady Cat Powers, Boulder, CO

A THIEF IN THE NIGHT – AND THE DAY

Tazzy (short for Tasmanian Devil) is a Red Tabby that just appeared at my house. Although she has quite a temper, i.e. her name, we fell in love with her because she was always so affectionate. She will get in your lap and lay her head on your shoulder in a very loving manner. On the other hand, if you look at her wrong, she is just as quick to pop your face and then love you. She always seems to catch you off guard with her behavior. She doesn't seem to want to hurt you and it can create quite a humorous situation. It seems I'm the only one in the family that she hasn't popped.

She also collects small objects around the house and hides them behind the bathroom door; pens, my razor, bathtub toys, bathtub stopper, and toilet tissue (when tissue is placed on the side of the tub instead of the holder) along with other objects.   One time I found a bath toy placed in the middle of my pillow and my razor under the cover. No one was home when this happened. When you move these articles, she moves them back. She does this late at night, or when we're not home, and make sounds as if she is calling her babies. (We still have two of her first and only litter.)

A friend, who is a veterinarian, said that it sounded as if she was bonding with me since practically all the objects she collects seem to be articles of mine or have been handled by me. She also wants to be in my lap when I am at my computer. She makes her "mothering" sounds then too. Tazzy has a way to make you feel better when it seems the world is falling in around you.

Mary Dotson, Fletcher, NC

What's your fetish???

Graphic by: DESIGN SEVEN

Welcome to Club Neurotic. Please get to know our charter members:

Fish in aquarium, *Jackie, Glendale, CA*

Shiny lights & VCR sound, *Coony & Notty, San Jose, CA*

Crabapple game, *Muffin, Longmont, CO*

Pettridge Farm cookies, *Munson, Hartford, CT*

Water, *MCKENKITTY Baby Love, Litchfield, CT*

Chases crumpled paper, *Sam, St Charles, IL*

Milk jug rings, *Tippy, Syracuse, IN*

Ice, *Spoon Buckley, Lawrence, KS*

Truck, *Jake, Lawrence, MA*

Recliner lover, *Shadow, Maynard, MA*

Running water & boxes, *Chelsea, Baltimore, MD*

Eating acrylic material, *Muffin, Clemmons, NC*

The Discovery Channel, *Suzanne Sugarbaker Deyton, Winston Salem, NC*

Posing for camera, *Mitsu, North Bergen, NJ*

Taking toys to bed, *Bandit, Paramus, NJ*

Dressing-up, *Sable, Staten Island, NY*

Shoe lace, *Harry, Warren, OH*

Loves cartoons & Discovery, *Joe, Bartlesville, OK*

Loves to travel, *Ahab, Wellston, OK*

Must have quiet, *Frisky, Cobourg, Ontario*

Must keep doors open, *Zonker Harris, Beaverton, OR*

Toy mouse, *Tango, Meadville, PA*

Fire in fireplace, *Schnutz Putz, Oley, PA*

Barbie Reebok, *Little Guy, Philadelphia, PA*

Drinking from sink, *Cee Cee, Columbia, SC*

Ice cream & sweets, *Whiskers, San Antonio, TX*

Another mirror fetish, *Madonna, Culpeper, VA*

Loves to watch birds, *Zack, Fairfax, VA*

Talking on the phone, *'Kitty' Roth, Richmond, VA*

Grated cheese, *Cassandra, Spokane, WA*

Bathroom watching, *Pepper, Sumner, WA*

Chapter Seven

Wild & Wacky

I s there no limit to what cats will do? Just when you think you've seen it all . . . along comes another crazy thing that some cat invents. And just why do they do these silly stunts? Do they get bored and look for a little excitement? Or maybe, like Madonna, they just want to have fun. Many who must live with these creative creatures, maintain the reason for this bizarre behavior, is solely to drive their human companions insane. Some say cats succeed in this pursuit more often than not. But achieving this goal may simply just satisfy one of the earlier theories: relief from boredom, fun, etc.

The range of activities that we might consider to be wild & wacky is so broad, this entire book could be devoted to it. Suffice to say that each cat is different. This is, most likely, part of our furry friends' master plan.

THAT'S NO WIFE . . . THAT'S MY CAT!

When is a Cat, not like a Cat? Answer: When the Cat behaves like a Wife! Examples of this type of behavior can be seen while observing my Siamese lady, IZABEAUX (of Ladyhawke)! She "presses" my laundry, while it is in the basket, nice and hot from the official dryer! She fetches things and bring them to me, gazes at herself, vainly in the mirror, yet, still takes time to smell the flowers! What more could anyone ask of a Lady Cat!

Most cat lovers will relate unusual behavior stories, and of course, I am no exception! Having bred and loved cats for so many years, I have witnessed a lot of "strange" behavior, yet I have never lived with a cat who will actually bring something back to me after I have thrown it! Sure, most cats will run excitedly after anything you may toss . . . but, how many will actually bring it back to you? Cats are usually "above" that sort of behavior! It is not in keeping with their dignity to "take orders" and retrieve something for a human! Perhaps, that is why I was so amazed to discover IZABEAUX not only running after the fuzzy pipe cleaner I had thrown, but to see her bring it back, drop it at my feet, and offer me an impatient MEOW that seemed to say: "Hey . . . what are you waiting for slowpoke, throw it again will ya!" Since I usually succumb to the requests and demands of my feline friends, of course I tossed it again! Much to my astonishment, once again she chased it, captured it in her teeth and brought it back to me! This was too much for me to believe, though my eyes told me it was true!

When I have exchanged cat tales with other cat lovers, most of them refused to believe that I have a cat who fetches! They would simply tell me that cats do not fetch! In addition to fetching, IZABEAUX also presses my laundry! Of course, she does not do the washing, as water is not high on her list of priorities! But, once the laundry is placed into the basket, she INSISTS upon jumping into it, stretching out and then, going to sleep for hours! By her doing this, all of the clean laundry is nicely pressed, including all Of the extra little wrinkles that IZABEAUX offers at no extra cost! By the time the laundry has completed its "dry cycle" in the machine, and is ready for

IZABEAUX of Ladyhawke

Solves pressing problems.

the basket, IZABEAUX's ready also! She waits for her basket of laundry outside the door, meowing impatiently, as ONLY a Siamese can! It is practically impossible to walk up the stairs with the basket, with IZABEAUX constantly trying to get into it! There have many times when the basket I carry up the stairs is filled with laundry and IZABEAUX! Oh my aching back!

Since most cats train their humans, we now realize that it's important for us to place a towel on top of the clean laundry BEFORE she assumes her pressing position, or, be resigned to the fact that we shall take her cat hairs with us wherever we go!

Not only does IZABEAUX fetch and press laundry, but she is extremely vain and will sit in front of the full length mirror staring at her beautiful image far long periods of time. She probably wonders to herself: "Who can that attractive cat be?"

Philosophy usually does not enter into a cat's consciousness, yet, somehow IZABEAUX has gained a form of cat wisdom, for she always takes time to smell the flowers, as so many humans fail to do in their lives! You may wonder what if any, incredible insights have come to me through experiencing life with IZABEAUX. She has taught me that cats do what they want, when they want, how they want, where they want, and that we humans had better accept that reality.

Lady Cat Powers, Boulder, CO

TANO - A DEVIL OF A SMART CAT &
SQUEAKER WHO ALWAYS GETS IN HIS LICKS

As a kitten Tano looked like a scrawny little bat without wings. An anthropologist who had worked in the South Pacific suggested the name for a black cat should be Ta-tan, which means Satan in Gilbertese. He was easily startled, sometimes for no apparent reason - giving rise to the suspicion that he was seeing things I couldn't. He also looked a little demonic at one time during kittenhood when two canine teeth protruded from the same place in his mouth where his "baby" tooth had not fallen out yet. But the kitten's persistent clamoring for attention and easy purr soon invalidated the devilish image, and with it the name. A few years later he even lost the remaining canine tooth when he fell off the second story balcony. I guess that purged any demon he had left in him. He had by this time grown into a beautiful, sleek, black cat.

Although both Tano and his "sister" Squeaker were easily trained using the scratching post, it was Tano who really demonstrated superior intelligence. At a young age he learned to fetch items thrown for his amusement, and he would signify the end of play session by dropping the toy in his water bowl. I really took notice when he learned to open the drawer in the table where his toys are kept. This trick required the ability to think sequentially, an ability I thought reserved for human animals. He stood on his hind paws under the table and pushed on the exposed back of the drawer until it opened a little. Then he climbed on top of the table and pulled the drawer out further until he could snag his toys. He enjoyed performing this trick for guests, who were usually impressed enough to toss his toy for him.

Tano's learning ability continued to surprise me. He even knows some commands. When I have had enough of his insatiable need for attention, which he demonstrates by rubbing against my hand and pawing my arm, I say, "that's enough, Tano; lie down," and he complies. He's one of those cats who drools when he is happy - an annoying trait which he mostly learned to control after I spent some time training him, "stop drooling."

Poor Tano and Squeaker have had to move with me 12 times in their 15 years. Cats would prefer to settle down someplace for life, and so would I, but it hasn't worked that way for us. Two years ago the move was particularly stressful since it involved an airplane trip and a 10-week separation from me. When we were finally reunited, I discovered that Tano had symptoms of diabetes. He became so interested in water that he would push aside the shower curtain and join me in the shower. After I was done, he stayed and licked the faucet until it stopped dripping. Sometimes he would even cry for me to turn it on again. As a physician, I knew diabetes was manageable, but difficult in the absence of biological monitoring. So I trained him to urinate in a cup.

It wasn't difficult. It was just a matter of putting him in the litter box, holding a cup in the proper place, and rewarding him with food after he performed appropriately. The compensation was all the more rewarding right before dinner time when he was particularly hungry. He quickly learned that when I put him in the box and held a cup under him, he should urinate. The veterinarians have always been entertained by this story, and they have always been amazed at how well he tolerates their poking and prodding.

For two years now I have easily monitored Tano's urinary glucose, and although he is aging, he is doing well on twice a day insulin shots. He never complains about his injections, and Squeaker even gets jealous because Tano is receiving special attention at this time. She doesn't seem to appreciate her "special attention" - a strict weight control diet and weekly weigh-ins.

Squeaker is not as smart as Tano, but she has her own endearing qualities. She loves to be around people, and will even put up with kids. She rolls onto her back with her paws up and purrs as her tummy is rubbed. Her purr is loud enough to get me to lift the blankets so she can curl up and sleep next to me. We both benefit from the mutual contact.

I take advantage of a funny reflex of Squeaker's to make it appear that she too can follow a command. When I scratch her back, she starts licking her chest. I say, "lick yourself, Squeaker," while I am scratching her, and she does so. Squeaker's tongue is often busy. She likes to lick my fingers, and she does a great job of keeping herself and Tano clean. Furthermore, she "talks" a lot; that is how she earned her name.

This predominance of oral behaviors is most clearly manifested by Squeaker's favorite activity - eating. I cannot leave food out or she will eat it constantly. If given a chance, she will eat Tano's food, too. To avoid having to watch her every mealtime, I put Tano's bowl on the middle shelf of the scratching post. He can still climb up there, but Squeaker - whether because of her weight or her arthritis - cannot. Sometimes she makes me feel guilty, until I remind myself she really does live a great life. Both cats receive (and give) lots of love on a regular basis.

Dr. Sharon L. Ludwig, Silver Springs, MD

SHE LOOKS LIKE THE PRESIDENT'S CAT

She lives in a white house too, and looks like the
    President's cat.
She's a black and white bright eyed beauty. In France
    we'd call her "le chat."
She stretches high and looks straight at you. (Li'l
    Orphan Annie's her name).
But the black shepherd dog she lives with doesn't
    realize her fame.

© *Marie Ballweg, Staten Island, NY*

MERLYNN: OUR LITTLE MAGICIAN

Here's some history about the uncommon cat I live with! She's a very striking tabby with unusual eyes that resemble an owl's; her fur is a very unusual brown/grey color with a sprinkling of silver and a silver undercoat.

While visiting a barn one day where my father-in-law kept a horse, my husband and I found this unusual kitten to be living in this barn. Apparently my father-in-l aw, while riding his horse one day, found this kitten to be abandoned along with a brother and sister inside a box along the side of a road; it infuriated me that someone could just toss out these three kittens like they were garbage. In rescuing them my father-in-law took them back to the barn where he kept his horse stabled. Upon seeing them for the first time we naturally wanted to take all of them into our home, but we already had three other cats living with us and the other two kittens seemed to be well cared for by everyone who boarded horses at this stable. It still upset us to leave them behind.

This one particularly unusual looking kitten left an impression on us too great to ignore, so we took her into our home. Soon after, we named her Merlynn for Merlin the Magician because right away she started displaying unusual tricks!!! Her favorite trick is to open the drawers under our waterbed and retrieve socks to play with which are her favorite toys; of course getting up in the morning is sometimes hazardous due to all of the open drawers!!! I then started discovering large piles of socks all over the house; they were everywhere including the couch, coffee-table, kitchen table, kitchen counter tops, bathrooms, etc. I then decided to let her have her very own drawer of socks to play with; I even put catnip in some of them!!!!

She's also very fond of moths that fly around the outside lights at night; she gets very excited if anyone goes near an outside door in the evening in the hopes that one of these small flying insects may inadvertently fly into the house. She then tears through the house trying to retrieve this unsuspecting moth whose unaware of its uncertain demise.

Merlynn the Magician – makes socks disappear

This very same, quite small mouse of a cat, loves to bully any other cat who may come into contact with her and as unbelievable as it may seem, all other cats, no matter what their size, seem to cringe, shrink, fear and run from this mouse of a cat!! It makes one believe the saying that "one's bark may be bigger than one's bite". Of course this is a very affectionate cat and gets along well with her siblings (most of the time)!!!

This same cat also likes to ride with me in my car; you can imagine the looks I get while driving down the road or filling up at the local gas-station!

All in all I'd say we really love our little magician even though her tricks can be hazardous at times; we're so grateful we found her in that barn not so long ago!

Donna Shomette, Kerrville, TX

"Queen of the Jungle"

Ashley is unique in appearance, as well as character. She was hand-picked by Denise out of four adorable kittens. She caught Denise's eye immediately and it was love at first sight. Ashley was on the top perch of the cage and decided she would look for a better sleeping spot. She then proceeded to march over the top of the other sleeping kittens and lain right on top of the golden tiger. No respect for her littermates! Denise knew she was going to be a "character" from this point on.

Ashley is an indoor cat, so she has learned to make her own "fun". We have a male Rottweiler that she terrorizes. It is quite comical to see little Ashley hanging onto the ear of poor "Ninja", the 120 lb. Rottie. She doesn't have to bite hard. All she does is put her teeth on his sensitive ear flap and Ninja lays immobilized, until she decides to move on. She only needs to hold her razor--sharp claws centimeters from Ninja and he decides to leave her be. She is queen. She insists on drinking from his water bowl as he looks on. She insists on speeding by him with tail erect and brushed out, when he is sleeping. She will scratch at his face and by the time he gets up to chase her - she is gone. Ashley is also very good at retrieving small items like rubber bands and milk caps for a game of catch. She also sits on her perch and will catch her yarn ball or catnip sack with one paw. The strangest thing she does is comb our hair when we get out of the shower. She insists on getting on top of our heads, licking the excess water from our hair and then combing it with her claws. Be careful if you move before she is finished or she will have her claws imbedded in your head.

She adores us - especially Gary. She will lick our noses until they are red from her rough tongue. Sometimes she will grab our noses with her teeth and just hold. Like Ninja, we are left immobilized or she will bite down. Ashley also needs to be fed on time. If she is not -- you will have a wildcat running circles at your feet. She will rush up your leg, mock-scratch you, then run away. She is really a joy. Her intelligence and character have certainly livened up our household!!!!!

Denise Muccioli-Brooks & Gary A Brooks, Nashua, NH

JAYNEE'S WORLD

At birth Jaynee was very tiny but had the best personality of her siblings. I remember holding her in the palm of my hand on her back. I was amazed how her little shoulders and front paws laid on her belly in a manner similar to that of a human infant's arms. We found that having a kitten in the house was very trying at times. Jaynee seemed to go through the terrible twos displaying many destructive tendencies including, but not limited to, curtain climbing, carpet and furniture clawing, and using the shredded paper for my ceramics as an upstairs bathroom. With some patience and a lot of love, Jaynee became a well behaved cat.

At an early age Jaynee displayed some interesting idiosyncracies. She liked to watch the Weather Channel and would chase Mario into the pipes during her favorite Nintendo game. She has an incredible appetite for miniature marshmallows - after she pounces on them to kill them first. She also plays a mean game of fetch doing impressive jumps and flips in the process.

Another one of her habits, besides making sure every throw rug in my house is rolled into a ball in the middle of the floor, is being a feline alarm clock. She loves helium balloons and will pull them around the house by the string until they pop.

Jaynee helps me write my mystery novel. She chases the eraser on my pencil and chews on it as I write out each scene. I guess she thinks I am so good I won't make any mistakes.

Like her mother Helen, Jaynee sits on her hind legs and eats a large piece of food holding it in her paws like a squirrel. And each will "guard" me while I'm sleeping. Both cats are constant companions to me and I don't know what life would be like without them.

Lisa M Blough, Windber, PA

THE KISSING CAT

"Indy" is my only purebred cat along with two household pet cats. I show him in CFA cat shows and he's gotten the reputation as the kissing cat!

He actually kisses them by licking them like a dog. He kisses anyone who comes up to him and asks, "Indy give me a kiss." He usually goes up and licks them either on the forehead or the cheek.

Indy was on a television news broadcast while competing in one of his cat shows. Indy can really get carried away with his kissing. A judge at the show, Ken Currle of Virginia, said Indy was really "buttering him up!" It's funny but sometimes embarrassing for me. At another show Judge Bob Salsbury of California commented about being kissed by certain breeds (head rubs), but had never gotten a head rub from a Maine Coon. When it was Indy's turn, a fellow exhibitor told the judge this Maine Coon gives real kisses. Bob gave everyone this look of disbelief, like sure this cat kisses. Someone then said, "go ahead -

Indy delights the judges © 1992 Chanan

put your face close to the cat and ask for a kiss!" Hesitantly, Bob looked down in Indy's eyes and said, "O.K. cat, let me have a kiss." Indy pushed his head into his face and then started to lick him on the cheek. He was surprised and pleased to be kissed by his first Maine Coon. Indy is a joy at home and always very affectionate with all our family members and even with close family friends. We don't know how he picked this kissing up, but we did have two dogs who lived with us and maybe he picked it up from them.

The Hinton Family, St Charles, IL

More wild and wacky cats and kittens . . .

Sleeps on horse, *Bunny, Alton, Ontario*

Nursed by dog, *Sarah, Basel, Switzerland*

Alarm clock, *Brodie, Kitchener, Ontario*

Hops like a bunny, *Cheyenne, Birmingham, AL*

Sings in litter box for hours, *Sniffles, Phoenix, AZ*

Takes brassiere to guests, *Daughter Cat, Prescott, AZ*

Purrs like train whistle, *Casey Jones, Arcata, CA*

Turtle for friend, *Zuñi, Beverly Hills, CA*

Heraldic knight, *Harri, Chico, CA*

Puts on masks to spook other cats, *Mo, Cutten, CA*

Knocks on door like person, *Homey, El Cajon, CA*

Sits like parrot on shoulders, *Bear, Encino, CA*

Toilet trained, *Dusty, Laguna Hills, CA*

Plays with python, *Sheba, San Jose, CA*

Uses toothbrush to groom, *Thaddeus, Simi Valley, CA*

Brushes with electric toothbrush, *Chelsea, Sunnyvale, CA*

Stalks clay bird, *Princess, Toluca Lake, CA*

Sings & yodels, *Sirvester, Weldon, CA*

Talks like a pigeon, *Rocket, Westminster, CA*

Flushes toilet, *Callie, Denver, CO*

Hates to dine alone, *Sarah, Ansonia, CT*

Watches TV for hours, *KC, Bridgeport, CT*

Erases answer phone messages, *Orphan Annie, Derby, CT*

Match-maker, *Annie, Derby, CT*

Another toilet flusher, *Cocoa, New London, CT*

Supercat, *Callie, Prospect, CT*

Long frog-like tongue, *Taffy, Vernon, CT*

Stamp lover, *Charger, Wallingford, CT*

Eats like a squirrel, *Gizmo, Waterbury, CT*

Sings in the shower, *Hopper, Waterbury, CT*

Attack-cat, *Ray-gun, Jacksonville, FL*

Cat-terrorist, *Lucy, Jacksonville, FL*

Eats at the table, *Tip, Pensacola, FL*

Perches on shoulder like bird, *Misty, Stuart, FL*

Gives midnight kiss, *Jingles, West Palm Beach, FL*

Uses toilet all the time, *Fremont, Alpharetta, GA*

Awake 16-18 hours each day, *Boy, Atlanta, GA*

Star-trek fan, *Pookie, Bainbridge, GA*

Gives big kiss for food, *Yellow Boy, Clayton, GA*

Lie-detector chatter, *Zorro, Norcross, GA*

Answers phone, *Kaz-A-Rooney, Riverdale, GA*

Rides horse & swims, *Giggles, Honokaa, HI*

Chases & bites own tail, *Max, New Plymouth, ID*

Hates men, *Cashmere, Elgin, IL*

Tells time, *Dorry, Melrose Park, IL*

Rides treadmill, *Nickie, Skokie, IL*

Brushes face with brush by himself, *EEE, St Charles, IL*

Opens refrigerator, *Tigger, Boonville, IN*

Tail has life of its own, *Myah Stoll, Mishawaka, IN*

Wraps around neck like fur-piece, *Misty, Madisonville, KY*

Likes to swim in the bathtub, *Sebastian, Ayer, MA*

Joins anyone in the shower, *Dimples, Dudley, MA*

Takes off lid to peanut butter, *Jammer, Worcester, MA*

Ninja kitties, *Bentley & Jasmine Bibette, College Park, MD*

Brought watch & bra to owner, *Stimpy, Deerfield, MI*

Opens & sleep in drawers, *Buckeye & Sparty, Farmington Hills, MI*

Olympics inspired gymnast, *Kiki, Lake City, MI*

Types on typewriter, *Smokey, St Clair Shores, MI*

Bike riding cat, *Maudie, Hardin, MO*

Does aerobics, *Rascal, Kansas City, MO*

Runs can opener, *Seth, St Louis, MO*

Thinks he's a dog, *George, Nutley, NJ*

Hops to imitate ferret, *Bamama, Piscataway, NJ*

Operates answering machine, *Cat, Rockaway, NJ*

Likes to be spanked, *Elwood, Las Vegas, NV*

Plays hockey with water bowl, *Pixie, Brooklyn, NY*

Color changes: eyes & body, *Buggs, Endicott, NY*

Turns on clock-radio in middle of night, *Otis, Larchmont, NY*

Gets leash for walk, *Ling Ling, Liverpool, NY*

Raised by turkey, *Snooks, Medina, NY*

Harp player, *Tuxedo, New York, NY*

Kisses on command, *Bimbo, Poestenkill, NY*

Sits at dinner table, *Kitty (Boom), Staten Island, NY*

Knows his curfew to exact minute, *Slick Hanners, Cleveland, OH*

Wraps exposed feet with string, *Margin, Fairborn, OH*

Alarm clock - knows weekends, *Bam Bam, Fairborn, OH*

Vegetarian cat, *Priscilla, Jackson, OH*

Sits & watches TV like a person, *Spunkey, Stillwater, OK*

Flying squirrel & boxer, *Tigger & Taz, Johnstown, PA*

Another great kisser, *Toby, Newtown, PA*

Still another toilet flusher, *Mortimer, Pittsburgh, PA*

Chews gum, *Tazmanian Devil (Taz), West Chester, PA*

Sits like a human, *Chapman, Cordova, TN*

Jewelry thief, *Lucy, Humboldt, TN*

Can pick out biggest currency, *Kazz, Kingsport, TN*

Sings scales, *Hiker, Roanoke, TX*

Goes into other room to cry, *Adam Hiatt, West Jordan, UT*

Likes to take bath, *Mr. Stretch, Arlington, WA*

Fetches darts, *Peach Tootie, Janesville, WI*

Dart player, *Pastie, Manitowoc, WI*

Another that answers the phone, *Prancer, Moatsville, WV*

Penguin-Cat, *Sterling Silver, Morgantown, WV*

Chapter Eight

Lap Cats Extraordinaire

N o image is more typical of the average cat than the notion of a feline friend curled up in one's lap – totally relaxed and oblivious to all about them. Or so the belief goes. Lap cats extraordinaire are <u>anything</u> but average. They seem to possess a sort of cosmic energy that transcends the present. While appearing to be lost in space, they are at the same time, keenly aware of life around them. With uncanny perception they sense the thoughts and the needs of the fortunate humans who surround them. How else can we account for the stories revealed in this book?

Here is where cats as pets really shine. Many other animals do tricks, are great companions, and are fun to be with. But cats are more than that. They're our alter-egos. They see what we don't. At times we are blind and miss the obvious. Through the eyes of a cat we gain a new perspectives on the world about us. What a great gift it is to have a cat!

SIAM'S DAY

Good Meoooowing!

The alarm woke me up before I was ready. Purrr . . . I'd like more time to cuddle up in the covers and purr; but, here we go - out of bed. Rise and shine! The floor is cold! I'll sit on the rug and watch my breakfast being prepared. If I roll and look cute, I might get it sooner. Sure are a lot of bright lights and something sure smells good. Wait - wait - wait - finally I get my dish - ummmm. It's good. I was hungry. Now I'll play ball and they will watch me and I can get a lot of attention. Guess they are busy now so I'll look out the window and watch for a bird or squirrel and sometimes I even see another cat - worse yet, a DOG, but we won't talk about that.

Time to play hide and seek. I'll hide behind the corner and jump out at them (pounce). Now we run and play and chase each other from room to room. I can hide behind the bed or in my sack.

It's fun to put my ball under the ice box and bookcase and reach under with my long arm and pull it out. Sometimes I can't reach it, but they come to my rescue. Mew (thank you).

There goes that noisy phone and I won't get any attention, so I'll walk around crying loud and they can't hear to talk. Then they will hang up sooner. Well, it worked (See how smart I am? Can you believe they say animals are dumb?)

Time to look out the window again. A car is coming in the drive. Oh boy! Someone is coming to see ME. I like to get company. They come in and talk and talk to me and make a fuss over me. That is fun and we play with my ball and string, Oh - now they are leaving - goodbye.

I hear the mailman coming. When he brings our cat magazine, we sit down right away and read the articles, look at the pictures and it doesn't work when I try to sit on the pages. They push me off.

Well, it's quiet now so guess I can take a nap. I'm not going to sleep 80% of this day though. There is too much to do for fun. Just a quick cat nap. Yawn - ho hum.

Siam – ready for a purrfect day.

There goes the piano. How long is this going to last? Well it's time for me to put an end to this! It hurts my ears. I'm not getting any attention - POUNCE! These keys are hard on the toes. Well it worked. She quit playing and is holding me. Purrrr! (See - another smart "cat" trick)

Oh "NO"! They are getting ready to go away. Not that! What can I do now? Well, I'll try rolling and putting my chin up and laying on my back and looking so adorable, they just can't bear to leave me. It didn't work this time. One good thing happened though; before they left, they fed me. Now I can take another nap. It will be quiet.

zzzzzzzzz - Later:

Good I hear them coming! I run to see them and meow and purr and they will pet and hug me and talk to me. Purrrrr

They are happy to see me too and you know what? They are going to take my picture. Oh, how I love that. I pose and look so cute and get so much attention. They we play ball - have a good time.

Well, it's been a good day and it's bedtime now. I cuddle up and it's so warm. I get hugged and petted and talked to. Good night. Purrrr

This was a purrfect day! SIAM

Marsha Cross, Barberton, OH

MORRISA

My cat is named Morrisa,
By this picture you can see
She is as pretty as she can be!

She keeps her fur, colored orange and white
Very clean and shining bright,
By licking and bathing day and night
When I brush her she stretches with delight!

She rolls on her back for a tummy rub.
She only drinks water from a bowl in the tub!

She eats 9 Lives, canned and dry
Other brands she will seldom try!
Turns up her nose, tail held high, she stalks away
To go outdoors night or day.

She will reach with her paw to ring -
Three elephant bells on the back door on a string!

"Come on Morrisa", signals her to the front door to run
To get out on the front porch to swing and to sun!

Some visitors or strangers she will abide -
But at a vacuum cleaner noise she will run and hide!

Up high on the window sills by the hour she will stay
To look out in the yard at squirrels or birds feed and play.

One stormy night, her "Meow" woke me to put windows down
The wind and rain was in gust all over town!
A watcher, a protector, a fire alarm if needed she is around
An amuser, a friend, a welcomer and often a clown!

When I am making my bed she plays "Hide and Seek"
She will jump up and crawl under the sheet!

When I sit down to watch T.V., read, relax, make a lap
She comes to cuddle close, curl up and take a nap!

She sleeps on the foot of my bed at night
Steps all over me to wake me with a kiss in the morning light!

She was born in Atlanta, April 1983
Brought to Alabama in June, company for me!

A more lovable, smart, ruler of my home than she -
Could never be found on land or sea!

My cat named after "Morris" - MORRISA!

Martha Kilpatrick, Reform, AL

SUCH A GOOD TRIXY

Four years ago my niece, Jean, felt I should have kitty company. Looking forward to making a good choice, she drove to see a friend who had kittens to give away. Too late! There was only one kitten left - rather an odd looking creature, Jean thought. Thinking of the long drive to my home, she decided to take this strange looker.

Smiling, she placed the tiny little thing in my hands, and said, "The kitten is 6 weeks old. While covering the many miles to her new home, that tiny tyke cried and cried with various meows, soft and loud."

Half of her chin was white, making her face look like a little man sporting a partly white beard. Her double front paws looked like over-sized mittens. Her tail was so, so long for such a tiny body. I agreed with my niece - "this is an odd looking creature.

Making herself comfortable in my lap, the kitten looked up at me, paying no attention to the pretty girl who brought her. As I looked at her in her cozy position, she showed me the beauty that was hers. Her eyes! . . . So expressive from a lovely golden color. This bundle of fur was quite colorful. Half white was her throat, matching the white "beard" half. Her back paws were whitish tan. The rest was shades of black mingled with a cast of tan, white and light blue. What a beauty!

Within a short time she made herself QUEEN in her new home. She explored everything and everywhere. She enjoyed pushing down large bags of groceries so she could get inside. She sometimes made her napping quarters in a bag I'd toss on the floor.

What a frisky little one! Oh, "Frisky" is a good name for her, I thought. But every time I started to call "Frisky" - out of my mouth came "Trixy". Mmmm . . . full of tricks, she is. That's it! She shall be called Trixy. Wonderful how quickly she knew that she was Trixy.

Trixy liked to play, jump, hide and run around everywhere. She'd run down the hall onto the dinette floor, swiftly slide around the cabinet and run into the living room to jump onto the first piece of furniture she saw. Such an active, happy and so good kitty! One thing she would not be allowed to do - sleep in my bed. Of course, she had her own ideas. Up to join me as my head hit the pillow, I'd feel her long-whiskered, furry face touching mine. Cuddling up as close as she could, she'd knead my throat accompanied by her purring serenade. How could I turn her away? So I stroked her head. Trixy knew her QUEEN title.

Trixy is a very loving four year old now, quite pretty and very clever. She has her special meows, actions and looks. I think she tries some of her meows in English. "Do you want to go outside, Trixy?" "Meh yeh" is her answer with pleading eyes.

When I must leave the house, I tell her, "I have to go now, Trixy. You have to be a good Trixy." She looks up at me and walks into the living room, jumps on a chair and sits on the top of the chair back. There she spends her time looking out the window. This is fine for a short time, but if it's too long to suit her, she show's me she's hurt . . . when I come home, she turns her head away and ignores me for a while.

One of Trixy's pastimes, even after a long nap, is to make herself comfortable in my lap and nap again! Often when my lap is clear, she stands looking at me, and waits until I pat my lap saying, "Come, Trixy, come on." And she does. Other times when my lap is taken up by a lap board and I'm writing or sewing, Trixy simply jumps up, lands her front paws on my work, looks at me as if to say, "Get this stuff away, now. It's my turn." And I do.

Trixy did this so often, she made me feel I should rock her and after a while inspired me to make up a song to which she adds her purring melody and half-closed eyes:

Such a good Trixy!

Rock-a-bye Trixy, in Susie's arms.
Rock-a-bye Trixy, with all your charms.
Rock-a-bye Trixy, Oh I love you.
Rock-a-bye Trixy, I know you love me too.

You're such a good trixy.

Susan D'Avanzo, Guilford, CT

CLARABELLE THE TEACHER

Thanksgiving evening, 1989, leaving our car and walking into our condo (we were living in Guilford, CT), a beautiful Maine Coon cat ran across the parking lot and literally followed us to our door and into our hearts.

We discovered he was a stray and people in the condo area would feed him, etc... but no one was able to adopt him - so we did, very happily. He was the most wonderful cat ... very loving and affectionate; he would fall asleep in our laps - he turned die-hard cat haters into cat lovers (or at least Clarabelle lovers). He would jump across the rooftops of the condos - at best around 7 feet. He was an amazing hunter - bringing home birds of all kinds, mice, moles, bunnies ... but one day he brought home a full grown rabbit, nearly as big as he was (and he was pretty big - 13 lbs).

Probably the best story of Clarabelle is when our son was born (12/8/91). Clarabelle endeared himself to Robbie and vice versa. The first day Robbie was brought home, Clarabelle jumped onto the sofa where I was feeding him and started rubbing his face into Robbie's head (gently of course). He would cuddle into my lap when I would feed Robbie and fall asleep. When bathing Robbie he would jump onto a chair and very patiently watch me bathe him. When Robbie started crawling, Clarabelle would rub his face all over Robbie, and Robbie started doing it back to Clarabelle! Soon Robbie was doing this to his toys and to us, too. It was something Clarabelle taught him!

A Golden Soul

My son was actually "meowing" before he said "mama". I started referring to Clarabelle as Robbie's "brother"! Once when returning from a trip to Connecticut, Clarabelle was brought home from the cattery, and walked into our kitchen. Robbie, being very excited to see his "brother", crawled sooo fast after him (I don't think his knees hit the floor) then proceeded to "meow" and rub all over Clarabelle!

Unfortunately, he just recently past away from heart disease. We are still mourning our sweet Clarabelle.

Ann & Stephen Hallberg, Ligonier, PA

Suggested readings with <u>your</u> favorite lap cat in a comfortable position . . .

Purrs at 2 A.M., *Lady Tuppence, Mesa, AZ*

Saved from death row, *Oz, Montrose, CA*

Some-assembly-required kitten, *Jewelie, Rialto, CA*

Comforted in time of need, *Casper, Fairfield, CT*

Like human baby, *Shadow, Humboldt, KS*

Appreciates life, *Pinkie, Osawatomie, KS*

Found dropped by roadside, *Marissa, Marion, KY*

Stray needed someone to love, *Biscuits, Mandeville, LA*

Purr-fect friend, *Buttons, Cambridge, MA*

Kissing cat, *Sheba, Camp Springs, MD*

Simply loves me, *Katie, Mt. Pleasant, MI*

Interviewed human to pick home, *Samantha Van Dyke, Oak Park, MI*

Licks tears from eyes, *Simon, Rocky Mount, NC*

Liked only husband till he died, *Stubby, Skyland, NC*

King of the house, *Benjermen, Dickinson, ND*

Chose owner, *Rose, Concord, NH*

Changed lives, *Raggs, Delanco, NJ*

Tolerates tail pulling by two-year-old, *Fluffy, Forked River, NJ*

Light of my life, *Beau, Hackensack, NJ*

Faultless, Muffin, *Runnemede, NJ*

Permanent lap cat, *Tinker, Circleville, OH*

Most wonderful cat in the world, *Snowball, Westerville, OH*

Made her want to have children, *She-Wolf, McDonald, PA*

Picks favorite person daily, *Alexander Catnip, Philadelphia, PA*

Lap cat defined, *Mr. Pibb, Cordova, TN*

Constant companion, *Hannah, Memphis, TN*

Enduring friendship, *Toppy, Murfreesboro, TN*

Honorary teddy bear, *Atila the Hun, Virginia Beach, VA*

Chapter Nine

Catmunications

Catmunications refers to the many and varied ways cats communicate with their humans. The first and most obvious way is speech. As many of the essays submitted indicate, some cats have quite a vocabulary. All cats make a range of sounds – each one distinct – that allow us know what they want. A certain meow to be fed, another to be let outside, a shriek for a pinched tail, purrs of contentment and so on. But uncommon cats go beyond the ordinary. Some can actually imitate human speech. Felines with such abilities have unique words they use to get their message across such as calling their humans by name or asking for a favorite treat.

Body language is another way uncommon cats tell us what they're thinking. Some point with their paw to the object of their desires. Others mimic the body language of their human companions.

Uncommon cats are also great listeners. They understand what we are saying and rather enjoy listening in on our conversations. Many respond to voice commands and will do tricks when specified by word. For example handicaps are minimized by a blind kitty that loves music and a deaf cat that knows sign language.

Most amazing of all is the way many cats seem to read our minds. Without a word spoken, they seem to know what we want or what we are feeling. This is obvious by the way they respond to our needs. It's no wonder cats have become our #1 pet. We all like to be with someone who will be understanding and sympathetic.

JEZEBEL – A NEW PERSONALITY?

Jezebel is Quigley's full sister, but from a later litter. She is 18-1/2 years old, also a large cat - Siamese cross with brilliant blue eyes but a creamy gray longhair. She and Quig have always been madly in love with each other. Jez is also a very loving cat.

My sister, who used to share a backyard with me, had two cats also. I started getting very perturbed with her Penrod; I thought he was attacking Jezebel on a regular basis. I would hear spitting, hissing, yowling, but when I looked out, all I could see was Penrod padding back to his side of the yard - and Jez looking at me, playing the abused victim.

You can imagine my absolute astonishment to be at the back door one day when this altercation started. Penrod was sitting outside, about twenty feet from Jezebel, just looking at her - when she leaped to her feet, started whirling and yowling and spitting! For no reason! Penrod finally got tired of being a spectator at this strange sport and stalked off to his side of the yard. Jez sat back down, not having moved more than a foot from the original spot, and started giving himself a bath just as relaxed and unconcerned as could be. Since then it has occurred to me that maybe this was entertainment for me!

I haven't mentioned that Jez broke her leg before she was a year old and has lived to her ripe old age as a handicapped cat. Soon after we moved to Oregon she started showing a new side to her personality. One day I heard a fearful sound emanating from the garage. I found that Jezebel had trapped the neighbor's large dog (with a "mean" reputation) in the corner of the garage. It was his panicked complaint I had heard. My demure gray pussycat with the big innocent eyes was pacing up and down in front of him, swishing her long full tail. The neighbor came to get her dog who was practically a basket case, and couldn't believe that he was afraid of a cat! Once home he wouldn't leave his own yard for weeks!

Jezebel's new personality.

Jez has since shown great delight in stalking animals, no matter how big; her blue eyes stare them down as she comes closer and closer. Usually the animal falls apart, yowling for help! She then sits down and commences her bath, with just a hint of a smirk.

One day I stood outside my deck, watching Jezebel creep through the brush. I assumed she must be trying to catch one of the sand rats that Quigley had missed. She's never been quick enough with her game leg, to catch anything, which must have intimidated her. Suddenly I saw her freeze, leap forward and pounce on her prey - and toss it into the air! Watching closely I couldn't quite see what she had caught, but she would pounce, snatch, throw into the air - again and again! I picked up my binoculars and couldn't believe what I was NOT seeing! She had nothing! Was she doing this to fool me because she was ashamed and wanted me to think she could catch a varmint? Was it a joke? Maybe animals have a sense of humor?

Lillian Mason, Bend, OR

THE STORY OF TIGER & PANTHER

A secretary at work started bringing a tiny kitten with her to work. Everyone liked to pick the little thing up, but it really took to me. It would settle down and lie still in the palm of my hand. So when her friend had two other kittens to give away, she figured I was the logical choice to take them.

One was a gorgeous grey tabby with a half tail (part Manx), and the other was jet black. She brought them to work the day after the July Fourth holiday weekend. I took them home to my third-story condominium, and named them Tiger and Panther. Most people have just one pet, but I learned how much better it is for everyone when you have at least two in the same household.

The first night, because of the summer heat, I set up a sleeping pad in the living room next to an open sliding door to keep cool. My new kittens waited until I was lying down and then started the races. I think they were playing Indianapolis 500 that night. Around and around the living room they ran, and of course I was right on the track. Every time they raced around, they ran right up my back. Then, after the race was over, they took to biting my bare toes. For the first week or two, the time period from midnight until 4:00 a.m. was their prime play time. If it wasn't the races, it was professional wrestling or wall-climbing. (I had grass cloth on my walls, and they loved running up to the top of it near the ceiling.) I was beginning to wonder how much longer I could tolerate their wild nocturnal celebrations.

Then an amazing thing happened. They noticed that midnight to 4:00 a.m. was part of my nap time, and they changed their schedule to match mine. About ten days after I brought them home, they suddenly decided to go to sleep when I did and get up when I did. That was the end of their late night play period.

This was also when Panther became an alarm clock. Every morning at exactly 6:00, not 5:59 and not 6:01, but exactly 6:00, she woke me up. Her method was the tried and true nose touch. That's right, she climbed up on my chest and touched her nose ever so lightly against mine. This woke me up instantly every morning without making a sound. It was the most effective wake-up technique I have ever known.

I loved having them around the house. They followed me around, watched what

I was doing, and purred when I picked them up to hold them. When I shaved in the morning, they sat on each side of the sink, watching with fascination. When I sat in a chair to read, they snuggled up next to me. When I went to bed at night, they followed me and went to sleep at the same time.

We had a rule that bedtime was for sleeping, not for wrestling and leaping. Every once in a while, they would break this rule and it was my duty to escort them out of the bedroom. I hated to have to do this, but rules were rules. On these rare occasions, I would set them down in the hallway and close the door. The next morning I would always find them right outside the door. Even if they couldn't be on the bed, they wanted to be as close to me as possible. This was really touching, and made me feel even worse than I already felt about punishing them.

After a couple of months, I started taking them with me to the courtyard. I would put them in a laundry hamper and carry them to the elevator, down to the first floor, and out into the open area. They ran around the lawn and climbed trees while I read a book or sunned by the pool.

The coming of spring a few months later brought a new delight. A pair of Canadian geese decided to stop off for a visit of several weeks at our swimming pool. Tiger and Panther went crazy. They circled the pool, which was round, and tried to maneuver into position. The ducks saw this, and thought it was great fun. They used to swim to the edge of the pool on the opposite side from the cats, climb out, and dare the cats to pursue them. When the cats came running, the ducks dashed back into the pool, enjoying every minute of the chase. Once, when I returned after a trip to the third floor, I found both of my cats sopping wet. The geese had scored the ultimate victory.

On a number of occasions I had to leave Tiger and Panther on their own for a few hours while I took care of business upstairs. And on a number of occasions, when I was gone for too long, Panther came after me to tell me. I would hear her meow right outside my door. She would cross the courtyard to the atrium of my building, go to the elevator, wait for a human resident to press the button, get in and ride the elevator to the third floor, then get out and head down the hallway to my door.

Coming home was something I looked forward to. Tiger and Panther were always waiting for me, happy to see me back again. But one evening was especially memorable. It hadn't been a good day at work, and I wasn't feeling well when I arrived home. When I came in the door, the cats were napping on my bed. I headed straight for the living room and dropped face down to the floor to rest. When I opened my eyes and looked up about 45 minutes later, there were Tiger and Panther on either side of my face, like a pair of sentinels watching over me.

Tiger developed great rapport with other cats; Panther became very popular with people. But Tiger could warm to people also. Once a young man came out to lie in the sun by the pool. He was stretched out on his back with his eyes closed when it happened. With Tiger on one side and Panther on the other, both cats stood up and placed their paws lightly on his legs. He shot up on his lawn chair and let out a loud scream. It was hilarious.

When people came out into the courtyard, Panther ran to them and performed a kind of dance to greet them. She would run in front of them, roll over on her back, then stand up on her hind legs to be petted. (She didn't want them to have to lean over too far.) A woman once exclaimed, "This cat thinks it's a dog!" On another occasion, a young couple picked her up and carried her up to their upstairs unit. She just lay back in their arms without the slightest fear or suspicion.

Panther must have been one of the gentlest cats that ever lived. On one occasion a pair of girls about nine or ten years old picked her up and carried her around the lawn. They got a little rough, and you could tell by the look in her eyes that she didn't enjoy being treated this way. Yet she never once bit them or clawed them; she just waited patiently for about ten minutes until they let her down. Then she ran all the way across the courtyard to get away from them. She kept her distance from them after that, but she never left the slightest scratch on them.

People talk about having watch dogs to guard their property. But Tiger and Panther did quite a job of their own. One night about midnight, I was watching television when the two cats stood up, faced the front door, and started growling. When I went to the door to see what it was, I found a copy of the one-page association newsletter on my doorstep. Down the hall was the delivery boy in running shoes dropping a copy at each door. My cats had heard him approach my door wearing rubber-soled shoes on a carpeted floor above the noise of the television broadcast! (I think it was Johnny Carson.)

The following incident proved to me beyond any doubt that cats are capable of actions their human owners can learn from. To allow Tiger and Panther access to my balcony, I installed a glass panel with a special door just for them. Panther figured out how to use the door right away, but Tiger was having trouble. So I thought I'd give him a hand. I held him in front of the door and tried to push him through. He squirmed and pushed and stayed where he was. So I tried several more times. Each time he put up more resistance. It was becoming clear he wasn't interested in any unsolicited human assistance.

Finally, he lost his patience and took a swipe at me. His paw just grazed the tip of my nose and did no damage, but I got the message. Realizing he had to learn how to use the door at his own pace, I let go of him and went back to my chair across the room. I picked up a book and started to read. After a few minutes, Tiger came to my chair and jumped up on the arm. Then he placed one paw gently on my hand and looked up at me. When it became clear to me that this was his way of offering an apology, I was deeply moved. It's a moment I will never forget.

Douglas Topham, Woodland Hills, CA

. . . and who said President Reagan was the *Great Communicator*?

Talks all the time, *Dwezil, Fontana, CA*

Deaf cat knows sign language, *Amber Jean, San Francisco, CA*

Knows "vet" - reads minds, *Twinkle, West Covina, CA*

Understands conversations, *Stri, Fort Collins, CO*

Obeys voice commands, *Tipsy, Westminster, CO*

Knows "treats", *Daisey, Coconut Creek, FL*

Many different meows, *Cirrus, North Ft Meyers, FL*

Reads mind, *Secret, Palmetto, FL*

Imitated owner's limp, *Okeechobee Red, Sebring, FL*

Says "bless you" to sneezes, *Rambo, West Dundee, IL*

One talkative cat, Cecil, *Willowbrook, IL*

Understands English commands, *Solo, Topeka, KS*

Communicates like a child, *Babie, N. Adams, MA*

A talking cat, *Thumper, Arden, NC*

Understands English, *Riley, Elwood, NE*

Obeys voice commands, *Sir Lancelot, Portsmouth, NH*

Talks non-stop when she wants treats, *Taffy, Barnegat, NJ*

Blind music lover with large vocabulary, *Willie, Bayshore, NY*

Speaks different languages, *Marble, Douglaston, NY*

Obeyed words to eat, drink, & use litter box, *Holli, Endicott, NY*

Points to what she wants, *Feisty, Barberton, OH*

Expressive with face, *Cody Witt, Columbus, OH*

Says "I love you" & "mom", *Baby, Lima, OH*

Blesses when she sneezes, *Opus, Bristol, RI*

Says "Grandma" for treat, *Tinker Bell, Oak Ridge, TN*

Meow sounds like a chime, *Chimey-Ling, Dublin, TX*

Asks for water & treats, *JR, Stafford, VA*

Purrs & hisses at the same time, *Thumper, Richland Center, WI*

Chapter Ten

Who's Who in New England

CONNECTICUT

ANSONIA
Anne Kowalonek
Sarah
F, 1, Black, grey, tan
Longhair tabby
Insistent, playful, friendly, elegant
Sarah has been given this name because of its Hebrew translation - "Princess". She is not only elegant in appearance, but has this very insistent quality . . . her way or no way at all. She does not like to eat alone and will cry until someone comes to pet her while she eats.

Her playful side can get rough at times. She loves to hide and try to make people scream. Her favorite activity is terrorizing the neighbor's dog. In the midst of her elegance and tom-boy activities, Sarah is a carrier of feline leukemia, of which she shows no symptoms.

BRIDGEPORT   06606
Debbie Cerino, 606 Merritt St
KC
M, 2, Seal point
Himalayan
Loving & outgoing
KC - more commonly referred to as "Cases" came into our lives almost two years ago. From the first moment I saw him I fell in love with him - he looked like a little koala bear. In a short time he made himself

at home and quickly worked his way into my heart as favorite. His outgoing personality and undying curiosity makes every day an experience, yet his innocence and trust is endearing. "Cases" made friends with our other animals but has truly become my shadow. He seems to know my every emotion and always makes me smile when that seems impossible.

I honestly think KC believes at times that he is human. He'll sit with us for hours watching TV with himself propped up on his hind legs and resting on the back of the couch. Then at other times he transforms into a little dog bringing us toys, balls (preferably aluminum foil) and other things to play fetch or is the first at the door when the bell rings.

KC warms everyone's heart who comes in contact with him. Thank you Judy for bringing him into our lives.

CHESTER
Laurie I Blair
Mini
F, 6-1/2, Gray tabby
Domestic shorthair
Happy, often puzzled, snotty (but endearingly so!)
We spied the tiny, wet tiger kitten wandering blindly in the herb garden hours after birth. Born to a cat so anti-social my friends had owned her for five years without any clue of her sex, Mini had apparently been kicked out of the nest after a perfunctory cleaning and nursing -- her mother must have preferred even numbers, since Mini was one of seven in the litter. We

Mini contemplates her early beginnings

wondered . . . should nature take its course?

But Mini's cries were surprisingly loud and hard to ignore. I took pity on my friends, who were expecting relatives from Colorado and had planned a trip with them. I plunked Mini into a cardboard box and drove her to my house, where I later discovered I'd done almost everything wrong.

A heating pad or hot water bottle? Try a pile of dishtowels she might have smothered in. Formula? Feeding tube? Nope -- canned milk and one of my nephew's leftover doll bottles. Set the alarm for every two or three hours? I relied on hungry meowing to wake me up. Eyes opened on schedule, Mini (with great effort) trained herself and eventually she realized she is, in fact, a cat. This survivor's now fat, fluffy, spoiled and (discounting a small fold in one slightly frostbitten ear) quite sturdily beautiful. Would I do it over again? Sure . . . if my company would give me maternity leave for orphan kittens!

Gypsy

M, 16 dec, Gray striped tiger

Domestic shorthair

Joyous, loving, independent, fearless, determined

See story in chapter 3: Against All Odds

DERBY   06418

Chris Kowalonek, PO Box 128

Pandora (aka **Pandy**)

F, 12, Black

Mixed (part Persian)

Loving & mellow (finally!)

I was five weeks old when I got my mommy. I was fresh and beat on my big cat brother. He was 17 pounds and I could flip him. I slapped food from my other cat brother's mouth - then caught it in my paw and ate it myself. I loved to lie on the porch rail and spit on people from the second floor. If someone sat on the couch, I scratched or bit their legs. No one wanted me but mommy. My brothers died and we got a black sister cat. She stands up to me. Now we are pals and I'm an old loving, mellow fat cat.

Annie

F, 11, Black

Mixed (part Bombay)

Lovingly spiteful

Annie came to me as a 6 year spayed black female with a balding tummy. Fur never grew after spaying.

She's fearless - befriending anyone - except another cat. When things don't go her way, the spitefulness surfaces. Her favorite thing to do is urinating wherever she wants.

One year I had guests overnight from a folk fest. A guest put his sleeping bag on her spot - the biggest puddle. Horror! Wash it? How? The nice lady at the laundry helped him. Then they became friends . . . and now it's many thanks to my black bundle from a glowing, happily married couple! Annie the match-maker!

DERBY

Terri Kowalonek

Orphan Annie

F, 1, Brown, black, tan

Unknown

Highly animated

Orphan Annie beat the odds and lived despite being abandoned on a busy road. Although she weighed less than a pound when I adopted her, almost a year later she weighs a healthy ten pounds.

Annie loves to sneak up on me from behind. My scream is her reward. Her favorite hiding places include the shower and the kitchen sink, where a dripping faucet is an open invitation to take a drink. Another hides out is the top of the refrigerator, where she enjoys sending magnets flying across the kitchen floor. Other activities include swinging from the spider plants, bathing the mouse toys till the fur falls off, and listening to the answer machine until she erases the messages.

EAST HARTFORD   06108

Jennifer Williams, 33-B Orchard St

Garth

M, 2, Orange, dark orange & white

Tabby

Kind, loving, but spoiled

My cat is special because I know he loves me. I can tell.

Sometimes when I'm moving things up and down the stairs, he'll follow me because he wants attention. I love Garth very much. Garth knows when I need comfort and when I don't. (He will still beg for "loves.")

Garth has the cutest face. Garth knows how to pull the shade up all by himself. All you see is the tail sticking out and then the shade will go up. Garth will cry all the time until I come home. I love Garth very, very much.

Randy [owner: Crystal Marie Williams]

M, 9 months, Calico & white

Tabby

Very friendly and playful

My new cat, Randy, is a joy in my life! Every time I reach to pet him, he starts to purr immediately. I don't need an alarm clock! Every morning I wake up to Randy licking my face, happily. Randy enjoys being petted, but hates to be held like a baby. I once had my friend over, and she noticed a scratch on my arm. She asked, "What happened?" I said, "Kitty, Kitty." Randy is not all that nice! He can be very vicious. He scares away my sister's cat, Barth, who is almost 2 years older than Randy.

I am very sad to say my poor little kitty is going to a farm because we can't have more than 1 cat in our house. I will miss him very much! He is my whole heart! Well I must go! It is time for Randy's daily scratch behind the ear!

FAIRFIELD   06430

Barbara M Crowe, Curiosity's Cat - 565 Kings Hwy East

Casper

M, 6, White with orange points

Himalayan Flame Point

Quietly affectionate

In 1987, while living in Florida, Casper came into my life through the kindness of a doctor. I was struggling with a bout of depression after being divorced and quite lonely. At the time I didn't have any animals and he asked me if I wanted Casper. All I had to do was contact the breeder and he would be mine.

At first I was doubtful because I knew that breeders don't often give cats away. At any rate, I met with her and my dream became a reality. He brought back joy into my life and as I look at him each day, I am grateful for him.

Sasha

M, 1, Seal point

Himalayan

Gentle and warm

When he is in what I call "his love mood", he will want me to hold him. He will then climb up toward my face and place one paw on one shoulder and the other paw on my other shoulder, purring softly.

I never owned a cat who would behave in this way. Usually they caress on one side or the other. This position enables him to look you right in the eye with an almost human-like quality.

GREENWICH   06831

The Coviello Family, 104 Pemberwick Rd

Baby

F, 6, White/orange/brown (Calico)

Calico

Independent, plays hard to get. Loves us on her terms. She's human !

My son Andrew Jr., brought our cat named "Baby" in off the road in 1987. "Baby", does her business (#1) in the toilet, which she probably learned from watching my mother, "Grace". Mom, had two back surgeries in 1984, and it was difficult for her to feed "Baby". In 1988 I invented and patented the "Easy-Care Pet Feeder", a Healthcare/Pet Care Product, that enables all people to feed their pets at the proper level in relation to their size, and without the need to bend over whatsoever. It received media attention in newspapers such as Gannett, Greenwich Times and other local weeklys. The Feeder received many endorsements throughout the United States, and will be a wonderful way of life for all people and their cherished pets. This invention was chosen for inclusion in Who's Who of American Inventors 1992-1993. I hope to have it on the market very soon.

GUILFORD   06437

Susan D'avanzo, 281 Nut Plains Rd
Trixy
F, 5, Tortise shell w/ black whiskers
Domestic shorthair
Lover, soft music fan, happy, plays, jumps, explores.

Trixy ran her race track, rolled over, walked in the grass, sat in the garden. One morning she walked down the driveway, looking like a queen. "Come here, Trixy," I called, but she walked in front of the mail box. Luckily she didn't cross the street. She walked up the next driveway, stopped, looked at me and ran into the bushes.

Half an hour later, Trixy's "Mee-ow" sounded at the door. I let her in, stroked her gently and said, "Trixy, you are now an 'indoor kitty'." Surprisingly, it wasn't long before she was happy in her new life style.

See story in chapter 8: Lap Cats Extraordinaire.

HARTFORD   06103

Harold T Yamase, 1 Gold St #23E

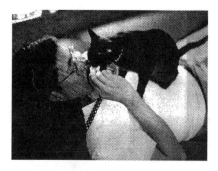

The Cookie Munster at work.

Munson
M, 1, Chocolate Brown
Burmese
Shamelessly undisciplined, spoiled, but loveable.

I affectionately refer to Munson as the Cookie Munster. Whenever I am lying on the sofa munching on sugar cookies, Munson rushes over, sits on my tummy and nibbles away on the other side of the cookie. This has become a habit and we eat cookies together. He is however, very particular. It has to be Pepperidge Farm Sugar Cookies. He will not eat any other kind and I have to eat the cookie with him. If I leave him a cookie on the floor he won't touch it.

LITCHFIELD   06759

Kathy Kittredge, 120 Marsh Rd
Champion   MCKENKITTY   Princess Spring Elsa
F, 2, red
Abyssinian
Extremely active, into everything

Baby Love (left) & Spring
give pause for thought.

As the owner of 7 extremely active Abys it becomes necessary at times to confine them. We have a Tokyo cage - very large and high (4 feet high). We confine them sometimes at meals because Spring, for one, sits on my shoulders and steals the food on the way to my mouth. She uses her paws and can scoop up the food. Spring is many times the first cat confined in the cage because she is usually the first in trouble. Spring is our only cat who taught herself how to open the cage. She uses her nose to push up the bar until the door falls open and she jumps out. Spring can also open doors and cabinets. Spring was the first to ride on a person's shoulder.

MCKENKITTY Baby Love
M, 2, Red
Abyssinian
Active and into mischief
Baby loves to watch the water drops drip down the side of the sink when I do dishes. Unfortunately, I do not do dishes often enough for Baby because he loves playing with the drops so much. I keep a water bowl on top of the counter for the cats. Baby has taught himself to make his own drips. He cups his paw. dips it into the bowl, then walks to the side of the counter and drops the water. He then jumps on the floor and watches the drips run downward and tries to catch them.

NEW LONDON   06320
Kelly A Troland, 179 Montauk Av Apt #8
Cocoa
M, 3, Brown, tan, white
Longhair, Mackerel
Playful, shy & timid with others
I have known Cocoa since he was a newborn, as I knew the person who gave him to me; I may even have witnessed his birth. I entered him in his and my first T.I.C.A. cat show held at Connecticut College in August 1992; he did not win an award, but he behaved very well and earned an impressive amount of points. He has mastered the art of flushing the toilet repeatedly, to my dismay, although sometimes I get a laugh over it - this is his bizarre distinction and one of his favorite "games" besides pouncing on and biting my fingers.

He is big brother to Ben, my short-haired, black & white, good-natured male, 2-year old cat; they are not biological brothers.
Ben
M, 2 approx., Black & white spots
Short-hair
Affectionate, friendly, and easy going
I adopted Ben this past summer as he often fed on my porch and I began to see him everyday. I believe he sought shelter in the water drainage area under the sidewalk.
He is a wonderful companion for both Cocoa and myself. He and Cocoa often pick on each other during their game of pounce and tackle. Ben, having not yet been neutered, is very obstreperous; he makes quite an array of vocal sounds like nothing I've ever heard before, while sitting on the window sill or desperately trying to claw his way outside.

NEWINGTON   06111
Caro & Forest Platt, 604 Cypress Road
Zorro
M, 2, Black
Shorthair
Rambunctious
We thought we'd let the cats talk about themselves. "I love to give my mommy and daddy hugs. I stand on my hind legs and reach up with my front paws; then I meow to get their attention. Then they pick me up and I put my front paws around their neck. While expressing my love I'll knead their neck, purr in their ear, and occasionally "drool" all over them. Mom and Dad call me a devil because I like to share what they eat - especially if the food is left unguarded on the counter. Shouldn't they share and share alike?"
Snowy
F, 2, White w/ black spot on head
Longhair
Affectionate & vocal
"I'm special because I am a little princess girl with long white hair and a small black patch on my head. (I've thought about bleaching it, but Mommy says 'NO'! I love hanging around Daddy. Dad makes a great vehicle - I ride on his broad shoulders and get a nice view. When I went to show my daddy that I love him, I suck on his earlobes. For some reason Daddy gets mad at me when I wake him up at 3 a.m. when I'm sucking on his ears. Mommy thinks it's funny."
"My sister Missy would like to say a few words too. She's a 3-1/2 year old girl cat - a grey & black Tabby with beige belly."
"Hi, I'm Missy. I allowed Mom & Dad to find me one night when I was 1-1/2 years old. First I tricked the vet into thinking I was pregnant, so I got more food. Then when I was supposed to be spayed I shocked everybody as I already had been spayed. Now I run things at home. To show my mom how much I love her, on Mother's Day 1992 I brought home a present - a freshly caught chipmunk. I guess everyone loved the present, since my parents and grandparents got so excited when I came through the cat door with my 'gift'.

NORWALK   06850
Virginia L Bossone, 6 June Avenue
Mittens
M, 16.5 dec, black & white
Very affectionate, funny & loyal
Mittens was my faithful companion and friend for 16-1/2 years. We were devoted to each other and never were there two beings so one. He would wait for me each night when I got home from work, he would sleep with me and was constantly by my side. He would wake me in the morning with a snorting sound to get my attention; if that didn't work he would knock something off my dresser or use the dresser handles as door knockers till I got up. He was affectionate and unique in his own special way and I greatly miss him in my life.

PROSPECT   06712
Rachele Patrignelli, 71 Putting Green La
Callie
F, 1, Dark gray - tiger
Affectionate & vivacious

Callie – Supercat

She can leap tall counters with a single bound (and a running start), fly through the air with the speed of light (right into the wall), and wrestle a six-foot Christmas tree to the ground. She's our Supercat, Callie.

Callie has a distinct personality as well as exceptional hygiene; she hops up into the kitchen sink for her daily shower (and to play with the water).

As for intelligence, Callie has been decorated for learning to operate the dog biscuit

dispenser before the dog did. A+! Our holy terror is a bundle of joy!

SOUTHPORT   06490
Judith A. Byman, 642 Kingshighway West
Amber
F, 2, Cream
Himalayan
Sweet, intelligent, human-like
Amber was so tiny at birth (1-3/4 oz.) that she wasn't nursing her mother. As a breeder I knew immediately that Amber was going to require "hands on" feedings and around the clock care. I used an eye dropper rather than tube feedings because I felt it was safer. Since October 9, 1990 Amber has traveled with me every day. In the beginning it was in the interest of her survival and now it is for the wonderful companionship she brings to my life.

In those early days and weeks she was secured in a tiny insulated special designed carrier and placed inside my leather jacket when we traveled outside. As the months passed she developed into a healthy intelligent feline. I sense that she thinks she is human as she uses little throaty sounds in communicating with me. And since I've talked to her so much during her 2 yrs. and 2 mos. she has a wealth of word association that I have not seen before. I've owned and cared for cats as well as many other animals in my lifetime. For the last few years I've owned and breed Himalayans.,

STORRS   06268
Carine Alma, Celfron Square, Coogan 2F
Noah Alma
M, 1.5, Black & white
Domestic shorthair
Outgoing & social, sensitive, affectionate
Noah has a sensitivity that is truly unique. Noah has helped me overcome many bouts of depression. Whenever I feel depressed, Noah jumps onto my lap and cuddles next to me. He also rubs his face against mine and gives me a kiss. When I have a bad dream, he runs into my room and jumps onto the bed to be near me. Noah also assumes cute postures. Usually I end up laughing at Noah's melodramatic poses. If he were human, he would surely be a Thespian of the stage.

STRATFORD   06497
Joni Gaines & Mike Zito,   82 McGrath Ct
Camille
F, 2, Black
See story in chapter 4: The Tricksters.
Claude
M, 2, Black and white
At first glance you might think that my
brother Claude is nothing but a bird watching, sister chasing, water out of the faucet
drinking, eggplant scallopini eating, pineap-
ple leaf chewing bully. But on one special
night he revealed his true colors. Our
humans were changing their clothes to go
out for the evening. I took the opportunity
to sneak into a forbidden closet for some
fun and exploration. All of a sudden, the
door slammed behind me. I didn't think
much of my dilemma until I also heard the
front door close. The humans had gone and
I was trapped!

I spent the first few minutes climbing
around on some boxes and swatting the arm
of a bathrobe. After all, a cat is nothing if
a cat can't keep her cool. But after a while
I started to get scared. I climbed clothes
looking for an escape route and I tried
desperately to dig my way out. It was then
that I heard Claude on the other side of the
door. He took on my fight. He tried to
rescue me by opening the door on the other
side. At one time we even touched paws,
and that made me feel a lot better.

Now usually when the humans come back
home, I'm the one who greets them at the
door. Claude tends to hang back, eventually
making his entrance (usually yawning as he
does). But this night, Claude was like a cat
possessed. As soon as he heard the key in
the lock, he ran downstairs. He started
racing all around, yelling his feline head
off. Even the humans knew something was
wrong. Claude led them right to the closet,
jumped on the door, and scratched it.
Freedom never felt so wonderful.

From that day on, Claude is more than just
my brother, and more than just a cat. He's
my hero.

TORRINGTON   06790
Ned Rozbicki & Staff,   100 E Main St -
Box 419
Blackie (Mr. Black)
M, 3, Black

Domestic longhair
Gentle, trusting, affectionate
Mr. Black ("Big Guy") had matted fur, an
ulcerated cornea in one eye, infection in the
other, and a broken tooth when he came to
the back door of our law office. Unknown
to us, he had been hit by a car, leaving him
with a permanent pelvic injury.

After extensive medical treatment and
loving care, Mr. Black has become part of
our staff, welcoming clients who are en-
thralled with this gentle giant. His most
endearing habit is to wrap his paws around
our necks and give us great bear hugs, his
head on our shoulders and purring loudly.

Miss Julie (The Noodle)
F, 1-1/2, Black/brown tiger
Domestic shorthair
Mischievous & cuddly
"The Noodle" came to our law office
through the back door, winning our hearts
with her wide-eyed stare and loving personality. She was thin to the point of emacia-
tion and could not meow.

A year later, she has blossomed into a
chubby, charming, vocal companion who
entertains our office staff and clients with
her Dr. Seuss-like antics. A favorite one is
her unique habit of drinking water by
placing both front paws into her water
bowl, dragging it backwards across the
floor, spilling most of its contents, and then
drinking the remainder with ALL four
paws in the bowl.

TRUMBULL   06611
Esther Mechler,   106 Booth Hill

A Tiger with a ROAR!

Tiger

M, 19, Grey, brown, black

Sweet, gentle, affectionate, smart

Tiger was special because he was such a happy cat. His purr was so loud it could be heard throughout the house - I still have a tape cassette of his purr - more like a ROAR! He used to wake us up at 5 A.M. with that purr as he greeted the new day. Tiger had several serious illnesses during his long life but only in his last few days did his purring stop. He lived to be 19.

VERNON   06066

Christine Church, 10 Russell Dr.

Taffy

F, 9, orange and white

Domestic Shorthair

Extremely friendly to all humans and animals

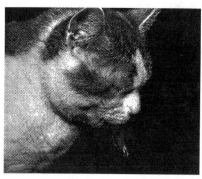

A most uncommon tongue

Taffy has the longest tongue that I have ever seen. After eating, Taffy licks almost her whole face with this tongue. Her long tongue and her "croaky" meow are responsible for Taffy having such nicknames as "Lizard Lips" and "Frog Cat."

Teisha

F, ?, Tabby

Maine Coon Cross

Shy, innocent, sweet, quiet

Teisha is blind. I adopted her after she had a rough start in life. She manages to find her way around - as long as things are not moved around. One time, I removed her water bowl to fill it and I watched her as she felt around for it with her paw (like a

person feels their way around in the dark). Teisha is shy and sweet. If she wants to be petted, she'll bat at my leg with her paw.

WALLINGFORD

John & Sally Gervasio

Charger (Moose)

M, 6, Gray Tiger

American shorthair

Smart, energetic companion

The Philatelist

The cat who loves stamps - When Charger hears you tear the perforations on stamps, he charges through the house to you so that he can lick the stamps. Then he will use his paws to press the stamps onto the envelopes. Charger loves to bat around crumpled stamps taken off incoming mail.

Victoria (Woobie)

F, 2, Gray & tan

American short hair

Round & loving

Every night Woobie comes to my ear and squeaks good night and then goes to her usual spot resting against my ankle.

WATERBURY   06704

Thomas Gignac, 138 Hope St

Gizmo

M, 3, Black, small white patch on chest

Longhaired domestic

Gizmo is everybody's friend

Gizmo is Hopper's little brother, by 1/2 a year. Gizmo helps himself to the can of Pounce treats once we open it for him. He reaches in with his left paw, scoops one up with his paw and puts it right in his mouth. The treat never touches the floor. I think he's part squirrel!

WATERBURY   06705-1648
Sarah Haines, 11 Richard Ter
Mittens
F, 15, Gray and white
American shorthair Tabby
Fussy and a perfectionist

Mittens – Cat Meteorologist

She came from Essex, Connecticut. Mittens
is very acrobatic. She arches her body on
the banister, when a toy slides towards her.
She loves to perch on top of open doors -
a cat's view to the world.

When we had a tornado, she knew something violent was coming. Her heart was
beating like a stampede. She ran for the
cellar, until it was over. She'd make a
terrific cat meteorologist. She is totally
spoiled with love. We have a bond of love
and trust.

Puff [owner: Katherine Haines]
M, 2, Dark & light grey
American longhair Tabby
Mischievous, cute, lovable
Puff is an unusual cat. He is grey with a
white mask around his eyes, with a raccoon
appearance. My friend's cat had a litter of
kittens - he was the only longhair. He
knows when my bus comes home. He loves
to play hide and seek and tag. His favorite
toys are a crumpled paper, toy rabbit's foot
and milk bottle strip. He sits up on his hind
feet to lick the spoon from cat food. He
loves to snuggle and is fascinated with
bugs. He is my best friend.

WATERBURY   06708

Debbie & Jim Hughes, 925 Oronoke Road
- Unit 36A
Smokey
M, 14, Grey
Domestic shorthair
Very possessive & a free spirit
Smokey is a very special cat. When he
came into my life he was nothing more
than a farm cat. He somehow managed to
work his way up to being a king. He has
somehow accomplished stealing the heart
from anyone that meets him.

He has a very unique way of letting you
know he wants something. Instead of meowing, he stands straight up on his two
hind legs, draws his two front paws together moving them up and down in a begging
motion. Smokey will always be dear to
many of our hearts!

WATERBURY   06704
Karen M. Worden, 178 Hope St
Hopper
F, 3.5, Black, small white patch on chest
Long haired domestic
She thinks she's a prima donna!
Hopper was born in the back of my boy-
friend Tom's garbage truck. The back of a
garbage truck is called a hopper and that's
how she got her name. If you wave your
hand and say "Hi Hopper" she says "Hi"
back (she meows).

If Hopper hears someone coming to our
house, which she usually does before we
do, she growls and runs to the front door.

The only other thing Hopper will eat besides dry cat food is Green Giant peas in
butter sauce, which she loves.

When you whistle Hopper comes and jumps
on your lap. She also likes to sing in the
shower! Hopper will accompany me with a
chorus of meows whenever I sing in the
shower and has done this since she was
small.

Mandy
F, 8, Calico
Calico
Timid but loving
Mandy was abused and homeless when I
took her in. Now she's spoiled rotten. One
day, to get her to eat, I made a game of
sliding and throwing dry cat food across the
floor. She would catch the food with her

paws and put it in her mouth and eat it. When I'd throw it, she would catch it mid-air. She would make a great goalie!

WETHERSFIELD   06109

Greta Johnson, 81 Crystal St

Kristy

F, 14, Black, brown, rusty

Tabby - very silky fur

As a kitten she found me! Having a barbecue she was meowing at the corner of the property when we found her and fed her. Later that evening we were watching television and she came around to the front door, propped herself up and meowed and meowed. What started out as a one night comfort to the kitten has continued for 14 lovable years and still going on. She loves to sit in my lap and massage my belly with her front paws while purring and even drooling at times. She is devoted to me, after all these years. She still does not respond to anyone else quite like me.

Smokey

M, 8, Gray

Domestic

He is the "man" of the house - protecting the house and the property. If another cat dares to bother one of his family (6 other cats and a dog), he runs over and starts to "beat up" the strange cat. Being affectionate is another trait - he will "hug" my arm as I hold him. Far be it from Smokey to allow me to oversleep - he will come over and lightly tap his paw on my face. He also likes to have conversations - as I talk he will meow in response.

MASSACHUSETTS

AYER   01432

Bonnie Snow & Gary Petit, 38 Jackson St Apt #1

Sebastian

M, 1, Grey/black

Tabby?

Spaz, hyper, independent

Our cat Sebastian was an abandoned kitten found in the wild by my fiance's brother when he was approximately 2-3 weeks old. We took him in and he became best buddies with our brother and sister cats Bud and Daisy.

Sebastian enjoys sitting in a full bathtub of water and playing with a straw and trying to swim. His favorite toy is a fur mouse that he will retrieve when thrown. That's right, our silly cat plays fetch! He is crazy but cute and keeps us happy and on guard!

BOSTON   02127

Shannon & Brian McNeil, 7 Dexter St Apt 2

Kato

M, 2, Black w/white spot on chest

Bombay cross?

Very playful

Kato – up to his old tricks

After 10 months he began learning tricks like: lay down, give left or right paw, jump through 6 inch hoop, jump to a 2x4 post - stand on top - then jump down to a specific spot. Sometimes he wants treats and he will start doing tricks and get your attention as he is doing the tricks. He will come up to me and give me a paw or sit up like a circus lion and put both paws in the air like an indian "How" welcome.

He also jumps on top of his 2x4 post on all fours and meows then jumps down to a spot . . . and will continue this until you give him treats. If you don't give him a treat after he performs a command, he is stubborn and just lays there.

Kato has learned a new trick. He jumps up to the 2x4 post, walks across the rope attached to another 2x4, turns around and will walk through a hoop returning on the rope to the 1st 2x4 . . . and will jump through the hoop from the top of the post to a spot on the couch.

BUZZARDS BAY   02532

Laurie Lawson & Robert Williams (fiancé), 3030 Cranberry Hwy Lot 30

Maggie

F, 3yr 7mos, Black

Appears to be part Bombay

Demanding & impatient

Maggie was never one to be coddled or hugged. She loves her "combies" and massages. She is very intelligent and has invented many games. Her favorite is fetch and she will even growl like a dog when you try to take her toy away. She can hiss on command (if in the mood). To get my attention she will whack her tail against the wall; if that doesn't work, she will call out "Mommy" (Meow-eow); and if all else fails, she will proceed to climb the drapes. If I am tired and want to go to bed early, she will grab and bite my legs all the way. If it is cold, she will sleep on my stomach under the blankets. She is truly one of a kind, a treasure. She is my baby.

Sebastian

M, 9 months, White w/ grey tiger stripe spots & raccoon tail!

Unknown

Sweet but spoiled

Sebastian was found by a friend of mine when his mother was hit by a car. Unfortunately, my friend's cat Sabath, was a carrier of FIP and infected poor baby Sebastian. We almost lost him twice to the disease; he has the neurological type which is always fatal. He is thriving on lots of love and attention. He loves to kiss your face and will hug you with his little paws. He is a miracle cat. He has no sense of balance and falls frequently; his brain damage is irreversible. I have never seen a cat with more determination than he. He tries to mimic everything his big sister Maggie does, unfortunately he is getting really good at the naughty ones. He is a very special cat and I would not trade him for the world. P.S.- My sister, Karen, calls him Katherine Hepburn because of the tremors he gets when he tries to move his head too quickly.

CAMBRIDGE   02139

Carol Sidabras, 18 Clary St #3

Buttons

M, 16 dec, Black

Happy, gentle, affectionate and smart!

My Buttons was a charming, devoted and dear friend. He had a special routine of greeting me at the door with a "meow" and a kiss. Buttons would then gallop to his scratching post, stretch his body and wait for me to come and play with him and give him lovins.

He was a terrific ball player, catching and batting his favorite foil ball in mid-air! Buttons enjoyed rolling and sliding across the rug like a snake while being petted. He would give me a gentle tap on my leg if he didn't have enough.

A truly purr-fect friend!

DUDLEY   01571

Linda Demers, 16 Michael Ln

Dimples

F, 2, Brown, dark brown, black & white

Mix - Persian, Siamese + ?

Playful and loving - a people pleaser

Dimples was born to love and be with people. She's not intimidated by guests who come to visit. Her blue eyes and distinctive brown markings make her one in a million. Dimples is very vocal like a Siamese although not a kitten anymore. She still tackles her catnip sock and ball with somersaults. She has an unusual habit of joining whoever is in the shower - she seems very attracted to water. She has made a very profound impact on our family.

LAWRENCE   01842-0834

Sandy J Picard, PO Box 434

Jake

M, 8, Brown and black striped

Shorthair Tabby

Eccentric

I found Jake as a kitten in the middle of the road after being hit by a car that failed to stop. Eight years and 18 pounds later he is still with me. He loves riding in my truck; he stares out all the windows leaving nose prints over about 98% of the glass and fur over 99% of the truck. He will not drink from a dish, preferring to daintily dip his paw into a cup to enjoy egg nog or milk. He always meets me at the door whatever the hour. He signs every card and picture himself by stepping on an ink pad. My Massachusetts license plate is named after him. ("JAKSTR")

Tiger

M, 13, Gray and black stripes

Shorthair Tabby

Eccentric

I had Tiger before I found Jake. Tiger greets me at the door only to escape out the door anytime it is open. He is my own personal alarm clock, using head butts to my face to inform me that he has decided it is time for me to wake up. If that doesn't do the job he has a yowl that would wake the dead and he is smart enough to sit far away so I have to sit up to holler at him.

LEOMINSTER 01453

Carol Kenyon, 123 Winter St

Herman

M, 7, Gray/black/white tiger

Lovable house cat

Loves all people, loyal, very special

My boy Herman came to me on Sept. 10, 1986 while I was working at Fotomat. A customer took him out of her trunk(!) and I adopted him.

After doing some work, I brought Herman home. To keep him apart from my other babies, I put him on the porch with food, water and a litter box. It was a nice September day.

Herman is a loving sweetheart. That Christmas my brothers came up. Herman climbed into my brother's lap, unusual for a kitten to do with a stranger. My brother started an argument. I closed the door to my room. My other brother came to the door saying, "He wants to come in." Herman was at the door. He was saying, "I love others - but I'm loyal to Mommy." It was a beautiful gift. Herman is very special to me.

MAYNARD 01754

Robert A. & Angela M. Derosa, 40 Great Road

Shadow

M, 13, Black

Domestic short hair

Outgoing, not at all shy. Thinks that is

human.

Our cat Shadow is totally in love with our recliner. Since Bob is the only one that uses the recliner he receives all of Shadow's attention on the subject. Whenever Bob is sitting in 'his' recliner Shadow must and will sit in the cradle of Bob's arms for hours! If Shadow feels that it is time for Bob to sit in the recliner he will follow him everywhere crying and crying until Bob either picks him up or sits in the recliner. Although it appears that Shadow is a one person cat, you guessed wrong. I am equally the subject of his affections but luckily have no involvement in his recliner fetish.

We are very sorry for the person that left Shadow at the animal shelter where we adopted him 13 years ago because he is some cat!!!

NORTH ADAMS 01247

Maura & Todd Sumner, 667 Curran Hwy

Babie

M, 7, Black with white spot on chest only

Mixed

Affectionate, loving, funny, intelligent

He's been raised as our child. Our whole family treats him as such. When my parents call, he talks in his own cat vocalizations. Some meows can almost sound like words. He sleeps with us. On cold nights, he sometimes sleeps under the blankets with only his head sticking out on the pillow. Come morning, he knows what time we should be awake. If ignored, he'll lay on our necks to make us get up. After getting up, he goes to the cabinet where his "num-mies" (cat treats) are kept so he can have them for breakfast while we eat.

PEABODY 01960

Maria & Craig Preston, 17 Warren St

Conan

M, 9 months, Brown, black & white

Maine Coon

Playful, unique

Conan is very special to us because of his unique personality. We think he has an uncommon habit because he enjoys drinking only out of the bathroom sink. He will sit by the door and meow very loudly until someone walks by and turns the water on for him; or if you just mention the word "water" to him, he'll just perk right up and run to the bathroom. The water will just run down the side of his face, just enough to get in the corner of his mouth; but he won't care, because for some reason the running water just excites him.

We think the world of Conan. He's a very special part of our life.

WORCESTER   01609
Karen Kovalic & Richard Leaton,   WPI Box 2125 - 100 Institute Rd
Jammer
F, 1, Grey & black tabby stripes
Tabby (shorthair)
Lovable, playful, "sugar & spice and a little vinegar"
Jammer is a quite capable cat. She discovered how to open the pantry door which opened up a whole new world. She learned how to open the lid on tightly sealed jars of peanut butter, and found a liking for "Chips Ahoy" cookies. She actually brings the bag of cookies up to the table to eat. Of course she only does this when left alone.

Jammer also enjoys playing fetch with an aluminum ball.

Furthermore, she learned to open oak drawers on the dresser and removes everything so that she can have a supplemental bed. Nonetheless, we love her.

MAINE

RAYMOND   04071-0523
Betty Welch, PO Box 523
Muffy
M, 17 dec, Pumpkin and white
Maine Coon
Intelligent, conversational vocally and bodily
Muffy was a tiny flea-bitten ball of fur when we got him from an animal shelter. Rather than let him run freely, we hitched him to a line with a pulley like a dog. He was our "watch" cat. He allowed no other cats or dogs in the yard. When his line got caught, he usually could free himself. If not, he'd howl until we helped him. Muffy preferred raw tomatoes to meat. He loved

walking on a leash, through bushes and all, which always left me with scratches on my legs. I didn't mind because he loved our walks.

RUMFORD   04276
Elaine Foley, PO Box 294
Roach
M, dec, Black
Domestic shorthair
A good & kind cat
My youngest son Keith found Roach on the street. So Roach is a stray. He was a good cat and I miss him. My grandkids enjoyed him. When my youngest grandkid fed him, she used to sit by him and eat cat food with him.

Roach kept me company. Roach was always there when I needed him. He always sensed when something was wrong. Roach gave joy to my daughter, grandkids, and whoever else crossed his path. They say black cats bring you bad luck - they are wrong - they bring joy and happiness. I had the cat neutered. I think Roach was lucky to come into my house and world.

Then one day our joy and happiness fell apart when Roach was diagnosed with a tumor in his head and had to be put to sleep. It was hard to get over. I miss him.

RUMFORD   04276
Tampsa Treadwell, 239 Pine St
Kahn Anthaney Touchette
M, 7, Black, white, gray
Siamese
Playful & very short tempered
My cat has many characteristics that others of his family had. His dad had blue eyes like Kahn, and when his temper got extremely mad, his eyes turn red. All of his paws have white on them and he is very playful. He has a distinct, really neat thing about him: on his chest is a lot of fur that comes together to look like a tuxedo. He also sleeps all day long and prowls almost all night. He comes up to me in bed and licks my face.

RUMFORD CENTER   04278
Tonya Cunningham, P.O. Box 132
Tiger
F, 9 months, White, black, silver, brown,

tan
Domestic shorthair
Warm, loving and affectionate
Tiger is very special. She likes to lay down with me and put her delicate head on my pillow and stretch out. Once I was eating chunk turkey and Tiger was sitting on the floor near me. I dropped some and I saw her in it, so I threw it away. When I was not looking, she was dragging it out of my garbage can. What a scrounge! And one night I had London broil and she licked it. She is good. My little brother Peter bought her Christmas presents. Two books, a mug, a note pad and a door hanger. She is very special. She got spayed in November '92. That is why Tiger is special to me.

Miki
F, 9 months, Black
Domestic shorthair
Cold, not too affectionate
Miki is special because she just attached right on to us. On Halloween she was in her kitty room with her sister Tiger. Miki's eyes glow even in the light. She grooms my Tiger. They lay together on my bed. Miki meows if you touch her.
I measure Miki each month. I took out a measuring string and it was moving and Miki dragged it. One thing Miki enjoys is going under my bed and ripping anything in sight. She also makes calls to Tiger. This is why Miki is special to me.

NEW HAMPSHIRE

CONCORD   03301
Ann Zerder, 4 Liberty St.
Rose
F, 6, Calico; orange, white, grey, & black
Definitely a "mama's girl", loves a warm spot and a good sleep. She's my shadow! (always by my side)
We met six years ago as I was getting into my car adjacent to a busy highway. As I was sitting down into the car seat and about to slam the door, a beautiful calico kitten jumped into my lap! She cried with hunger

and the need for a loving companion. I knew right away that she'd be my little girl! My life has never been the same since! Once an avid traveler, I now only go on vacations where Rose is also welcome! I spend as much time as I can with Rose for she truly is my best friend!

NASHUA   03060
Carol Longbottom, PO Box 7906
Callee
F, 4, White, brown, and silver
Mixed
Reserved, very appearance-minded, very ladylike
Callee is very special to me because she can massage me by kneading whatever parts of my body she feels need it. She is double pawed (polydactyl) front and back; she has a pronounced "thumb". She also plays fetch & carry and is an auto bird watcher from "her" window. Her fetch & carry in a ring from a milk bottle, supervised of course, and she will play as long as you are interested. She does enjoy test smelling whatever jar, box, or package you open. Also she enjoys grazing on her pot of kitty grass or my chives on the window sill. She's more of a one person cat and tends to rather like to watch than to participate.

Shadow
M, 7 months, Totally grey (nose & paw pads too!)
Mixed
Very lovey-dovey, out-going
Shadow is special because he was not wanted, along with 2 other litter mates. When I rescued him, he had ear mites (badly), fleas, plus a bacterial infection that later almost cost him his young life. The money I have spent to bring him health is nothing compared to his very loving self and the chuckles he gets from me and his antics. He does eat in a very different way; he takes food, no matter what it is, cups it in his "hand" and puts it in his mouth, water too! He is also the "official kitty greeter" of the household, a title he enjoys.

NASHUA
Denise Muccioli-Brooks & Gary A Brooks
Lady Ashley
F, 5, Grey & white

Domestic longhair
"Queen of the Jungle"
See story in Chapter 7: Wild & Wacky

PORTSMOUTH   03801
Bonnie-Jean Brown, 16 Hillcrest Est
Sir Lancelot
M, 4, Grey, cream
American tabby
Trusting, loving, unusual

Sir Lancelot – at your command

Lancelot is like no other cat I've seen. He obeys voice commands like "stay", "go to your room", and "come". If he wants to go outside, he runs over and taps the doorknob. He travels everywhere with me on a leash and loves people and attention. He's done just about everything - canoeing, bicycling, flying, and sledding. He's been in a car, airplane, and a moped - everything but a train. He loves chasing waves on the beach and our dog. As a kitten he used to ride along in my pocket . . . now he rides on your shoulder.

There's more to this cat than meets the eyes.

Bright Eyes [owner: Edward Brown]
M, 10, Black & white
American mix
Motherly, loving

At six months of age he was found under a bridge presumably in an attempt to drown him. He had a compound fracture of his right front leg and a tear in his ear. Over the years he's lost his top right fang, most of his teeth, and suffered a broken jaw. Despite this rough beginning, he loves everybody and mothers every animal brought into the home.

He's devoted to my granddaughter who's an infant. They'll play together on the floor where he'll allow her to pull his ears, fur, and anything else she grabs. When most cats would pull away or scratch, he purrs and moves in closer.

RHODE ISLAND

BRISTOL
Sharon & Patrick Swist
Opus
F, 1.5, Black & white
Domestic shorthair
Very picky about choosing human friends

Opus is a very happy cat. She wakes us up for her breakfast every morning, and is reluctant to let us leave for work. When we come home, she's right there to welcome us, rolling around and purring as if to say "Welcome home!"

The most spectacular way that Opus shows her love is when I sneeze. She may be occupied or taking a nap, but she always "blesses me" by squeaking out a special chirrup. She doesn't bless my husband, just me.

I wouldn't trade her for anything.

EAST PROVIDENCE   02914
Ruth Lynn, 40 Irving Av #207
Cookie
F, 6, Black/white
American shorthair
Love and companionship we have together.

Cookie has special sensitivities. One time Cookie alerted Ruth to trouble by meowing at her and running into the kitchen. Ruth paid heed to Cookie's beckoning and discovered that the pilot light on the stove was out. Ruth called the Gas Company to relight it, and the repairman later told Ruth that she was lucky Cookie had alerted her!

Cookie enjoys visiting the patients at the attached Health Care Center. Ruth says many of the Alzheimers patients do not remember her name, but they do remember Cookie's name! Cookie's efforts are obviously appreciated.

One smart Cookie

EXETER   02822

Kim Jacques & Joe Kirtlink, 155 Yawgoo Valley Rd - Apt.25C

Boots

F, 1yr 5mo, Black, tan, orange, and white

Domestic short hair

Affectionate, verbal.

We were only to buy fish. When I saw her, I fell in love. This one little kitten of three, sitting in the litter box of a pet store cage, quietly. Now, Boots is family. Each day I learn more about her and myself. I understand each meow when she "talks" to me or answering a question. She's somewhat playful, and very loving. Her favorite thing to do is to curl up under a blanket that's set up like a tent and fall asleep with me, whether I'm in bed or watching TV. Boots brings much happiness.

Tahra

F, 10 months, All white with a grey strip down center of head.

Domestic short hair

Inquisitive, frisky

While outside, a stray white puffball came bouncing towards my boyfriend. When picked up, she'd bite just enough for defense. Her name came to us calling her "Little Terror". Now she's a lovable "stay-puff marshmallow kitty" (nickname). She loves to play, eat, and sleep. She'll play with anything in sight. She eats crackers, Doritos, and even cantaloupe! Her favorite

is popcorn. She sleeps like a normal cat except on occasion we find her sleeping with our two foot, four inch Savannah Monitor. Tahra is a very interesting cat. Having her around keeps us smiling and on our toes.

NEWPORT   02840

Emily Harding, P.O. Box 974

Rudy

M, 4, Blue mackerel tabby

(apparent) Maine Coon

Loyal, friendly, outgoing

See story in chapter 4: The Tricksters.

VERMONT

WINDSOR   05089

Lois Wheeler, HCR 71 Box 164

Munchkin of Star Route #2

M, 9, Grey-black-white

Ragdoll

Hyperactive, funny & lovable

My Munchkin came into my life to fill the void left by the death of my "Patches". He is the only cat I ever bought, after having cats in and out of my life for over sixty years. He has been a comfort and a joy; he doesn't like to be held but cuddles against me during the night. He gets into mischief a lot of the time. What a funny cat he is! My next booklet will be written about him.

Patches

F, 16, Black-yellow-white

Calico

Cantankerous, vocal & spoiled

She came into my life as a kitten about 8 weeks old left in the rotunda of the State Hospital at Northhampton, Mass., where I worked as a licensed practical nurse on the grave-yard shift. She lived among the patients for three years on the disturbed wards. I boarded her for two years with an employee friend of mine from the day shift. Then she came to live with me for eleven years. I wrote a booklet on her life to cope with the grief of her death, "Patches - A Very Special Cat". After 10 years I miss her still!

Chapter Eleven

Who's Who in the Mid-Atlantic

MARYLAND

BALTIMORE   21221-6019

Carol Bostwick, 702 Hyde Park Rd

Chelsea

F, 2, White & blue

Affectionate, clumsy & curious

Chelsea is a large cat who likes to drink water directly from a faucet. Her preference is to drink cool, running water. She'll sit on the vanity every morning waiting patiently for the water to be turned on. We only have a problem when she hogs the sink and I'm trying to brush my teeth.

Chelsea also loves to lay in boxes . . . any kind, any size. It's funny to see her trying to fit into small boxes and half of her body is hanging out. It wasn't so funny the day she sat in a cake box that had a large birthday cake still in it!

Zoé

F, 2, Tabby in white/brown

Loveable, sweet & cuddly

Zoé is a tiny cat who loves people. I guess it's because she was bottle fed. We found her abandoned when she was about three days old. A lot of time was spent cradling and hugging her which made her very affectionate . . . so affectionate that she gets right up in your face, purrs really loud and then licks you on the nose. She's so adorable - except of course when she licks you in the middle of the night while you are sleeping. Sometimes it's hard to get her to stop because you don't want to hurt her feelings.

BALTIMORE   21236

Andrea Head, 4 T D Dunhaven Pl

Ms. Yukey

F, ?, Gray/white

Tabby

Affectionate, curious, mischievous, energetic

My tabbys, Mr. Doós and Ms. Yukey, have a unique way of letting me know they're thirsty. When the craving arises - both cats simultaneously jump up on the bathroom sink and perch themselves in front of the faucet to meow!! No doubt they've trained me that this is the signal for assistance with turning on the spigot. Then it's . . . Bar's open, drinks on the house as usual!

Mr. Doós

M, ?, Black/white

Tabby

Mellow, loving, cautious, impulsive

Mr. Doós is included with Ms. Yukey.

BALTIMORE

Alma Homrighausen

Clancy

M, 8, White/orange

North American domestic

Macho "8-year-old kitten" with maternal instincts

See story in chapter 3: Against All Odds

Scary

F, 16 dec, Gray and white

North American domestic

Timid, but full of ESP

Elizabeth, a recently adopted kitten, escaped to a neighbor's yard where Scary was sunning herself atop a brick wall. As soon as she saw the kitten, she jumped down and began making even smaller circles around Elizabeth, driving her to the hole in the fence so I could catch her when she came through. The next day, when Elizabeth went too far up the fire escape, Scary raced up behind her, jumped ahead one step, turned quickly, and hissed Elizabeth down to the ground. Scary could sense when a vet visit was due and had to be trapped with a trout net.

BALTIMORE   21221

Jennifer Petty, 705 Hyde Park Rd

Toby

F, 13, Tortoise-shell

Proper, affectionate, & superior

Toby is a special cat because she came into our family when I was only one year old. She has been a great role model for me. She regards herself as an upper-class cat who thinks running around acting like a normal cat is beneath her. Occasionally she does bat a toy around, but her favorite thing to do is to sit around looking dignified. If she were a person, I think she would be royalty. Mom refers to her as the "Queen."

We have other pets but she rules the house. When we go out for a little while and one of the other pets has not behaved as she thinks they should have, she meets us at the door and meows and meows as if to give us a full report on what went on while we were away. I think she knows that she is a beautiful cat (and she is) because she's always acting prissy.

BALTIMORE   21227

Kathy Spittel, 2919 Georgia Ave

Kitty

M, 1, Orange & white

Mixed

A " people" cat

Kitty rolls over and over to greet people coming into the house. He wakes up and greets me each morning by sitting on my lap while I'm in the "bathroom"! Kitty also drinks out of a glass rather than a water bowl. We also have a 9 year old Chesapeake Bay retriever, and Kitty has always slept next to him or out on the open floor like a dog, and they often share their din-

ners with each other, and wrestle together. We've often said Kitty thinks he's a dog, and that he loves people and loves to be handled, and his favorite playmate is our daughter Hillary.

BALTIMORE   21221

Legore Titus, 1505 Galena Rd

Garfield

M, 12, Red classic tabby

Household pet

Sweet, affectionate, and slightly cynical

Garfield – a bit of a cynic

Garfield is very affectionate in the morning and evenings - I suspect because that is breakfast and dinner time. His stomach rules his life.

He has lived a hard life when it comes to his health. Garfield has the world's best vet, Dr James Orrell, who has always pulled him through bouts of F.U.S., asthma, and knee reconstruction. He has somehow, through all this, retained his sweet nature.

He has, however, become a bit of a cynic. Whenever he becomes invaded by younger sister cats or dogs, he is very cynical about the whole thing - but his heart of gold always wins out. And he loves them all (well maybe not the dog) . . . but these are the things that make him special.

BALTIMORE   21221

Christina Young, 1503 Galena Road

Jennyanydots

F, 2, Red/brown/white

Patch tabby household pet

Loving and very intelligent

I feel that Jennyanydots (Jen Jen) was truly a gift from God. She is a very affectionate and loving cat - more so than my other two. She follows me around the house no matter where I go or what I do. She is cute and knows it. She knows how to turn on the cuteness when she wants something from me - especially treats, and it works every time. She has even taught her sister to do it, so now when I go into the bedroom, which is where I keep the treats, the two of them double team me. And I just can't stand it, so they get what they want.

Jen Jen has even gotten her sister Funny Face to let her guard down a little and actually play. I never thought I would see that. Jen Jen loves to play with milk jug rings and if she looses one, she knows where I keep them and has figured out how to help herself. She is truly a wonderful friend.

Funny Face

F, 6, Calico

Household pet

Fit for a Royal Family

Funny Face is the star of our house. I show my 3 cats in cat shows. But Funny Face really shines. She has won 2 Morris Awards and many Rosettes.

She is beautiful and knows it. I have never seen a cat so dignified. I think she believes she belongs in the Royal Family. She rarely plays with toys or the other cats - especially if you are watching her. She feels she is too ladylike to lower herself. In fact sometimes she is downright snooty.

But she is a sweet and loving girl without an aggressive bone in her body. And I love her very much.

CAMP SPRINGS   20748-3913

Donna B Scheungrab, 6805 Tall Oak Dr

Sheba

F, 5, Black & white

Mixed

Investigative, demanding, loving, loyal

One way Sheba shows affection to those with whom she feels comfortable and safe is to give them kisses. If someone Sheba trusts gets close to her face and makes kissing noises, she will lick their lips!

Since Sheba is an exclusively indoor cat, she cannot kill mice, birds, etc. to bring home as presents like many cats do. Instead, she attacks her toy fur mouse until she feels it is sufficiently "dead", and then she comes yowling with it in her mouth and drops it at a loved one's feet.

COCKEYSVILLE   21030

Frank & Christine Frisch, 1M Reldas Court W

Axl Rose

M, 3, Grey, black & brown

American Tabby Shorthair

A very mellow and sweet cat

Axl is special to us in so many ways, but one in particular comes to mind: the love that is shared with the three of us. For example, when we feel bad, he knows how to cheer us up in his special way with his head rubs and purring - or talking to us when he is hungry or wants to play. The love runs so deep for our Axl and the happiness he brings us.

COCKEYSVILLE   21030

Debbie Smith, 7-C Reldas Ct

Tigger

F, 2, Orange tiger

Domestic

Playful, friendly, and lovable

Our two year old cat, Tigger, is very special to our family. Besides being lovable and playful, she does some interesting tricks. When she wants my attention, she will sit up on her hind legs and "scratch" at the air towards me, similar to a dog begging. When she wants to play, she gets her favorite toy, her toy football, and drop it at my feet or on my lap. I throw the football across the room and Tigger retrieves the toy and drops it at my feet or lap for me to throw it again and again!

Anyone for football?

ate it. She had oxygen, fluids and Mucamist (antidote for Tylenol toxicity) for a whole weekend and part of Monday in late Jan/early Feb 1993. She is well and back to normal.

A Ninja Kitty

COLLEGE PARK   20740-2479
Barbara & Richard Furlani, 4800 Berwyn House Rd #322

Bentley

M, 2, Tabby w/mostly white

Maine Coon/domestic shorthair mix

Affectionate, curious, acrobatic, comical

Bentley, "Ent" for short, is a very special cat. He is the acrobat of the household doing four-footer door jamb jumps, four-foot leaps to grab his kitty tease. He plays, what I call, "Ninja Kitties" with Jasmine Bibette. They spin, run, leap and chase each other through the apartment. He enjoys stealing pens from the table, Barbara's purse and tubes of mascara from her purse.

Our little fluff ball was entered in one TICA cat show last November and took home a rosette from one ring as the fourth best longhair household pet. He is the upcoming star of the story *Bentley: An American Plume Tail*, due in spring of '93 issue of *I LOVE CATS*. The story was written by Barbara Furlani and a sequel is on its way soon.

Last, but not least, is Bentley's language. He trills the most beautiful notes, "Breeeeewowwwwoweee" or "rrrreeeeeelllllll". Our little "Ent" is very special.

Jasmine Bibette

F, 10 months, Torbie w/white

Maine Coon/domestic shorthair mix

Playful, curious, talkative

Jasmine is very special because she is alive now, through the grace of God. She found a fallen Tylenol on the floor and somehow

She is playful as ever and enjoys her "boyfriend" Bentley's company. They are so cute together and trill and sing and play their "Ninja Kitties". She also loves to beat up the bathtub faucet every day. Jasmine doesn't like to be held and will let you know by growling.

DUNKIRK   20754
Jennifer Girardi [daughter], 2705 Apple Way

Oscar

M, 1.5, White & black

Affectionate, playful, loving, loyal

Oscar came to us as one of 5 abandoned kittens. His purpose was to mend our daughter's broken heart from a boyfriend break-up. Shortly after arriving, Oscar and my husband were in the recliner. Unbeknownst to him, Oscar got down and crawled under the chair. Dan got up. The chair snapped into an upright position. Oscar's head got caught. The snap was so forceful, he got a concussion and his head lay tilted to one side (for 2 months!) Dan disposed of that recliner.

The Vet had doubts of Oscar's survival. When he finally came home, every night I gave him his medicine, then he would snuggle into my neck and go to sleep. Since then, at bedtime, we still snuggle, and once, when I was injured, Oscar never left my side.

Trinket [owner: Jo Girardi]

F, 10 months, Calico

Playful, VERY curious, fearless and amusing

Purrs constantly. "Trinket" got her name because she was a tiny Mother's Day gift from my daughter. However, considering her interest in *t*elephones, maybe she should have been named for the telephone operator, "Ernestine"!

When she hears the wall phone ring, she jumps on the kitchen counter and stretches her paws up the wall, trying to get the phone. When the standard-type phone rings in the bedroom, she tries to stick her head under it . . . looking for the bells, I guess. There is also an answering machine attached to this phone. When she hears the buttons on the phone, she starts walking on it. When the calls are done for the day, frequently you can find Trinket retired under the table . . . the one that holds the telephone.

ELLIOTT CITY   21043

Amirah Rahim, 7978 Brightmeadow Ct

Rose

F, 1, Blue point

Siamese

Very inquisitive

Rose is special because she can (and likes to) floss her teeth. When my mom calls "wanna floss?", Rose bounds upstairs and jumps on the bathroom counter. My mom has to tear a really long piece of floss so that she and Rose can share. As my mom is flossing her teeth, Rose grabs the other end of the floss and drags it through her teeth with her paws. After she is done, my mom gives Rose a cup of water and says "empty that when you're done." When Rose finishes drinking she pushes the empty cup in the sink. That's her way of emptying it. Rose was not trained to do this (except for emptying the cup). She just started doing it. Rose looks forward to flossing each day.

KENSINGTON   20895

Kristen Keppel, 4030 Glenridge St

Gandhi

M, 1.5, Black with copper eyes

Bombay

Affectionate, playful, energetic, and immensely loving

Gandhi's swift rise to international recogni-

The first male Bombay born in France

tion ever since birth hasn't for one minute affected his sweet personality and craving for affection. He's the first Bombay male born in France, in the seaside port of La Rochelle. His father, Bagheera, and mother, Opium, were imported from the United States. Before deciding to own me, Gandhi appeared on French TV5 veterinary special and posed for a national cat magazine. Gandhi subsequently decided to own me - an American in Paris - an accompany me all over the world. Together we've been all around France, Switzerland, and the United States - all before Gandhi's second birthday! His favorite spot is the Pope's Palace park in Avigrion, but no matter where we are in the world, I can count on waking up to find him keeping watch beside me.

LANHAM   20706

June Hogan, 9901 Greenbelt Rd #203

Billy

M, 4, Black & white

American longhair

Very curious, given his past, a little nervous, a little bit of a bully, too, with my roommate's cat.

Billy loves to help me answer the door and the telephone. He also lets me know if I've forgotten something on the stove. I've burned many eggs, but never had a fire!

In the past year, I had three operations and he always kept my spirits up, especially when I wanted to give in. He seemed to know when I was feeling down. He still does.

Recently, during my Christmas vacation, when I had him neutered, I was able to stay with him at home afterwards to take care of him. I feel a little better knowing that I repaid some of the love and affection he's shown me in the last two years.

MOUNT RAINIER   20712
Louise Holton (Co-Founder, Allies Cat Allies), PO Box 397
Adam / Morgan
M, 2.5, Black & white
Alley cats (domestic shorthair)
Formerly feral - now sweet & loving

Adam & Morgan (top) climb to new heights

HELPING AMERICA'S ALLEY CATS
This is the story of Adam and Morgan, two black and white alley cat cousins from Adams Morgan, Washington, D.C. They are very special cats because their capture led to the first national organization to be formed in the United States to help other alley cats and kittens like them.

First, Adam's story: Very wild when I trapped him as an 8 week old kitten, it took two days to tame him! He just loved the petting and the food! Adam has a wonderful nature, he is very sweet and gentle, and two years later, he just loves everyone and has lost most of his feral instincts. His markings are very unusual, he looks like a black and white cow!

Morgan is more feisty. He took a little longer to tame and still has some feral instincts left. He's addicted to being petted, and will jump on me from every angle no matter what I am doing! He is very demanding for affection and cannot get enough!

POTOMAC   20854
Dianne Schaeffer, 13305 Beall Creek Court
Nathan

M, 17, Black with white chest and toes
Parents were stray farm cats
Friendly, loving, very tolerant of all people and animals
Nathan was raised in a houseful of cats, dogs, and children. He was most attached to his mother, Natasha. When Nathan was 8 years old, Natasha was dying at age 10. Natasha spent her days on my daughter's bed with Nathan often at her side, grooming her. No type of food I made would interest Natasha, but every day about 4:00 pm Nathan would bring a freshly killed mouse to the garage. I would carry Natasha down and Nathan would watch his mother eat the mouse. When Natasha died, Nathan sat on her grave for weeks mourning his mother.

Mikey
M, 3, Black and grey tabby
Long haired
Very loving, trusting, friendly
Mikey is a very special cat who belongs to a very special girl. At 4 months, Mikey underwent a very delicate operation and at 1 1/2 years had an eye injury. My daughter Laura, who was 10 years old when she got Mikey, took excellent care of him and spent hours reading Mikey stories while he recuperated. When Laura was diagnosed with dystonia and was in and out of the hospital for tests and operations, Mikey returned her devotion. Every time Laura came home Mikey stayed by her side, cheering her, consoling her, and strengthening a very special bond of love.

SILVER SPRING   20901
Sharon L Ludwig MD, 10307 Ridgemoor Dr
Tano
M, 15, Black
Domestic shorthair
Smart, attention-loving, hyper-vigilant
Squeaker
F, 15, Red tabby
Domestic shorthair
Sweet, gregarious (with people), not too smart
See story in chapter 7: Wild & Wacky.

SILVER SPRING   20906
Carol E Sawtell, 15311 Beaverbrook Ct Apt 3-B
Tiger

M, dec, Grey stripes
All American kitty cat
Funny, loveable, curious, very smart
See story in chapter 3: The Good Samaritans.

Gypsy
F, 5-1/2, Grey, gold, black
Maine Coon
Independent, sweet, sleepy
We were lucky to come just in time at the animal shelter. She had been declawed and was an ideal apartment kitty. She has trained us so that we operate on her schedule. Unfortunately she does not like to ride in the car, so she stays at our son's home when we travel. But she adapts well. We have had her for almost 3 years.

NEW JERSEY

ABSECON   08201
Jean & James Thumhart, 27 Mattix Run
Jezabelle
F, 2, Orange/white
Tiger
Playful & cuddly
Jessie, as we call her, is very, very special. I found her as a stray kitten and decided to bring her home for my new husband, as I already had 2 "one-woman cats" of my own.

I don't recall how we discovered her special skill of fetching, but she fetches "Starlite" candies. She will only fetch if it is thrown from our bed, and she will bring it back onto the bed! Our other two special ladies, Tigger and Cheetah, await the treats Jessie has earned for them all!

Although I brought her home for my husband, she is very much a mamma's girl and loves to snuggle anytime I sit still - even in the bathroom!

Tigger
F, 5, Tan/black
Tiger
Independent/chatty
Tigger has been my best friend for the past 5 years. I got her while I was living in Missouri. Both her parents were barn-"mousers". She is quite large in size - as

though she goes outside (but never does).

She has moved to Colorado and three times to New Jersey - staying with me in hotels and traveling in the car. She talks a lot, especially while I'm on the phone - she thinks I'm talking to her! She waits on the bathroom counter each morning to be brushed and loved. She truly is my closest and dearest friend.

BARNEGAT   08005
Patrice Horton, 27 Capstan St
Taffy
F, 13, Black. rust, tan
Tortiseshell Calico
Sweet, gentle, loveable
Taffy is a people cat. She loves to sit on my lap while I'm watching TV and have her head scratched. She taught me the game of fetch the bread twist tie. After she sampled several slices of bread (through the wrapper) she brought me the twist tie. I threw it - she got it and brought it back!

Taffy also thinks she's a mountain lion. Quite a jumper, I usually find her on top of my kitchen cabinets. When I'm getting ready to go to sleep, she "talks" to me non-stop - "Hurry up! I want my treats." I love her!

BASKING RIDGE   07920
Barbara Koberlein, 11 Bradford Ln
Rascal
M, 15, Orange/white
American Shorthair
Easy going, lovable, out-going
Rascal is 16 pounds of pure love and affection who thinks he's the king of his harem. Eight years ago a kitten was tied up in a box and left by a garbage can. Fate soon brought her into my life. She was deformed and cripple so she could not stay in a shelter and no one wanted to adopt her. When I brought Tippy home, Rascal adopted her. He washed her, protected her, loved her. She slept snuggled against him; she was safe. Tippy quickly became one of the girls thanks to the "Big Guy" who was her Guardian Angel.

BAYONNE   07002
Jerri Zdancewicz, 119 W 19th St
Rusty

M, 5, Rust & white

Part Maine Coon

Calm & personable

Rusty was found outside in the rain. He went through surgery and treatment for a long time with the vet. In spite of all this, he emerged with a warm, lovable nature. He loves to be petted - loves to lay on my bed and sit on my chair. He is soft and furry and has adapted well to our household. Because of this he definitely is a special cat to us. We love him very much.

Midnight

M, 3, Black with white spot on belly

Part Norwegian forest cat

Lovable

Midnight was found as an outside cat. I fed him outside and decided to take him in. I was afraid he would not adapt well to my other cat . . . well, they tolerate each other.

"Middy" is very lovable with people and loves to be petted. He loves watching TV on the couch. He is soft with long legs and a bushy tail. We love him!

BRIDGEWATER   08807

Sandra Campbell, 502 Milltown Rd

Spunky

M, 2.5, Gray and black Tabby

DSH

Quiet & very loving

Spunky has gourmet tastes

There really are two Spunkys.

Spunky the normal cat loves to run, play with fake mice, watch the birds and fax machine. His taste in food is up-scale: pasta only with tomato sauce, bean sprouts, cauliflower, grapes, peanut butter, and, his favorites, watermelon and cat food.

The volunteer Spunky visits nursing home residents. When Spunky is "working", he's a charmer, curling up in laps and napping, giving unconditional love and attention to his friends.

Spunky is a Delta Cat, and we are a Pet Partner team. We were recently honored by being asked to represent Pet Partners at a jewelry promotion at Bloomingdale's in New York.

CLARK   07066

Bonnie Masters & Mary Jane Costa, 22010 Gibson Blvd

"Buster"

M, 4, Blonde

Mixed/domestic

(Human!!) nosey, Don Juan, athletic, persistent & superior - spoiled too!

With the grace of a cheetah and the speed of light, he will charge through the rooms, into the kitchen. Like a baseball player stealing home, he glides across the floor with the greatest of ease! Wasting no time at all, he pulls open the cabinet, exposing his favorite delicacies!! While admiring his greatest "Evel Kenival" stunt, sticking his chest out like a decorated soldier, he babbles for our approval!! Purposely ignoring his cries for attention, we sneak around the corner, only to hear this crashing sound as if a box of cereal had just expired!!! No matter what ...... he always gets what he wants!!!!!!!

"Spanky"

F, 4, Black & brown Tabby with party-white stripe

Mixed / domestic

Extremely sensitive, independent, needy & fearful, loving & caring

Like her brother, Spanky was an orphan: unlike her brother who craves attention, she is independent. In order for us to vacuum, one of us takes her into the bedroom, lays on the bed and surrounds her in stuffed animals. The TV is turned up loud, to muffle the sound and our arms embracing her like a newborn. This ritual forces us to become creative, like getting down on all fours with a brush to clean our carpet. Whatever it takes to avoid her greatest fear, we're willing to do because she's our little girl.

DELANCO 08075

Agnes M Scaramazza, 413 Kansas Av

Raggs

M, 4.5, Gray w/silver

Domestic longhair

He has a split personality.

After our Persian of 16-1/2 years died, it took four years to finally convince my Dad to get another and Raggs was it - 6 weeks old and a holy terror, biting and scratching. My parents wanted to get rid of him, but I said he'll grow out of it. He is mean but in a nice way and a real comic.

My Dad was laid off for awhile and Raggs was his enjoyment away from the worrying. Our lives have been happier now that he's here and we wouldn't think of sending him away. It's amazing how an animal can change your life.

FORKED RIVER 08731

Jacqueline Keiper, 4 Orlando Circle

Gizmo

M, 6, Black, silver, brown

American shorthair

Playful, protective, affectionate

My Gizmo has a very strong personality - from the day I brought him home, we knew who was boss. He sleeps at my side each night and whenever I move, he makes sure I know I disturbed him by meowing in my face and patting my cheek.

He has also over the years developed strange eating habits. This past Christmas he decided he liked milk chocolate. He now steals chocolates. If he gets caught, he walks away rather indignantly.

Fluffy

M, 5, White

Longhair

Affectionate, loving

Fluffy is the most loving and tolerant cat in the world. My best friend's 2 year old loves to play with him. Unfortunately he pulls Fluffy across the floor by his tail. We've tried to stop it but Fluffy seems to enjoy it. Fluffy is also the family clown - always managing to fall off whatever he happens to be laying on.

GLASSBORO 08028

Janice Saltenberger, 128 S Main Apt B

Azrael

F, 6, All black!

4th generation generic alley cat

Loyal, friendly (to me), loving, adaptable

My best friend and most cherished companion is my girl-cat, Azrael, a.k.a. The Rasta Girl, a.k.a. The Acid Cat. She is both vocal and physical in expressing her love for me. See, in the mid 1980's we found Pooketha, an orange/white, sickly, half-drowned wretch of a cat in an empty lot. Her black/white/orange/mottled daughter, Mog, was a loyal member of our family, for many years, who enjoyed jumping from floor to our shoulders or licking the milk from our cereal bowls (which Azrael does now).

Mog's daughter, Muffin, belongs to my father now. When I was a college sophomore in the fall of 1987, Moggie had Azrael, who I brought with me from New Jersey to West Virginia. She has moved with me into at least 6 different homes in both states since then, leaving at least one son, Scratch, in West Virginia.

Azzie, like her mother Muffin, enjoys drinking from the bathroom sink ("watering the cat"), jumping to the highest seat in the apartment, usually on top of the refrigerator and loving me very much. She now rules the roost over Gabriel, Pixie, Badger, and the 6 or 7 strays who live around my apartment.

HACKENSACK 07601

Jane Prosser, 25 Grand Av Apt 2E

Beau

M, 8, Gold & white

Domestic shorthair

Very gentle, sweet & loving, & beautiful

My cat, Beau, is a "golden cat". Every morning when the sun rises, he jumps on my window to look out. He is very sweet and affectionate. Every night, he follows me to bed and "makes bread" or "kneads" on my white sheepskin rug next to my bed. I pet him and he purrs - he has done this ever since he was a kitten. He waits for me to get up in the morning (usually on my bed), and we have breakfast together. While having my morning coffee, I let him out on my balcony to see what kind of day it is. He is my faithful friend and follows me all around. Beau, like his name, loves beauty. We have a very pretty apartment and he is very content here.

At Christmas time, he loves to sit next to the tree and bask in the glow of all the gifts. He loves to play with his ball and catnip toys. Sometimes Beau likes to sleep with my mother, whom he loves, too. He likes to spread his affection around evenly. He is a very clean cat and really very beautiful. Beau is the "light of my life."

HILLSDALE   07642
Alison & Keith & Brian Whitman, 4 Lesa Lane

Maximillian

M, 3, Red

Abyssinian

Outgoing, affectionate, adventurous, curious

Max performs all the normal Abyssinian tricks such as fetching, climbing great heights and leaping from the floor to a standing person's shoulder. However, he also likes to play catch with both paws. His favorite toys are plastic rings, small foam balls and scrunched-up pieces of paper. If these are thrown above his head, he makes sensational leaping catches as a soccer goalie would. He also jumps from the floor to the top of an open 7' door. He will sit watching his owner through the glass shower door, waiting for her to emerge so he can jump onto her shoulder and rub his head all over her wet hair. The owner has learned to reach for a towel as she gets out of the shower.

Veronica

F, 4, Red

Abyssinian

Ladylike, well behaved, loving

Veronica, who has the same mother and father as Max, does not perform the same athletic feats. However, she is obsessed with rolled socks and packets of artificial sweetener which she steals and carries all over the house in her mouth.

Both cats have learned to growl when anyone comes to the door. They also have a strange reaction to the sound of a comb cleaning the hair from a brush or the strumming of high G on a guitar. They both retch violently as if choking.

JACKSON   08527
Catherine Demko, 25 Rhode Island Dr

Brutus

M, 4, White and orange-yellow

Domestic shorthair

Shy, a loner, and dumb like a fox!!

One afternoon I saw our cat, Brutus, chasing a squirrel in our backyard. As I watched mesmerized, I then realized that they were only playing tag with one another. After an extensive workout, the squirrel went over by one of our trees and started digging furiously for nuts. Brutus studied the little guy very intently from the sideline. Suddenly, our cat started digging right next to the squirrel! It looked like he was trying to help. I don't know if either one found any treasure, but when the squirrel left, Brutus came inside, ate, and then promptly took a nap!

Daisy

F, 1.5, Brown, black & white striped Tabby

Domestic Shorthair

Smart, talkative, lovable, comical, and a bit of a fighter

A woman came to adopt one of our kittens. Daisy and Samson were left. The woman immediately fell in love with Daisy, but Daisy had no intentions of going anywhere under any circumstances. She fought us both tooth and nail and clawed her way out of the makeshift carrier. She hissed and spit, did a feline war dance, then ran and hid from us. Samson quickly settled this problem by jumping into the box. When they left, Daisy peeked around the corner with the biggest smile on her face, then surveyed her domain with the "I belong here" attitude.

LAKEWOOD   08701-6487
Helen L. Onderlinde Jr., 711 A Dorchester Dr

Samantha Socks

F, 2, Grey/black w/white front

Domestic shorthair

Talkative, nosey, lap cat, & bossy

Samantha came to our house as a 8 week old kitten from Jersey Shore Animal Center. Together we battled a U.R.V. she came down with. Amazingly, at 10 weeks, she knew what medicine was and spit it all over me.

Sam is boss of the house, knows the routine and cons her way into getting her own way. She loves to dip her paws in my bath water and lick them dry. Sam is an indoor cat only, but chases the birds window by window through the house. This is her favorite game - so much so - she'll skip meals.

A real bird lover

She is spoiled rotten and shows it and knows it . . . and knows she is loved very much.

MONTCLAIR   07042
Robin Engle, 30 Franklin Pl
Squint
F, 4.5, Calico tabby
Domestic
Playful & devoted
Squint joined the family while I was pregnant. She and her litter mates would all sleep packed together on the top of my belly! Black and orange tabby colorations on her face made her look like she was squinting, thus her name. Squint likes heights and our shoulders. She'll perch there and ride around! Being a very small cat, only 5-6 pounds, that's OK. She gets to my shoulder by leaping, unannounced, from wherever she happens to be - floor, bed, mantle! She has startled us (and houseguests) several times, but she has never hurt anyone!

Wiley
M, unknown, White
Domestic
Crafty & wiley!
Wiley was a stray. My neighbor thought he was mine and returned him. My fiancé said he'd take him home. Before Tim could get him, Wiley left. One year later, Wiley

returned. Tim did take him home! After we married we moved to another town. Two years later we bought a house one mile from our first apartment. One day Wiley disappeared. Our old neighbor called to say she had a visitor. It was Wiley! For the next year he made regular visits to her. She would feed him table food, then call us to come and get him. Wiley is no longer with us. We're sure Mrs. M. decided he liked her home (and food) better!

NEW BRUNSWICK   08901-2710
Ann Ledesma, 49 Comstock St
Bupka
M, 9, Ebony ticked tabby
Half-Burmese, half-mixed breed
High-strung, sensitive, loving

The official greeter

When my family comes from Europe to visit, our extra-toed tabby, Bupka, is our official greeter. He goes right to them, snuggles up, hugs necks, and follows them everywhere. He seems to know when humans need a special loving touch. His tricks with his big many-toed paws make everyone smile; for instance, he takes cat treats from the container and puts them right into his mouth! Relatives have told me that when they first came here they felt nervous and disoriented - until Bupka helped them over the rough spots and made them feel they belonged.

NEWTON   07860
Peggy & Joe Capp, 1 Hicks Ave Apt 1
Bud
M, 12, Black/brown/white
Mixed

Always happy/curious

We adopted Bud at our local ASPCA when he was a kitten. Within a short time, we started to notice he was running into door frames or walls when he would play. Our veterinarian discovered that Bud had inherited a disease that was quickly causing him to go blind. Bud's other senses have more than made up for his blindness. His hearing and sense of touch are so acute, that he barely seems impaired. He is also very intelligent. In five minutes we taught him to climb up and down from a window perch. He investigates everything.

Two years ago, Bud also developed diabetes. Now he eats a special diet and receives an insulin injection daily. He is always happy and has given us so much love. He loves to be hugged and talked to and petted. We will never know another cat like bud.

NORTH BERGEN   07047
Patricia L Allegretta, 9052 New York Ave
Mitsu
M, 1.5, Champagne
Burmese
Playful, comical, sensitive, lively, clever

Can you imagine a cat that fetches pipe cleaners, balls, and various toys? Well, that's Mitsu! Not only does he fetch these articles, but he then cries to inform one to throw it again so he can fetch.

He also poses for pictures. When he sees the camera, he sits and looks right at the camera.

Finally, Mitsu responds to his owner by blinking his eyes when his owner, Pat Allegretta, says "Mitsu, I Love You".

NUTLEY   07110
Bette Baer, 633 Franklin Ave - Suite 146
Kelly
F, 13 dec, Calico
Longhair
Friendly, loveable

My Kelly was the prettiest little Calico cat, predominantly black with a black mark down her nose. She loved me so much and when she wanted to show me how much, she would climb up on my lap, walk up my arm to my face and go crazy while licking my lips. It was like she was kissing me.

She was always there for me and I was

there for her - holding her beautiful face in the crevice of my neck when she took her last breath.

George
M, 4, White - champagne on back
Shorthair
Scaredy-cat

My George is such a handsome boy who thinks he's a dog, since he once lived with dogs. All I have to do is call him and he comes running to me and sits down in front of me as if to say, "Yes, you called?"

He sleeps with me every night on the covers between my legs and wakes me in the morning by washing my hair with his kisses. He is extremely jealous and possessive of me and hates it when people knock on my door because the scaredy-cat must go hide.

PARAMUS
Patti Pecoraro & Keith Massimi
Bandit
M, 3, Black & white
American shorthair
Perky & attentive

Our cat Bandit is an extraordinary and beautiful animal. His tiger tail toys are his biggest joy in life. He carries them in his mouth wherever he goes while playing with them. When he is tired, he even brings them in his bed and uses one as a pillow while hugging it. When he awakes, if we mention the word "treat" he perks up and will stand on his hind legs and tap our hand for the treat to fall out. We taught him that when he was 8 months old. We adopted him from Bergen County Animal Shelter at that age. He was so sick and now is as healthy as an ox. All in all, Bandit is the best thing that we could ever have!

Buster
M, 5, Grey & white
American shorthair
Wise & bold, affectionate

Buster is our cat we took in from outside. He has been around for awhile, and looked like he had a very tough life. We cleaned him up and gave him a lot of love. He is very trusting now and likes to lay on laps while purring loudly. He doesn't ever go out now. A window open is all he prefers. We also taught him the "treat" trick like Bandit does. He is the elder in our house and the other cats respect that. If he doesn't want to play, he lets them know and they listen immediately! We really adore him!

The Elder Statesman

PISCATAWAY 08854

Carla Shoppe, 26 Lenox Ct

Bamama

F, 3?, White/gray

Domestic shorthair

Peaceful, mellow - little playful

I first found her in the woods; next found a home for her 3rd batch of kittens; then had her fixed. By this time she was so used to my apartment, she wouldn't go outside if you opened the door. She usually will sniff at the door, but if go to grab her - she runs and hides.

First she hated (hissed at) my ferrets. Five months later she started to play with Stingray (ferret) who would run up around the cat, tease her, then run away. Bamama would then hop like a ferret and follow her by hopping behind.

When my alarm goes off in the morning, she jumps up and gently taps my face with her paw until she sees me get up. The Cat Alarm Clock! She also watches TV for periods of time.

Spider

F, 1.5, Black

Domestic shorthair

Adventurous & outgoing

He prefers to be carried upstairs. When he's carried, he puts his paws around your neck like a baby and hugs you. But outside he runs, puts his head to the ground - eyes wild - then runs up and tries to tackle you - by the same motion of paws around - but around your ankles or legs.

He loves riding in the car, but if he's in a cat carrier in the car, he cries and digs (like he's trying to dig a hole to get out!)

PITMAN 08071

Margaret D Wilkins, 33 Woodlynne

Starman

M, 3, Seal Point

Himalayan

Easy going - take me anywhere

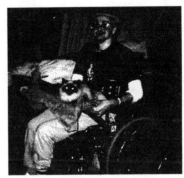

Pet therapist

Starman is special because he does "pet therapy". He visits people in nursing homes, retarded children, people in wheel chairs and paraplegics. He has been visiting homes since he was 8 weeks old. Starman was three, May 18, 1993.

I have seen Starman bring people out of depression and hopelessness. One time, while visiting an old man who was dying, a nurse asked me to put Starman in the bed with the man. When I did, the man smiled and spoke for the first time since he had been placed in the home. He is a special cat.

RIDGEFIELD PARK 07660

Lotte De Roy Van Zuydewijn, PO Box 438 - 118 Bergen Av

Stringfellow de Roy van Zuydewijn

M, 18 months, Orange stripes, white bib and white feet

American shorthair (real breed unknown)

Very adaptable and affectionate

See story in chapter 3: Against All Odds.

ROBBINSVILLE   08691
Francine Mayer, 306 Meadowbrook Rd
Nooc
M, 4, Grey w/white
DSH
Very affectionate & friendly to all
I've had many cats over the years, sometimes up to 4 at a time! Once in awhile one
will stand out as being "special". When that
extra special cat "Coon" passed away at 15
years old, I thought it would be a long time
before I was lucky enough to find another
"special" cat again.

We went out to get a kitten to replace the
void "Coon" had left in my heart and
named him "Nooc" (Coon spelled backwards). My 4 year old daughter was constantly with him and it was clear to see a
strong bond was occurring between the
two. Nooc never let her out of his sight and
at bed time he would climb onto her, knead
and suckle on her nightgown till they both
fell asleep. It was quite a sight to see this
kitten on her suckling away noisily!

We mentioned it to our veterinarian and he
thought it might be because the kitten was
taken away from its mother prematurely.
We were told he was 6 weeks old when we
got him, but our vet seemed to think he
was more like 4 weeks upon examining
him.

We all thought he would soon outgrow his
unique behavior, as any kitten would upon
being weaned. But at 4 years old, he still
continues his nightly ritual of suckling her
nightie! My daughter loves the "special"
treatment even if it means changing into a
dryer nightgown in the middle of the night!

Some of his special traits are that he runs
to the door to greet everyone (even strangers) much like a dog would. He is very
friendly, and always wants to be the center
of attention. We've had 4 new cats since
Coon's passing, and Nooc by far has
earned the reputation of being our "special"
cat in the household in his own special
way.

Coon
M, 15 dec, Classic tabby w/white
DSH
"I'm the boss"
[See Nooc's story above.]

ROCKAWAY

Ginny Aboyoun
Cat
M, 2, Mackerel stripes
Mix
Maniac
From the start Cat adopted Rocky our Pug
as his new mom. "Cat" tried unsuccessfully
to nurse from the dog. He did however,
learn how to sit and shake hands. He never
quite mastered cleaning himself but does
often join one of us in the shower. His
favorite toy is a Q-tip. He will play with
one for hours. His best trick is disconnect-
ing the answering machine. We thought the
machine was to blame until we caught Cat
red pawed. He had stepped on the record
button and left the incriminating message of
a jingling bell and loud purring.

RUNNEMEDE   08078-2002
James Saltenberger, B2 Presidential Ct
Apts
Muffin
F, 8, Silver grey
Mixed
Loving
When Muffin was at the Vet for spaying,
they called and told me that she was ready
to be sent home. When I got there, the help
didn't want to let her go with me. They
said they had never had such a loving cat
before.

I live alone (divorced) and she is such a joy
to be with, really a faultless cat. I can't list
a single problem with her - unless purring
too much bothers you.

SALEM   08079
Penny L Crissy, # 30 Jericho Rd
Percy
M, 2, Silver classic tabby
Scottish Fold
Affectionate and docile
This letter is to tell you about my Percy.
What makes him so special to me is that he
sits around our house like a little person,
and he will stay that way for hours. He
watches t.v. that way, too. He also has his
own high chair that he sits in like a child.
Friends that come over can't believe it. At
the present time, 7 cats share my home and
everyone's personality is completely differ-
ent, but we all live together in harmony.

My cats are the loves of my life, and I will never be without a few.

I do enjoy a nap after a good meal

WESTVILLE   08093

Theresa McEvoy, West Park Apts - Apt A-3

Willie

M, 2-1/2, Black, gray & white

A nut, picking & fussing

I got Willie when an ex-neighbor threw him out into the hallway - so I brought him in. Somehow I just spoiled the cat. I try to get him to the vet, but I have a little trouble controlling him. He has calmed down a little bit now.

Willie will jump around and is a fast runner. He loves to purr and meow all the time. When people come to the door, he runs and hides underneath the chair or somewhere else. Ten minutes later he'll come out to check out the person. He's an indoor cat and loves to look out of the window to see everything. He even likes to run to the window - back and forth - when neighbors come to the window.

NEW YORK

ALBANY   12206

Susan Clover, PO Box 6779

Sugar & Honey

M, 3, Tan and white

Quiet, passive, kissable

My cat, Sugar & Honey, saved my life! I had been sleeping in the parlor in the morning. At about 8 am, my boyfriend had gone to work. At about 9 am, Sugar & Honey awakens me by licking my face. I get up - I smell gas! My boyfriend had forgotten to turn off the gas burner and the wind blew out the flame!

BAYSHORE   11706

Rose Knight, 156 Third Ave

Willie

F, 2, Black and white

Mischievous, lovable, angelic sunshine

Willie was born blind, but she doesn't know it. She has a large vocabulary and always lets me know what she wants. Willie loves music; she plays the chimes in my kitchen. She sees through her ears; they rock back and forth when she is studying something. Her sense of smell tells her who is who. Willie has six playmates (cats). They all treat her as special as I do. Willie is very gentle; her playmates have learned not to use their nails when playing with her. Cod liver oil is Willie's favorite treat. Her hair is like rabbit fur. Willie rarely leaves my side.

BRONX   10462

Ann McManus, 780 Pelham Pkwy S #A6

Johnnie

M, 1, Grey, white

Abyssinian/Tabby

Friendly & curious

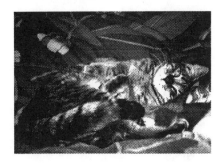

I won't get up till the coffee's ready

My cat Johnnie, or "Long John Silver", was found near my building, and right away he was very friendly, purring and rubbing on your leg. He was accepted by the other cats and even adopted by an older cat, Dusty, who had already adopted a kitten before. Johnnie behaves more like a little brother than a cat. He would be bratty one minute and sweet another. His favorite foods are cheesecake, potato chips, donuts, and eggs. Sometimes he likes coffee. He likes to watch birds by the window sill with his "father" and "sister" cat family and sleep on my bed at night too.

Dusty

M, 3, Grey

Russian Blue

Loves everybody and silly

Dusty is special because he loves everyone. Though he was a stray, he is very friendly. He adopted a female kitten - Kitty who is now one year old, but she is still groomed by Dusty. He likes to jump up and put his paws around people's necks, as a hug. Whenever there is a visitor, Dusty must get petted by them. He likes to stretch, plop, and then roll over - which is the way he lays down. He likes to sleep under covers, with just his head sticking out.

Nikki the hearing-ear cat

BROOKLYN   11214

Inga Ammon, 126 Bay 25th St

Nikki

F, 3, White & grey & black - like tiger striped

Common

Very alert and smart

Nikki knows I'm deaf and she wakes me before the alarm does by putting her paw on my chin. Also when someone knocks on the door, she comes to me and walks to the kitchen like she is saying "someone is at the door". She is a real smart cat - also lovable.

BROOKLYN   11219

Rita Bagala, 1035 64th St

Popeye

M, 3, Tabby stripe brown/black

Tabby

"Doglike", loving, playful, demanding

Let's play ball

Poyeye's stray mother Munchkin was pregnant, hungry and very affectionate in January 1990. He was the runt of four, and got extra attention from me because of it.

As a kitten he'd watch me walk my dog Brandy, till finally I took him along, on a leash. He loved it! One day after playing ball with Brandy, Popeye brought me the ball and waited. I threw it laughing and he brought it back! We "play ball" every day now. He wakes me mornings by digging in between my right side and arm and kneading my upper arm, meowing indignantly if I am not "accommodating". Brandy has since passed on, but Popeye, Munchkin and sister Pixie are very happy together.

Pixie

F, 3, Black & white

Tuxedo

Devilish like her name

Pixie's favorite game is knock hockey - always using her water bowl as her "puck". She's not happy till she's helped "wash the floor".

As a kitten from a litter of four, she won

my heart when at four weeks, she climbed onto the bed, nestled into my neck, and fell asleep. Her two sisters live together in Virginia, and Pixie's mom and brother live with us. She earned her name by acting impishly, and talks incessantly. She's my sweet little airhead!

BROOKLYN 11229

Marlene & Ira Berkowitz, 2828 Kings Hwy Apt 6G

Shani

F, 8-1/2 mos, Gray tabby w/blond highlights

Domestic shorthair

Bundle of love who just loves to play, though is a bit more clingy to "mommy" (Marlene) than her sister. She is a happy kitten with her tail in the air all the while purring.

Being the baby of the two sisters (in personality, that is), Shani just loves to be held and loved by "mommy". She will actually stand up on her hind legs, lifting up her front paws, and then squeaks (her meow) for me to pick her up. She then curls up in my arms, on her back and goes to sleep.

Together, Shani and Rivke will break in the bathroom door, while I'm showering, by standing one on top of the other and pushing in. Both sisters are very loving with one another (and their parents), falling asleep while hugging one another.

Shani & Rivke love the water

Rivke

F, 8-1/2 mos, Gray tabby w/mink highlights

Domestic shorthair

Bundle of love who is the more maternal of the two. She also tends to go to people more easily, talking to them, with her tail in the air.

Rivke is very protective of her sister, Shani, with her running to lick Shani whenever she might yelp. While both eat their canned food from our hand, Rivke is quite fond of homemade chicken soup, having been nursed on this (due to illness).

Both Rivke and Shani love to go to the sink, but Rivke sticks her head under the faucet. Rivke also loves to jump for foam balls, catching them mid-air with her front paws. When Rivke's collar comes off (while playing) she has carried it in her mouth to be put back on, meowing to "mommy".

BROOKLYN 11202-0045

Bernice Thomas, Box 022083

Cheryl Jean

F, 3, Flame Point

Himalayan

Friendly and affectionate

Cheryl Jean is a third generation trick trained cat. She is extremely dog-like. She follows me everywhere; she's leash trained, comes when called and she like all of my cats can do 20 or more tricks. I breed Persians and Himalayans for intelligence and gentleness. Cheryl Jean is the perfect example of what my breeding program represents. My cats are never under any circumstance given food as a reward or treat. My cats are intelligent because they want to be intelligent and they want to please me.

Angel

F, 3, White

Persian

Friendly, affectionate, intelligent

My cats are highly trained. They jump through hoops, over hurdles, they come when called. Angel can "sit up" on command. All of my cats are leash trained. Why are my cats so uncommon? Because they accomplish these things without the use of food as a reward!! My cats are highly trained and they enjoy pleasing me. What is the most difficult trick I ever taught my cats?? Synchronizing my four Persians and Himalayans to jump through hoops!! This is extremely difficult and requires cats of superior intelligence.

CANTON   13617
Robert & Mary E B Latimer, R3 - Box 295
Rufus
M, 8, Mostly grey w/white markings
Unknown
Aloof, demanding, at times aggressive, independent
Rufus is our eight-year old house cat. Until two years ago, we didn't know he was uncommonly intelligent. He has found a way to come and go as he pleases! He enters the garage through a pet door, then through the furnace-room to a small door that he can open into our living room, by simply pushing it open with his nose. When he wants to go out, he has learned to open the small door by pulling on the knob, keeping it open by quickly putting his head through the door - and out he goes! The tiny door was made for easy access to fireplace wood.

CENTRAL ISLIP   11722
Christine Catalano, 45 Adams Rd
Shadow
M, 14 dec, Black & white tuxedo
Domestic shorthair
A gentleman and a charmer
Shadow cared a great deal about his "family", which included another cat (Willow) and myself. Although he was timid with other animals, he was quite courageous where we were concerned. One day, Shadow and I heard a cat's terrified cries outside. It was Willow, cringing in fear on the terrace because a big tom was threatening her. Shadow became frantic, throwing himself at the screen door, trying to get out. I let him out to see what he would do (planned to intervene if necessary). Shadow planted himself between the tom and Willow, while I called to her from the open door. She ran inside to safety. Meanwhile, Shadow tried to face down the tom, but looked more and more uncertain what to do. I called to him, and after the tom scratched Shadow's nose, he came bounding back as well. The next day, Shadow continued his "terrace patrol" as usual, and the tom never returned.

DOUGLASTON   11362
Paula Manjoras, 242-51 51st Av 2nd Fl
Marble

M, 2, White / dark gray
Domestic longhair
Human - a flaky south-paw

I'm Bronxese

Marble was found in an alley in the Bronx. He was one of 5 beautiful kittens. People always ask me if he is some special breed because of his beautiful face and long hair. I tell them he's Bronxese. I don't know where he developed his gift for gab. He "talks" to me in different sounds and inflections. He also comes, sits, and begs on command and eats his food by scooping it up in his left paw. He turns the doorknob when he wants to go out on his leash. He greets me everyday when I come home with a forceful headbutt. He's quite the companion.

ELMIRA   14905
Sue M. Rogan, 712 West Water St
Kai
M, 9, Red Point
Siamese
"Laid-back", shy with strangers, tenacious
Gentle stroking or scratching are okay, but this guy prefers more vigorous caresses! Kai likes to be "thumped" from head to toe - one flat hand on each side. He accompanies this unusual
"affection" with loud purring and tail-puffing, moving back and forth so I don't miss a spot! I sometimes worry about injury since Kai really loves very earnest "thumping". He complains bitterly in his un-ignorable Siamese voice if I forget this nightly routine! Unusual behavior? I think so! I wish I had a camcorder to capture his

hilarious "startle reflex" - a slight foot movement when he's unaware results in a spectacular stiff-legged jump about two feet off the floor!

Mairu

M, 11, Seal Point

Siamese

Very affectionate, unpredictable, aggressive

An urgent call! Another dash to the cattery from which the "star boarder" had escaped over two weeks ago! However, the fugitive had disappeared once more. After coffee and condolences, I headed sadly for my car. Two glowing eyes appeared across the street. "Mairu, is that you??!" A flurry streak flung himself into my arms. Redolent of manure, scratched nose and skinny, he meowed my tears away, promising nevermore to roam. But now, pushing twelve, he still eyes the door. Maybe I should have named him Marco Polo!!

ENDICOTT 13760

Barbara Korbler, 516 Woodford Av

Holli (Daze Mischief)

F, 9, Black/white/tan tabby

Mix - longhair, silky fur

Friendly, a sweetheart

Daze knows how to get ready for bed

When my husband and I were first married, we kept the door to our bedroom shut at night so our three cats (his, mine, and ours) were excluded. One night, as I was washing-up before bed, I heard Rudy talking to Holli. She was lying on the bed and he was warning her: "If you want to stay the night, you'd better make sure you don't want anything to eat or drink, and that you don't need the litter box. Once we close the door

- that's it!"

I heard her jump down off the bed. She walked out toward the kitchen, where we had a bowl of dry food available. A few minutes later, I heard her scratching the walls of the litter box. As I looked out into the hallway, she came wandering down into the bathroom, where she took a drink. After she finished, she walked back into the bedroom and jumped back up on the bed.

ENDICOTT

Stacey & Bill

Buggs

F, 1, Calico like w/orange stripes

Mother: tiger - father ?

Loving - playful

When we went and saw the litter of kittens, we picked her out because she had green eyes; but when we picked her up and held her the eyes turned blue. Now that she's an adult her eyes don't change as often but her coloring has. She's Calico colored but her mother was an orange tiger, so she has orange stripes which you can't see unless you're looking for them; and on one side her whiskers are black and on the other side white. She is a big part of our life. She fills it with love and joy. Although she hasn't done anything unusual, she's ours.

ENDWELL 13760

Erma Parisella, 608 Lowell Dr

B F ROSS

M, 9 months, Black with wide gray stripes

Shorthair

Fascinating, bright, independent, loving & cuddly

My cat is special because he retrieves as well as any dog. His record is 32 retrieves with 3 short pauses. He chases only Dum Dum lollipops!

B F Ross was rescued when he was 4 weeks old. His foot was broken and had healed improperly. It stuck out at an angle. Dr. Allen performed corrective surgery and they named him Broken Foot. I added "Ross" making him extra special.

B F Ross licks my wrists and elbows and neck if there is a scent of perfume. One day I sprayed Chantilly on my toes. Yup! -- He licked them -- silly cat!

Mike

M, 3, Orange Tiger

Shorthair
Unpredictable, independent, "cool"
Mike goes for walks with total strangers.
He gently wakes me up EVERY morning at
4 am (5 am - DST). He does all his indoor
sleeping - flat on his back - legs usually
straight up! And he does his sun-bathing on
top of anybody's car or van - belly-up! If
you bend over for whatever reason, Mike
is on your back. Stay bent for any length of
time and he's fast asleep. Stand up fast and
his claws are in your backside!
P.S. Mike loves chicken soup.

HENRIETTA   14467
Elizabeth M Noce, 1546 Erie Station Rd
Regan
F, 14 dec, Blue Point
Himalayan
Intelligent, beautiful, unforgettable
See story in chapter 2: The Good Samaritans.
Francis
M, 19 dec, Red
Mixed
Loyal, loveable; a friend, he loved life.
[included as noted above]

HURLEYVILLE   12747
Kris Conklin, PO Box 109
I just call her **"Kitty Girl"**
F, 4 approx., Orange/white tiger
Domestic shorthair
Loving, friendly, very intelligent
See story in chapter 2: The Good Samaritans

KIRKVILLE   13082
Ann M Parody, 7190 NYS Route 298
Oscar B. Parody
M, 3.5, Orange/white
Domestic shorthair
Temperamental but lovable
Oscar, an 'only' cat, was adopted on December 10, 1989. Since then, he has become very habitual. Oscar greets me each
afternoon by meowing, rubbing against my
legs and leaping into my arms to give me
'kitty kisses'. After his hellos, he sits on
the living room floor to stare at me until I
pick up his favorite toy, a feather teaser, to
play with him. When he's tired he flops

onto the floor, paws dangling in the air, a
cue for a tummy rub. At bedtime, Oscar is
never far behind. He climbs onto my pillow, kneads my head and falls asleep.

Anyone for a tummy rub?

LARCHMONT
Gerry & Ed Muir
Otis
M, 7, Orange (with white feet)
"Persian tabby"?!
Brave as a lion, sly as a fox, more fun than
a barrel of monkeys!
Otis is our rascal redhead -- gorgeous,
greedy, good-natured and articulate. His
distinguishing marks: a white freckle under
his nose, a brown thumb on his right hand
and a giant raccoon's tail. When bored
overnight, Otis attacks our clock radio and
rocks the room with music. (He claims he's
looking for WCAT.) Yes, Otis can talk.
Sample vocabulary: "Hi." "Out." "Hmph."
"Who -- ME?" The year Otis arrived, our
son started college in August. Our dog died
in September. Our daughter got married in
October. Then Otis joined the family,
filling the empty nest with nonstop love and
laughs ever since! We couldn't live without
this guy.
P.S. My maiden name is Morris, but Otis
is definitely smarter than that kitty!

LIVERPOOL   13090-1726
Joseph Wilson, 6511 Ealing Ct
Ling Ling
M, 5, Black & white
Maine Coon
Regal & arrogant

I'm ready for my walk – are you?

Ling Ling is a large (nineteen pound) cat with long hair, large tufted feet and neck ruff. He will meow softly as a kitten for attention and does not hiss but rather growls at his adversaries Not a lap cat (no way). He flops down on my feet, on his back, fore legs stretched out, to be rubbed on his chest (my dog). On command "sit and stay", he will - to be hooked up to his collar and lead for a walk or to be hooked to the wire and pulley (dog run).

MEDINA   14103
Trudy L. Moyer, 12241 Million Dollar Hwy

Spooky

F, 3, Orange & black

Dark Calico w/ split face orange & black

A mama's girl; smart & elegant attitude.

Here are a few things that make my cat Spooky special. Her looks are one. She's a dark Calico, with a split face, with one side black and one side orange. A typical Halloween cat. She will cry in the morning while I'm looking out the front door, so that she can look out with me. So I have to pick her up to let her look out. She's fascinated with the outdoors. For playtime she will find the littlest thing on the floor and bat it around like a crazy cat, and to end it, she has to mess up every rug in the house. Her favorite trick is me patting myself on my chest, saying "Spooky come on". And she'll jump into my arms. She also sleeps next to my chest every night. She feels content.

Snooks

M, 6, White, gray

Seal-point Siamese

Garfield personality, very mellow

Snooks is a very special and lucky cat. He was raised by a pet turkey (Percy). His mother left the kittens in the turkey pen. The turkey thought the kittens were his. Whenever the kittens would run toward the road, Percy would gobble and the kittens would come running back. When Snooks was 2 years old he got hit by a truck and now only has 3 legs. When he was 2-1/2 he was neutered. At the age of 3 he had feline urological syndrome twice and is on M-caps for life. Now he is strictly an indoor cat that has bright blue eyes, the markings of a seal-point Siamese and weighs 15-20 pounds. But he thinks he's the king of the house and has a very mellow attitude.

NEW YORK   10010
Dorothy Breen, 40 Waterside Plz - Apt 20H

Beauty

F, 3, Silver & black w/creamy tummy

Scottish Fold

Shy, sweet, absolutely adorable

Beauty is special because she just is. I say God named her because he made her so beautiful. No other name is appropriate. When I'm watching TV she watches also. Usually on her back with her front paws folded. Sometimes she tries to catch the movement on TV.

She kisses me goodnight and then goes and curls up on the bedroom chair. She also wakes me in the morning. And she loves cream and always asks for it when her dish is empty. My life is richer since Beauty.

Whiskers

M, 13 dec, White & black striped

Domestic shorthair

Gentle. He was my gentle man-cat.

Whiskers picked his own name. He was 2 months when we got him and he was in an Irish household, so we were trying to find an Irish name for him. He was in the kitchen eating Friskies on the naming day. He ran into the living room with Friskie crumbs on his whiskers. I said to my husband, "Oh, look, Friskie Whiskers." He (the cat) smiled first at me and then at my husband for picking out a very appropriate name for him. He died at age 10 from inflammation of the stomach lining.

NEW YORK   10013-4777

Denise Shane, 182 Hester St

Maxine (a.k.a. Max)

F, 4.5, Tri-color: blue, cream, white

Calico - domestic shorthair

Polite, gentle & empathetic

Two years ago Max fell out of my window due to insufficiently fastened screens - 5 stories to the cement sidewalk below. She survived, suffering a fractured hip and other less serious injuries. She was an excellent patient, recovering fully.

Recently, I was injured and wrote the following:

"My cat Max is my best nurse. Last year, I took care of her when she broke her hip. Now that I am laid up with a bad back, Max takes care of me. She sits on the bed with me all day and meows if I'm out of bed too long. Sometimes a cat is a girl's best friend." [published in *Why I Love My Pet, National Enquirer*]

Patient turned nurse

Dusty

F, 3.5, Grey-mackerel tabby

Domestic shorthair

Curious & Quirky

Dusty is unique because of her way of looking at things. She does not enjoy being looked down upon because of her stature, instead she finds a high perch from which she can look down for a change of perspective and to measure up her friends, guests, etc. The rest of her reasons are obviously food related, but who knows.

NEW YORK   10023

Janet Waggener, 134 West 72nd St

Tuxedo

F, 12-1/2, Black & white

Domestic shorthair

Sweet & non-aggressive - an artistic "fraidy-cat" who can't stand to leave home.

Tuxedo performs own composition

Tuxedo, named for her looks, is also appropriately named for her talent: she plays the harp.

Around 7:00 each morning, she awakens her owner with a "Breakfast Concerto" on a large concert harp. In the evenings she asks for a snack by clawing or teething the strings of a smaller folk model. While some of her compositions resemble those of John Cage, others consist of more classical melodic fragments repeated over and over.

Between meals she plays with no agenda other than her own evident enjoyment. She helps her person practice by playing duets and believes that any music on the household sound system is controlled by her tail-baton.

She claims several harpists from Juilliard as colleagues and friends.

Pixigatto

F, 1-1/3, Black & white (tuxedo type)

Domestic shorthair

Wired neurotic who tries.

Pixigatto was rescued from a 48-cat household to keep Tuxedo company (after Tuxedo's sister died).

She saved Tuxedo from severe depression just by appearing, and is slowly learning to tolerate HUMAN contact.

She invented "fetch", or so she believes, and will spend as much time as her person can tolerate chasing and retrieving a fur-covered button. She either bats the toy back, or spins and leaps to catch it out of the air in her teeth. Perhaps she's a reincarnated baseball player.

P.S. She WANTS to play the harp, too, but Tuxedo won't let her!

NORTH TONAWANDA   14120
Lori Kilburn, 1748 Ruie Rd
M.Y.O.
F, 3, Ruddy
Abyssinian (Grand Premier)
Outgoing & assertive

An Abyssinian named M.Y.O. (mine, yours and ours) is one of the few cats registered and certified as a Delta Pet Partner in the pet assisted therapy program. We work with a not-for-profit group called "Friends From the Heart" in Buffalo, New York. . . bringing smiles or therapy to many people in nursing homes and human service organizations.

When M.Y.O. is home relaxing and waiting for breakfast, she has learned how to step on the answering machine. This triggers voices to make sure her owner is up and ready to feed her on M.Y.O.'s command.

POESTENKILL   12140-0130
Lorianne K Winslow, PO Box 130 Main St
Bimbo
F, 2, Gray & white
Domestic shorthair
Aggressive dog-like character; watch-cat

Hi, my name is Bimbo Winslow. I'm just an energetic bundle of fur. My parents call me a watch cat, as I growl at strangers that come. I also do it to my parents. They think they're fooling me, but I know who they are. I just keep them on their toes.

I also follow them around all day just like a dog. I don't think they can tell the difference. Mom and Dad think they trained me to come on command . . . pssst . . . don't tell them, but I come because I want to. After all I get what I want each time - love, patience and understanding. Of course that dog treat and catnip are nothing to pass up. I'm not stupid.

Another trick is to give kisses on command. I have two kinds of kisses I give: regular (lick) and nip kiss (special). My nip kiss is special cause I know the tone of voice Mom uses when she expects a nip kiss.

Peaches 'N Kreme

F, 4, Calico
Longhair (domestic)
Lovable

Hi, I'm Peaches Winslow - older sister of Bimbo. I'm the lovable sweet cat. I don't think I'm as much of a problem as my younger sister. I'm very timid when it comes to company. As soon as a car pulls in the drive, I'm running upstairs as fast as I can. Sometimes I get going so fast I slide on the dinning room floor and miss my cat door to go upstairs. Then in my excitement, I almost get stuck in the door. Mommy laughs but I just give her a dirty look and be on my way.

Mommy's a sucker for my big green eyes. It's shortly after I find comfort in her room, that she's up there giving me hugs and kisses. Boy do I have her wrapped around my paw or what! One thing about my mom is each one of us four sisters get equal time. We've decided to keep Mommy anyway.

POMONA
Paul And Jane Zippilli
Scarlet
F, 5, brown and white
American Shorthair (Tabby)
Attentive, conversational, active, maternal

Can you help me to my seat?

Scarlet is a very special cat for many reasons. She lives with my husband and me and our two other cats, Gambler and Eastwick. Scarlet is a very attentive cat. She comes to the rescue when Gambler and Eastwick have a scuffle and we pretend to be crying. She always has to be in on any conversations. She will take "her" seat at our kitchen snack counter and pay close attention to everyone.

Scarlet stays close to us day and night. She is very special to us. She is very loyal, loving, and intelligent. Scarlet is also very vocal and demanding when she wants attention. She loves for my husband and I to play with her. Her favorite toy is a little white furry mouse which she will chase and retrieve for as long as we can keep throwing it for her. She opens cabinet doors, then peeks in as though she needs something from inside. Scarlet's photograph has appeared in Cat Fancy magazine twice, and a photo of both Scarlet and Gambler was in the 365 Cats Calendar of 1990. We love all three cats with all of our hearts.

PORT CHESTER
Sheryl Badolato
Wagner
M, 1.5, White/smokey gray
?
Loving, playful, creative

My cat was given to me the day before my husband and I got an accepted offer on our first house. At that point he was my good luck charm. It's hard to pick out only one story when EVERY DAY he makes us smile. One day my father and brother were changing the dryer vent in the house. The dryer was away from the wall enough for a cat to fit through. A few moments after the old vent was removed, Wagner stuck his head out of the hole in the wall to be greeted by the three of us outside!!

POUGHKEEPSIE   12603
Kim Borell, 9 Mainetti Dr
Daisy
F, 23.5 dec, Black & white
Domestic shorthair
Caring, loving & devoted to the end

The night that Daisy died was the first time ever that I felt left behind. Daisy was with me for 23-1/2 years - since I was 5 years old.

When she was a kitten I taught her to come to me when I whistled. I could whistle for her, not knowing where she was, and she would come running. Daisy followed me almost everywhere and if I would get too far ahead of her, she would cry and I would wait for her. Above all, when I cried

Daisy would listen and understand, like no one else. It was not easy for me growing up with juvenile rheumatoid arthritis. Daisy was, in many ways, my strength - and I think she knew that.

Daisy – my strength

Even on her last day she tried so hard, weak as she was, to walk to me. This time though, I had to be strong for her. I held her close and told her that it was ok for her to close her eyes - that I would be all right and I would always love her - always.

SPENCERPORT   14559
Barbara & Edmund Woods, 5 Rene Dr
Maxmilian Maximus Woods
M, 9, White
Longhaired White & odd-eyed
Affectionate but arrogant

Max the Cover Cat

Max was a cover cat for Pedigrees Catalog. He demonstrates high intelligence by:
1. pressing the phone buttons or computer

keys to get attention.

2. leads guests to food, opens cabinet and places paw on the food container.

3. with human parents he places his paw on their mouth to indicate hunger.

4. critiques piano students by lifting his tail vertically and leaving the room when they make errors.

5. sits in his own chair at the table and draws food toward him with his paw.

6. demonstrates affection by hugging parents and friends with both paws wrapped around their necks.

SPRINGWATER 14560-0317

Barbara A Carney, 7978 School St

Miss Kitter Kitty Carney

F, 3, All white short hair

Mixed breed, "Barn Cat"

Very smart

Tricks are my trade

My cat does tricks. She sits up, gives me her paw, and kisses me when asked. I tell her to lie down, stretch out, and roll over, and she does. I say, "Get in the baby buggy." - she hurries in. I say, "Get on the clothes hamper." She digs on the bedroom door to get to the hamper. When I tell her to say, "MEOW!" - she does. I put treats on her paws - she won't touch them until I pet her head. I say, "Smack out loud!" Her mouth moves around and around and you can her smacking loud. (She should be on a commercial . . . smacking for cat treats.)

Miss Katter Katty Carney

F, 2, Gray tiger - short hair

Mixed - "Barn Cat"

Playful & loving

She was also a barn cat. She was about 3 months old when I got her. She is very affectionate. She is a gray tiger named Miss Katter Katty Carney. She does tricks: sits up like a dog and stretches out when told to. I say, "Lay down!" - she does. I put food on her paws and say, "Don't touch it!" When I pat her head, then she eats it. She does tricks like a dog. Maybe she thinks she's one? Miss Katter Katty is playful . . . and she loves me.

STATEN ISLAND 10314

Marie, Pat & Frank Ballweg, 87 Woodward Ave

Li'l Orphan Annie

F, 11, Black - with white chest & legs

Domestic shorthair

Smart, alert - loves to show-off

She was found at the age of four-weeks in a barn on Staten Island, N.Y. She knew how to defend herself and put her front paws in a punching position like "Little Orphan Annie" did in the comic strip. Thus there was no question as to her name.

Today she enjoys life with the Ballweg family in window sills and on captains' chairs, overseeing activities; especially in the kitchen. She has learned several tricks - sitting on her hind legs for several minutes and rolling over two times upon request. What a pal!

See poems in chapters 1 & 7.

STATEN ISLAND 10301

Jeanne Ferrantino, 460 Wooddale Ave

Sable

F, 2.5, Black

Cornish Rex

Loveable, mischievous, sociable, friendly, "all around sweet-heart".

Sable, my cornish rex is so sweet, even those nasty cat haters love her! Sable is extremely sociable and loves company. When the doorbell rings, she runs to the front door. When our guests are comfortable on the couch, Sable adopts a knee for the evening! Sable loves to play dress-up for the holidays. Friends look forward to the funny Christmas cards Sable patiently poses for. One cold winter morning, Sable stole my heart when I saw her sitting on the floor with her front paws atop the baseboard heater, purring, purring, purring

- she'd found heaven on earth!

Even cat-haters love Sable

STATEN ISLAND   10309

Philip Gebbia & Rebecca Sandbek, 65 Burton Ave

Kitty (Boom)

F, 4 dec, Black/white

Domestic longhair

Sweet & gentle

Kitty (Boom) began life in a cold horse stable. As a hungry, dirty, but sweet cat; she was fed by hand by Phil because the big cats ate all her food. Her sweet personality won Phil's heart - so one wintry day she came to live with us.

Such table manners!

Kitty's most unusual trait is that she joins us at every meal. As a young cat she was curious about what went on at mealtime; tail to one side, sitting on her haunches, with her paws resting on the table, she sits and watches.

Her nickname "Kitty Boom" comes from her grand entrance into a room. She walks in and "Boom", lies down hard. Kitty also comes when called (usually!)

Postscript . . . On March 17, 1993, Kitty had to be put to sleep after a brief illness. She died quickly of renal cancer. My heart is broken, as she was in my life only a short time.

WOODSIDE   11377

Diane Moss, 41-46 50 St

Isis Ming Regina

F, 12, Cream colored w/ dark brown points

Siamese/seal point

Shy and subtle, whose passionate purr is a paean of love and joy

Isis was abandoned by a garbage dump in Valhalla 12 years ago with her friend Saki. She is a dainty and demure creature who adores Saki and grants him full permission to rule the roost.

Saki recently spent a day in the hospital for minor surgery and after his triumphant return home that night, Iris passed by and gently greeted him with an almost invisible touch of her body. She always mourns his absence from home, however brief.

Watching them at play, witnessing their somewhat fierce fights and seeing them peacefully nuzzle as they sleep together, envelops me in a tender, loving bond with these wondrous animals.

Saki Wu Chang

M, 12, Cream colored with dark brown points

Siamese/seal point

Bold, bossy, wildly funny and enormously possessive

Saki is a macho seal point whose accelerated antics always let you know when a full moon is in bloom.

I recently thought that he had fallen out of a window because he couldn't be found anywhere and it seemed to be the only available route for his disappearance. I frantically concluded that he had finally committed hari kari. But he had only leaped into a dish closet where he gave his ignominious presence away by rattling some of the utensils as he tried to fit his rather large self into a small place!

He is generous, gallant, affectionate, absolutely zany and a fabulous feline friend.

WYANTSKILL   12198
Liz & Frank Bonesteel, 209 West Sand
Lake Rd
Velcro
F, 2-1/2, Grey/orange
Grey tortoiseshell
Clingy & wild at times

Velcro in the news

Velcro is 2-1/2 years old. She was dropped
off in the woods near our home when she
was only 3 months old. She found her way
to us and immediately "attached" herself to
us thereby obtaining her name of Velcro.

She is very interested in everything that
goes on and in everyone she comes in
contact with. Whenever we travel, we
always find a pet store and bring home a
toy mouse. When we arrive home she
greets us and then paws through the carry-
-on luggage to find her mouse.

In the winter Velcro has to make sure that
when it snows, it is snowing at every window in the house (both upstairs and downstairs!) Her favorite game is "Where's
Velcro?" She jumps into a box and we
walk around saying, "Where's Velcro?"
When we get close to where she is hiding,
she crouches down until we pass by. As
soon as we pass by, up pops her little head
to see where we are and when we turn
around, she hides again. After a few times
of this, she jumps out and runs to us like
she is saying, "Here I am!"

Velcro is a great pet and a wonderful
friend. She wins the hearts of everyone she
meets, even if they aren't especially fond of
cats.

YONKERS   10710

Linda Stahl, 90 Spruce St - LB
Ginger
M, 1, Red/white
Stray
Silly, fresh, playful
From just strays, 10 weeks old, he kissed
my nose and fell asleep, adopted me, then.
Sits anywhere and everywhere he feels like
it, like a statue. Cries when you do not
play with him. Lovey-dovey when I come
home. Runs to bathtub to play. I pull his
tail and feet and he loves it.

He loves "Mr. Spider" (black & red toy).
Climbs up the walls, at nothing or a spot
on the wall. Rides on Sam (black & white
Persian stray) like a cowboy on a horse.
Attacks Stacey (grey 10 year old), then the
water bottle comes in use. Lets the mail fall
on his head. Eats string, rubber bands,
balloons, etc., which I now hid.

I'm in control!

Lets me know when someone or something
is outside by looking and crying. Has a
meowerr you would not believe. It is not a
meow, not a purr. It starts softly and goes
into a full blown meow and yowl combo.

PENNSYLVANIA

ALTOONA
Ginger
F, 1, Gold & white
Playful, independent, social, mischievous

Golden Retriever

Our cat Ginger, who is a gold and white long-haired cat, is special because she fetches a ball. When Ginger wants to play "fetch", she will bring her ball to us and patiently waits for us to throw it. When we throw the ball, preferable into the kitchen, she will retrieve it and bring it back to us. We play this game until Ginger or we become tired. We affectionately nicknamed her our "Golden Retriever" cat.

ERIE 16502

Barbara A Severance, 2202 Poplar St

Patches

M, 11, DLH Tabby

Norwegian Forest

He talked to you, hugged & kissed you

Patches was raised on a farm. Born in March of 1982 in Brookville, PA. A friend had given him to me when he was 8 weeks old as a surprise gift.

I took him for rides with me in the car. On occasion I gave him baths, in the kitchen sink. Even though I got soaked he gave me hugs, and I gave him kisses in return. After a bath he rubbed up against me and slept on my lap. At bedtime he slept inside my left arm. He got very sick, now he's resting in peace. I will miss him very much. He was my friend and my pal, and I will remember him always.

Misty Blue

F, 8 months, Black, sandy w/white

Persian/Himalayan

Highly energetic/imaginative

When I got my kitten he sat in the palm of my hand. He was born in Spartansburg, PA on March 15, 1992. She sleeps in the bathroom sink and plays with water there. She plays with the plastic ring off of a gallon milk jug.

Misty has turned into a junk food junkie. She likes pork rinds, mushrooms, pizza etc. She's a strange lovable friend and pal, with many more years of pleasure ahead. She's a real hot ticket.

FOLCROFT 19032

Tara Healy, 15A Grant Road

Nicky

F, 2, White, gray, brown, yellow

?

Mischievous, frisky, loving

Nicky is a sweetheart. She is loving and gentle to Tara ONLY (she tolerates everyone else). She doesn't go too far away from Tara. When Tara calls her, she does it the way you would call a dog - and Nicky responds. She does not respond when using a cat's call. What makes Nicky unique because she is a thief . . . There isn't a morning that goes by that Nicky hasn't carried something into Tara's bedroom. If Tara or the whole family goes out, you can bet there will be something in the girl's room. This could be anything from newspaper to a piece of candy from the candy jar. If nothing is readily available, Nicky takes napkins or bills from the bill box.

Dusty

F, 5, Gray - long haired

?

Quiet

Dusty is a one or two person cat - depending on whatever mood she is in. She is quiet and gentle, slow in moving. Dusty is not in a hurry to do anything or go anywhere - except when someone goes into the kitchen. Let me tell you she knows where her canned food is kept! She paws at the door until she gets it open then uses her paw to pull a can of food out. (The canned food is only used as a special treat once or twice a week.)

When you speak to Dusty she wags her tail - I guess to let you know she is listening. Dusty and Nicky get along well and their usual play time is about 10 p.m. We all love our cats are glad that they are part of our family.

HARRISBURG   17109
Vicki & Tom Gingerich, 4924 Wyoming Ave
Clinton
M, 9 months, Orange tiger striped
Domestic shorthair
He is high spirited, fearless and very loving.
Clinton is a little comedian. His little antics keep us amused everyday in spite of the fact that he has a virus and is on medication. He likes to play fetch with us. He is not afraid to interfere with our dog, Monty, when playing. Clinton (named after the new president) is a big eater and he likes to steal cat treats from our other cats, Lucy and Tyler, who are older than him. He also likes to steal meat off our plates when we are not looking. Clinton will always hold a special place in our hearts.

Tyler
M, 1.5, Black & white
Domestic shorthair
He is very affectionate.
I'll never forget that day in October 1991 when my husband and I went to the Humane Society of Harrisburg, PA. We came across a cage with kittens we liked. As the volunteer opened the cage, a black & white kitten grabbed onto the cage door as it swung open as if he was saying "please take me". We thought that was so cute that we decided on him.
Tyler just loves to lay around in his pet taxi carrier. He always watches when I'm putting on makeup in the morning so he can steal a Q-tip to play with.

HUNTINGDON   16652
Mary Ellen Shetrom, RR 4 Box 253
Tiger
M, 12, Black-brown tabby
DSH
Loving & caring about me
On April 8, 1988 I discovered a special cat. I had an aneurysm of the head. I had two cats and they tried to get in my room, but I wouldn't let them. I was gone from home about 45 days, and when I did come home, my tiger cat sat with his back toward me for almost two days. I had been wearing a bandanna on my head because I didn't have any hair. The next day I took my scarf off and he immediately knew I had come back home to him. He has truly

been my buddy - my friend.
Tausha
F, 9 dec, White & grey
DSH
Loving & funny
She forgave me immediately in spite of the fact I was gone so long.

JOHNSTOWN   15904
Kerrie Onderko, RD#3 Box 305A
Tigger
M, 1, Black, gray, white
Tabby
Friendly and cuddly and unique
Tigger is the son of Helen (owner Lisa Blough). One of his favorite things to do is play fetch. If you throw a ball he will get it and bring it back. He loves to go swimming in the
summertime and jump from tree to tree like a flying squirrel. Tigger doesn't think he's a cat. I'm not sure what he thinks he is. He's a very fun-loving cat. He loves people and people love him - especially that hair growing from his ears. And one other thing - he likes to chatter at the birds.

Taz
F, 1, Black, gray
Tabby
Attitude problem
Taz is Tigger's sister. They are like night and day. She doesn't like anyone, but me. She is definitely a cat with an attitude. But one thing she likes to do is sit on her hind legs and box. Loves to pick on her brother and perch on the chair ready to pounce. She's a one person cat and a great friend.

KENNETT SQUARE   19348
The R E Hutz Family, 401 Chandler Mill Rd
Ivan
M, 18 dec, Black & white
Domestic shorthair
Friendly; he had each member (4) of the family as his persons.
Ivan was the runt of the litter; born in a closet. We had lost a cat and were "looking" for a new male kitten. So I selected him when I found kittens available through a friend. What made him so special (he died in his bed of heart failure just a few weeks before his 18th birthday), was that

he indeed, lived 9 lives. He had many scrapes with other cats and animals and had his share of visits to the vet, but he survived two events that others might not have.

One due to his trusting nature in our ex-neighborhood was that he was hit in the rear by a car while sitting on the road - where it was O.K. to sit in the road - everyone knew each other's pets. The second was one spring when he disappeared for 3 weeks. After 2 weeks I began to fear the worst and asked UPS men if they'd seen him; went door to door. As it was spring, I was convinced he was locked in a garage and the owners had gone away for the holiday. After 3 weeks he came home - thin as a rail with his claws virtually destroyed.

I took him to the vet and he guessed I was correct that he had been incarcerated somewhere and had tried to get out. No one ever owned up to it. He had a tag, but he lived to come back to his people and live in the luxury of love until he died several years later.

KING OF PRUSSIA   19406

Susan & Lou Aceto, 200 Ross Rd

Lotus

F, 3, Sable

Burmese

People (us) oriented

Lotus is a purebred Burmese, but as the littlest of her litter with a slightly deformed nose (it's crooked), she would not be considered "show quality". But in our house she shines with personality plus.

She is always ready for a game of "fetch". She picks the toy she wants from her basket and the game is on. She prefers plastic shopping bag handles but also likes pelican feathers my mother sends from Florida. If she brings the toy back and is ignored she places it on our feet and "talks" about it.

Mikey, our other cat, is the prime target for "Hit & Run". He lays in the center of the living room floor and swishes his tail back and forth. Lotus hides, dashes across the room, hits his tail, keeps on going and makes repeated "hits" in this manner. He outweighs her by about 10 pounds but tolerates this very well. Last but not least is her ability to tell when it is 6 a.m. every morning without fail. Weekends included. Both cats will sit outside the bedroom door

and since she has the loudest voice she will continue to tell us to get up, it's breakfast time. Mikey sits by her and if she is not loud enough he gives her a little nudge.

Mikey

M, 7, Gray/white

Domestic shorthair

Friendly to all humans w/ food

Mikey is our 13 pound "pound" baby. Even at seven years old he still likes a cuddle now and again. When we got our Burmese it was touch and go as to who would be "boss". They worked it out pretty evenly.

There are two or three rough and tumble bouts during the day when anything goes. Lotus gives as good as he gets. Mikey can move pretty quickly for a "fat cat" but still can't catch Lotus unless she wants him to.

His favorite game is hide & seek. He hides under a cover and allows Lotus to pounce. Any toy will do as long as it moves and it is better if it's Lotus doing the moving. More than once our son found himself sharing his pillow with a furry head next to his. Also when Mikey lays along the back of the sofa and my husband puts his head back, Mikey will "comb" his hair with his teeth.

LIGONIER   15658

Ann & Stephen Hallberg, 332 E Main St

Clarabelle

M, 4-5 dec, Dark brown, tabby markings; white mask, mittens & boots Maine Coon

Loving, gentle, comical ... a golden soul.

See story in chapter 8: Lap Cats Extraordinaire

MCDONALD   15057

Beth Jankaowski, 215 Cherry Valley Rd

She-wolf

F, 5 mo. dec, Black

?

Quiet,, loving, very smart

Adopted this kitten from the Humane Shelter at Christmas time. She was so quiet and regal standing in the cage when others were noisy and active. I feel in love with her.

Soon we started going to the vet which slowly increased to weekly or biweekly. She never grew much or felt like playing. She rode on my shoulder and we talked and understood each other. Finally on April 15 she had an operation to find out what was wrong. She had F.I.P. and was put to sleep.

She was special because she made me realize I did want children. Now I have a boy and a girl because of the love of my cat She-wolf.

Tasha

F, ?, Black & white

?

Loving, protective

When I found Tasha she was starving. Having eaten a squash she was still so thin you couldn't tell she was nursing kittens. I put food out for her and she wasn't shy or skittish. But she was alert to the grass to her right. There I found three fat, clean, feisty kittens.

I found homes for all four cats but feel Tasha was an uncommonly good mother to have such clean and healthy kittens when she was so weak and hungry.

MEADVILLE   16335

Deborah & Greg Nichols, 757 Graff Ave

Tango

M, 2, White with red tips

Himalayan - Flame-point

Inquisitive, stubborn, very devoted to owners.

Has anyone seen my mouse?

His favorite toys are small, fake mice that closely resemble real mice. We keep his mice in a bowl in our pantry, which Tango can open up with his paw. Then he will bring us a mouse in his mouth and drop it at our feet. We will throw the mouse across the living room floor and he will bring it back to us repeatedly. We will usually get tired of playing fetch before Tango does. If we go to bed at night before Tango is

ready, he will bring his mice to bed to continue playing.

MORRISVILLE   19067-5155

Dorothy Schilling, 7031 Huber Dr

Abbygail

F, 10, Black & white

Mixed longhair

Quiet, reserved with strangers, loving with family

December 15, 1992 - my husband Dan was asleep on the living room couch. Abbey, who rarely meows, came running from the bedroom and stood in front of the couch crying. Dan paid little attention. She started toward the bedroom looking back at him - meowing. When he didn't get up, she ran back to him again, crying louder. She would take a few steps toward the bedroom, looking back at him, loud meows, a few more steps, more cries. Dan finally awoke and followed as Abbey dashed into the bedroom. There was smoke pouring from an electrical fuse box. My husband suffers from emphysema. If Abbey had not warned him in time, inhaling the smoke could have been fatal. We know Abbey saved Dan's life. She's our eight pound heroine!

MOUNT JOY   17552

Phyllis Zook, 348 Kelly Ave

Hoppy

F, 5, Grey and white Tabby

Sedate, quiet, loves her "Dad"

Our cat, Hoppy, has an uncommon relationship with our parakeet, Max. They're friends! (Hoppy is missing her back left leg.) Her favorite activity is to sit by the patio door and watch the world go by.

Max likes it there too. Hoppy is very attentive, but has never made an unfriendly gesture - even when the bird is flying around the room!

Max died recently, and sometimes I catch Hoppy looking for her buddy. I truly believe she misses her feathered friend.

MT TOP   18707

Pat Osisek, 3071 Alberdeen Rd

Charlie

M, 2, Platinum & gray

Part Siamese and calico

Playful, lovable, curious

Unlike me, my husband is not a cat lover. So when we married and I wanted a cat, my husband consented only if he could be trained like a dog. We both agreed and into our lives came Charlie, our cat, who is lovable, cute and very intelligent.

Charlie trained easily and now he comes to our whistle, sits, begs, lies down, rolls over and even gives his paw on command. Charlie is sometimes too intelligent because he now opens drawers to get his toys, open doors (ajar) to let himself out of a room and snoops in kitchen cupboards. Charlie is our two-year old terror, whom my husband loves.

P.S. Charlie's favorite quirk is licking ice cubes.

NEW KENSINGTON   15068-5240
Judy And Stan Zlotkowski, 151 Warren Dr
Hammy
F, 14, Dark gray, black - tiger
Prissy, reserved, loving, intelligent

Hammy was taken from her mother too soon so she doesn't meow, she squeaks. She was an outdoor cat for 11 years and became an indoor cat on the death of a family member. Adapting wasn't a problem. When we sit on our recliner she wraps herself around our neck and falls asleep; she thinks she's a fur piece. Most cats like catnip, but not ours. She likes rawhide shoestrings to chew and play with. Our cat is an alarm clock. She jumps on the bed, squeaks, purrs in our ear, and pats us on the face until we wake up.

Hammy – The Squeaker

NEWTOWN   18940
Nina Sokoll, 51 Kirkwood Dr
Toby
M, 6, Grey
Burmese
Beautiful, gentle & affectionate

My cat Toby is extremely affectionate. When I went to look at kittens at a local pet store, a Blue Burmese, climbed up the cage and tried to get my attention. The girl at the store said Toby was her favorite then scooped him up and handed him to me. She said, "Ask him for a kiss." When I did, he gave me one right on the nose!

Toby the Kissing Cat

Well it was love at first sight for the both of us! Toby left the pet store with me that day and has been giving kisses ever since! My husband has also taught Toby to fall down on his side and roll over on command!

OLD FORGE   18518-1730
Kathryn R. Legg, 330 Riley St
Thingy
M, 7, White with pink ears and nose
Short hair mixed
Thingy knows what he wants and lets you know it.

Ever since Thingy was rescued from the dumpster where he was left to die, he decided that I would be his "mother". Since Thingy obviously had very little, if any, loving contact with humans, he is in constant need of reassurance that he is loved. Every morning, Thingy and I have what I call "baby kitty and cuddle time". Thingy and I go to my room and I have to lay on my bed and say "are you ready to cuddle?"

Thingy will jump on the bed, wrap himself in a ball in my arms and I will have to scratch his favorite places. He will purr so loud and lick my hand. After about 5 minutes, his little eyes (one blue, one green) close and he drifts to sleep.

Catfish

F, 13, White, tan, brown-striped

Mixed

Catfish is easy going & gentle

Catfish has been a very loving, gentle cat since she was rescued from a plastic bag of kittens that were left to die in the woods. It is as if this gentle beast realizes how lucky she was to be saved. Catfish waits for my father to come home from his business every night. She will not come in until my dad comes home. Once he's home, she sits patiently for him to get his snack, turn on the TV and lie down on the couch. She then (even though she's quite large) jumps to the armrest of the couch, pats him on the head with her paw, gives off a big sigh and goes to sleep for the night.

OLEY   19547

Sandy Hill, RD 3 Box 41 Water St

Schnutz Putz

F, 1.5, Black, tan w/touch of gray

Tiger stripe

Curious, playful, affectionate

Schnutz Putz was a wild cat born outside, first seen by us on a bitter cold January morning in 1992, sitting outside our kitchen window. She was unapproachable at first; so we feed her food, milk and water for a little over a week. Each day she trusted me a little more till I finally caught her and brought her indoors. She hide for a few days; however by two weeks time she had graduated to coming up on the bed and most anyplace we were. She was so grateful to be warm finally and no more shivering.

She went to the vet for a routine exam and her shots. (After we nursed her back to health from a respiratory infection with help from our vet.) She loves all of our 6 other cats; loves to watch the fish in the tank; and wrestles with our 7 year old male Tiger Clyde all the time. (Lots of running and chasing.) Clyde accepted her on the first day in the house. She loves to sit in front of the fireplace and her favorite treat is shrimp tails with butter. Her real name is Marigold, but she immediately became my little Schnutz Putz.

Clyde (nickname: **"Bud"**)

M, 7, Black, tan, gray - white chin

Tiger stripe

Loving - most affectionate cat I've every known.

As a kitten, Clyde was accepted by me from my cousin as her child was allergic. I went to look at him and took him home right away. Of course he passed all his routine vet visits.

When I am hurt or crying and upset, Clyde always comes to comfort me by lying on my chest as close as he possible can and looking at me with those big eyes. Of course he does this during happier times too, for he loves to be close.

Helps keep the fireplace going

He loves to burrow under the covers on the waterbed and truly appreciates a nice fire in the fireplace. He sits as close as he can and if the fire gets low, moves in even closer letting us know it's time for more wood. He always helps build the fire by following along as the wood is brought in, watching in a supervisory way, until the flames are glowing. He likes to think we built the fire especially for him which is what we always tell him.

PHILADELPHIA   19135

Sandra Adcox, 7222 Hegerman St

Little Guy

F, 3, Gray, brown & black

Tabby

Playful & loveable

Little Guy plays fetch with clothes pins, paper, and anything you throw. She also has a Barbie Reebok shoe that she loves. If you ask her, "Where is your Reebok?", she knows what it is.

We bought Little Guy from a woman who takes in stray cats. At the start when we bought her, her name was Whiskers, but I always called her Little Guy so that is what she answers to. We love her and think she is a special cat.

Samanatha

F, 13-1/2, Brown, white, black

Calico

Loveable

My cat is special for two things. First she hugs your arm and buries her whole face in your arm. She also eats very strange foods. My cat likes to eat pizza crust and powdered doughnuts.

PHILADELPHIA   19135

Terry Colosimo (my mom), 7022 Hegerman St

"Coco"

F, 13.5 dec, Chocolate point ragdoll

Siamese/Himalayan

Very outspoken, lovable, needing constant companionship.

Coco was quite a feline. At feeding time she would wait by our feet and then escort us to her place mat - where she would bump heads with my mom before she was given her dish. She would stand on her hind legs and stretch up to nudge mom's forehead.

At other times while getting her exercise running through the house (she was strictly a house cat), if our living room door was wide open, this crazy cat would leap onto the chair adjacent to the door and then onto the top of the 2" wide, 7 foot door. She would cry until Mom came to her rescue!

Piccolena

F, 7, Black / with white under chin

?

Spooky / intimidated / playful

Piccolena got her name because she was the runt and almost died when she was born, hence the Italian name meaning "little one". She sits by her empty bowl when she's hungry and circles the table when we have dinner. She goes around until we share our goodies. She loves to play with a long piece of string, so when she's ready she finds us, cries very loudly, and then runs to

her scratching post where her toys are and waits for someone! She wakes us up in the morning by crying and if that doesn't work she reaches and taps us on the arm!

PHILADELPHIA   19145-0243

Liz Lord, PO Box 11943

Socrates

M, dec, White and grey

Blue Point Siamese

Affectionate, quiet

In our short time together, Socrates brought me great joy. Socrates was previously a stud and had not experienced much human contact. It took me a year to socialize him. He put his complete trust in me thereafter. When I was home after being involved in an auto accident, Socrates provided me with companionship and comfort. He even played substitute father to our new feline additions. Socrates succumbed to acute renal kidney failure only two years after we met. I miss him immensely, but he will always live on in my heart!

PHILADELPHIA

R Marvel

Abby

F, 9, Rust

Abyssinian

See story in chapter 5: Working Cats.

PHILADELPHIA

Regina Stone

Alexander Catnip

M, 1, Black & white

Persian

Sweet, lovable, courageous, mysterious

My feline Alex's favorite pastime is enjoying long siestas with his "chosen person of the day". He stretches his body, crawls under the sheets, lays his head on the pillow, and drifts off to dreamland.

Alexander also is very dramatic during play. Toys become prey, as Alex stalks slowly and almost parallel to the ground, before pouncing on them. His latest capture is then transported in his mouth back to a human friend for more to "fetch".

In addition, Alex loves to play "dead". A loving tickle on his belly quickly springs him back to life.

Samantha
F, 12, White
Mixed Persian
Sweet & mischievous
My cat Samantha has learned to use stubbornness to her advantage. Once she finds a suitable position for rest, nothing will motivate her to move. Even feeding time is done her way! If her bowl of cat chow is set down within "paws reach", Samantha won't budge. She will merely reach out her paw and pull the dish in front of her! Sammy's also been known to steal a bowl right out from under another cat's nose. At the end of the day, Sam offers kisses as if to say, "thanks for putting up with me".

PITTSBURGH
Nanette Allen
Punkin (Punk)

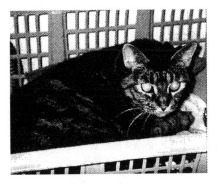

Punk in her favorite spot

F, 12, Brown/gold/grey w/white around eyes (like she has a mask on) Tabby
Very loving & talkative
Punk has a very unusual habit. She likes to sleep in my clothes basket that's in a closet in my living room. (If some of my clothes aren't in it, she won't sleep in it.) The closet is a double, bi-fold metal door closet. Each door measures 6'7" x 3'5". When the doors are closed, she uses her paws to partially open one of the doors and then uses her nose to finish opening it. She then jumps into my clothes basket. Friends have seen this and can't believe it. Punk is very special to me.

PITTSBURGH   15210

Jim And Cindy Tibi, 2024 Arlington Ave
Mortimer
M, 3.5, blue tabby
Alley cat
Curious, impatient, and playful
Mortimer is a "serious" cat about everything he does. He enjoys many hobbies such as: chasing our hands and feet; turning on and off light switches; taking toys from our other cats; taking phones off the hook, walking on the buttons and listening to the "beeps"; and flushing the toilet (his personal favorite). He's even serious about his naps (which are never very long). Mortimer is by no means a cuddly lap cat, as his schedule is so full, but he is fun and we love him lots.

PITTSBURGH   15210
Sara Tibi, 2024 Arlington Av
Miss Booger La Boop
F, 4, Black/gray
Lap cat, playful, loving, beautiful
Booger isn't a boring cat. She has many interests, such as her feet and tail. She rolls around and grabs her feet or tail. She has a special toy named Norman. She does a trick with me. When I stand up and pat my stomach, she jumps up and I have to catch her. Sometimes we play hide and seek. When she can't find me, she meows. Miss La Boop is known as a Blanket Buzzard. She likes to take the covers when you're trying to sleep. This describes my fun, loving, and beautiful cat.

Irma (Troll)
F, 3, Black/white
Funny, cute, lap cat
Irma is known as the Troll. She lays under my mom's rocker and when another cat walks by, she runs out and hits them. She reminds everyone of a wiener dog because her body is fat and her legs are short. Irma has a spot on her side and every time you scratch it, her tongue goes in and out. This is what my uncommon cat is like.

SAINT MARYS   15857-5004
Dyanne Schutz, P.O. Box 1004
Sheba
F, 5, Cinnamon, white, gray, and black
Calico Mix
Devoted, loving, responds to her name

Sheba – a great jumper

Sheba is a very affectionate companion. Each day begins with purrs and gentle nuzzles to wake me, starting our morning ritual. Next, belly rubs which she really enjoys, and begging for breakfast on her hind legs. Sheba's ability to leap with agility and land with grace is apparent as going outdoors requires her to jump 5 feet to a roof, scamper down a wood pile, tightrope a picket fence, and pounce to freedom. Her "many-toed" paws enable Sheba to bring in "friends" and transform my apartment into wild kingdom. Sheba awaits my return from work with love, and anticipation of "catnip dreams"!!!

TROY   16947
Dorothy Dehnel, RR 3 Box 983
Baby
M, ?, Black & grey
Maine Coon
Well mannered & lovable
Baby came to us a stray 9 years ago, in very bad shape. We kept him outside for 6 months and then gradually let him come in. He has no litter box but goes to the door when he wants out. Never goes on the furniture but sleeps on our laps or his bed. He was lost for 52 days in mid winter, came back and we nursed him back to health and is now a "stay at homer". Love shines from his beautiful eyes.

UPPER DARBY   19082
Sandee Chreiman, 115 Copley Rd
Scruffy
M, 5, Orange/white
Domestic Medium Hair
Very mellow, easy-going
Scruffy was dumped by his first owners when he was 3 years old at an animal shelter because they didn't want him anymore. He was then adopted out to a man that said he wanted him. The man dumped him out his front door (approx. 20 miles from his first owner's home) because he claimed Scruffy kept him up all night. Being a loyal, loving cat, he decided to go home - the only one he knew, with his first owner. It took him over 6 weeks but he finally made it. Tired, hungry, and now injured (his flea collar got caught under his front leg and became imbedded on his journey), he was once again dumped at the animal shelter (now with no chance for adoption). His fate - destruction, but NO WAY, not for this loyal, loving, now fat, happy, healthy, and strictly indoor cat because his owner (me) is as loyal to him as he was to those undeserving first owners. Scruffy shares his home with 4 dogs, 10 cats, 7 ferrets, and 1 rabbit - all very much loved with a home for life.

Thunder
M, 2.5, Silver/brown tabby
Domestic short hair
Super affectionate, friendly
Thunder is very special because he gives hugs - he actually puts his arms (paws) around your neck and hugs when you pick him up. Sometimes he will come to me and meow and then blink very slowly a few times. That means he wants a hug. Thunder can really brighten any rough day up. He puts his head on your shoulder and sometimes licks your ear or face. He is so affectionate; he even does this to the 10 other cats, 4 dogs, 7 ferrets, and rabbit he lives with. Thunder is from the SPCA. I think he knew what almost happened to him and he is just showing me how much he loves his life and the other animals he shares it with.

WEST CHESTER   19380
Linda Walnut, 273 Walnut Springs Ct
Tazmanian Devil (Taz)
M, 12 dec, Orange
Domestic shorthair
A one-person cat (and I was the one).
I once had a cat named Tazmo. His small head and big ears reminded me of the Tazmanian Devil. (I remembered it backwards!) Occasionally Taz would chew gum

without swallowing it.

One summer I had to work overtime thirteen straight days. On the fourteenth day I decided to visit a friend across the street. While sitting in her living room I heard a meow at the screen door. I opened it and invited Taz in. Instead of entering he turned promptly around and headed home. I told my friend, "I better go home and spend some time with my cat."

Sheba

M, 11, Black & white

Domestic longhair

Intelligent

Sheba is an intelligent cat. He knows "get down" and his name, which he learned quickly. Later we adopted KoKo. Sheba would watch KoKo and try to learn from her. She would carry a plastic golf ball in her mouth, so Sheba tried to pick up a small toy in his mouth, but he could not do it.

Sheba and I play hide and touch. We are both hiding and peeking around something waiting for the other to start daydreaming so we can surprise the other by running up and touching. The score is one to one.

WINDBER   15963-1335

Lisa M Blough, 312 5th St

Helen

F, 5, Beige, peach, white, brown

Tabby

Mostly mellow, but can be playful

In the summer of 1990 my younger brother, Tim, found a stray cat while walking from my grandmother's house. She was very scared and very pregnant. I fell in love with her the moment I saw her. My fiancee and I agreed to keep her on the condition that he could name her. The name he chose for her was Helen.

Helen immediately displayed incredible manners. She was most comfortable sleeping by my feet. Our personalities were completely compatible. We quickly became best of friends.

One day I walked outside and called her. I realized the time must have come for her to give birth. After 24 hours Helen showed up at my front door and was noticeably skinnier. Helen had five beautiful kittens in the back of the storage space under the front of the house.

Shortly after she had her kittens I got married and moved. When the kittens were weaned I brought Helen to our new home. Although my husband was a loyal dog fan, it didn't take Helen too long to win his heart.

In May of 1991, Helen gave birth to a second litter of three. Jaynee was the runt and the one we decided to keep.

Helen is often the "bully" with other animals in my neighborhood while Jaynee is very timid - but both will always be my little girls.

Jaynee

F, 2, Grey, white

Tabby

Very playful & energetic

See story in chapter 7: Wild & Wacky

Chapter Twelve

Who's Who in the Appalachian Highlands

KENTUCKY

ALVATON   42122-8705
Anita C. Stamatis, 1258 WG Talley Rd
Rugums
F, 8 months, Blue
Russian Blue
Playful, loving
Rugums has the bones in her lower front legs fused. This turns her paws 90 degrees inward from the elbows. Although many breeders would have put her down for this defect, she seemed healthy. My vet had me swim her in water every night for her first six weeks to build her strength. She is now 8 months and very healthy. She runs, jumps and sits up like a squirrel. Her favorite toys are whole almonds which she carries in her mouth or bats around like a hockey puck. If only all handicapped kittens had this choice. She's my friend and I love her dearly.

MADISONVILLE   42431
Ann Lynn, 1010 Pearl Dr
Stormy
M, 1, Black w/white under neck
Shorthair
Loveable, curious, frisky & mischievous
Stormy was found by a friend on the highway (a few weeks old) starving to death. He was bottle fed with milk and baby cereal. We got him at two months. He started out in the bathroom, so he liked water and didn't mind a bath - also likes to play with running water.

When he wants to be picked up, he puts his paws on your knees. He will bite on your finger like he was nursing . . . I guess because he wasn't raised by his mother. He enjoys looking out the patio door. My husband says Stormy can say, "MaMaw" (two short meows). He went from rags to riches.

Misty
F, 1, Black w/white under neck
Shorthair
Loveable, playful & sneaky
Misty is Stormy's sister, but doesn't like water or taking a bath. She is very sneaky. She gets into things, then runs and hides. When you hold her, she wants to be up around your neck, like a fur piece. She is very loveable, soft and cuddly.

I have always wanted a black cat, so I think God saved their lives for us. Our granddaughter loves Stormy and Misty very much. So Misty went from abandonment to being spoiled rotten - just like Stormy.

MARION   42064
Charlotte Beard, 106 Hillcrest Dr
Marissa
F, 1, Black with brown & gray
Mixed longhair
Friendly, loving, playful
Marissa was born May 1992 and dropped on the side of the road with three more brothers and sisters. A friend found them and all have good homes now.

This is my first house cat. I love her dearly. She has been spayed and front paws de-clawed. She is friendly to everyone - but only at her discretion. By that, I mean she'll usually go to people, only when she's ready, not if called, even by me. She comes every time at meal time. She sleeps with me and likes to sleep in the top of my hair. She has lots of toys, but prefers to play with new things she discovers in the house like ice cubes, rubber bands, bottle tops, and flowers.

She is afraid of large animals, but follows a friend's dog around (small dog). She loves me when I get home from work by jumping in my lap and putting her paws on my face. She's litter trained and will not use it if it is dirty. Hides everywhere. Plays hide & seek with me. Likes to play rough by wrestling & biting, but will calm down when I tell her. I eat yogurt in bed and she sits patiently and watches, knowing that she'll get the last of it.

PRINCETON   42445
Linda Crenshaw, 233 G C Crenshaw Rd
Matthew
F, 9, Black
Mixed
Kind, loving, very intuitive
Matthew was a stray with one broken leg and a badly mangled tail when we met. He was approximately 6 weeks old at the time. The vet had to amputate his tail and the broken leg mended. Three years later, we went through FUS and acute renal failure. The vet told me Matthew would not survive, but I could not give up on him and our vet was super.

The good Lord answered my prayers and this wonderful cat is still part of my life. Anytime I need to relax or need comforting . . . he is always there. If I have trouble sleeping, and he doesn't want to sleep with me, he will lie down with me anyway, until I begin to fall asleep. My husband adores him almost as much as I do. He's a very special part of our lives.

```
┌─────────────────────────────────┐
│                                 │
│       NORTH CAROLINA            │
│                                 │
└─────────────────────────────────┘
```

ARDEN   28704
Sheila Cotter Rogers, 8 Mulberry Ct
Scooter
M, 8, Apricot & white

Norwegian Forest cat mix
See story in Chapter 3: Against All Odds
Thumper
M, 4, Black & white
Domestic shorthair
Very confident yet needs attention
Thumper talks. When he was a kitten I would say "uh oh" when he was bad so now HE comes to me and says "uh oh" to tell me he's been bad, go see. He has said "water", "I'm hungry" and "no", and "Ma Ma".

He was given to me by my husband to ease the loss of my Scamper from a brain tumor. He looked like Scamper but refused attention from me. He only wants my husband and says "NO" when I get near. He will fetch and loves to play with milk jug rings, pompon balls, old vinyl cat collars, and earrings. He refuses to be told NO. This makes him "cute" to my husband and frustrating to me, but I love him anyway.

ASHEVILLE   28806
Sandra E Brown, 55 Nevada Ave
Morris
M, 11, Deep orange
Maine Coon
Most loving, attentive, endearing!!
I found Morris beside a busy interstate when he was 4 months old. From the moment I "rescued" him, he has been the most loving cat I've ever had! He loves everybody - even his vet! He is always in a loving mood! He HAS to sleep with me - as close as he can get! My other 4 cats will be in a chair or somewhere asleep. But not Morris - he has to be near me! He loves powdered-cake doughnuts and parmesan cheese!

If he's sleeping and I touch him - he "chatters" to me! He talks to me all the time. He has to sit on a stool beside the tub while I take my bath. When I'm eating, he takes his paw and pulls my arm to him - to see if I have something he might want (so cute!). I've been disabled and out of work and on Social Security for 8 years. Morris keeps my spirits up and gives me reason to go on day after day. He's the glue that holds our little family together.
Matthew
M, 2.5, Black

Domestic short-hair

Needs lots of loving!

I "rescued" Matthew from under a church - hence "Matthew" (gift from God). He is starved for love - was so poor and skinny - but now weighs 15 pounds - sleek and beautiful and GETS lots of loving. He runs his paw under any door that is closed - he wants IN! Morris and he are best friends!! He loves "people food" - mashed potatoes, lima beans, and spaghetti. Very sweet boy!

BESSEMER CITY   28016

Louise E. Simmons, 105 E Maryland Ave

Miss Kitty

F, 6, Calico

Tortoise Shell

Shy with others, frisky with me

One day Ms. Kitty kept dancing and meowing around my wheelchair to get me to follow her. When I did, I found my puppy had hung herself off the porch edge. I gave puppy mouth to snout resuscitation and revived her. After a vet trip and return home, Ms. Kitty "lick-washed" that puppy and stayed beside her for 3 whole days until the puppy started moving around. Ms. Kitty always lets me know if someone comes into the yard. She also follows me when I roll up to the library and to church. She leaves mice or an occasional bird for me on my ramp to let me know she loves me.

Bee Bee

F, 4, Chocolate point

Siamese

Possessive, playful

This beauty thinks I am all hers. She stays by my bed except when she senses I'm having a rough day - then she is either in my lap, riding in my wheelchair with me, or laying as close to me, on my bed, as she can get. When she wants out, she licks my chin; when she wants to be fed, she licks my nose. When she's just loving me, she wraps her soft paws around my hand and washes it. When I talk to her, she watches me and always meows at appropriate intervals, just as if she is answering me.

CLAREMONT   28610

Janet Dyson, 3663 Jinny Lane

Sammy Dyson

M, 1, Seal point

Siamese

Loving, mischievous, inquisitive

Sammy is an extremely loving & loyal cat. When my mama was terminally ill, there was always a seal point cheek pressed lovingly to mine. Many a day Sammy looked as if he had been caught in a rainstorm from my tears soaking his fur. To this day Sammy knows when I need to be comforted and is always there for me. His antics are a constant source of amusement! He can use his paws like jet propelled grappling hooks! Especially where food is concerned! He likes you to throw his toys for him and he will bring them back continually for more throw & fetch. Sammy is a constant source of love and amusement and friendship.

Jo-Jo Dyson

M, 6, Orange/white Tabby

American domestic shorthair

Intelligent, loving, protective

Jo-Jo is extremely intelligent. He actually got into my dog's stocking (without making any noise), retrieved my dog's bag of treats, and proceeded to have a party with my other two cats, Sammy & Fluffy. Jo is also a "watch-cat". If a stranger comes in and leaves our sight, Jo will attack them. This was made extremely clear when we were away and Jo proceeded to pen my cat sitter in the hall for thirty minutes (after she fed them of course). She said he was like a mini-mountain lion. Jo is a constant source of amazement for us.

CLEMMONS   27012

The Brady Family, 8815 Homewood Dr

Muffin

F, 3, Silver/grey mackerel

Mixed

Independent & cautious

Muffin is our #1 cat. She came to us at 13 weeks and has been feisty and neurotic ever since. Slow to show affection, Muffin knows and loves her family - plus she keeps our other two cats, Boris and Natasha, in line.

She has gentled since our move from Michigan to North Carolina and is smart enough to snuggle with her "mom" whenever possible. Her least admirable habit is eating acrylic material - beware of clothes left on the floor! Despite that, we all worship the ground she walks on!

Boris & Natasha

M & F, 2½, Brown classic tabby & black

Mixed

Gentle soul & the opportunist

These two cats came to us from the same litter at 5 weeks. Too young to leave their mother, they really bonded to us as family. Boris is sweet and laid-back. He is such a homebody that he will follow us all day.

Natasha, as black as her name suggests, is tiny and curious with big green eyes. She considers all high areas her domain - the roof, tops of cabinets, tall trees, and the like. Natasha and Boris both are shy with strangers, but purr like troopers for the family.

FLETCHER 28732

Mary Dotson, 1424 Cane Creek Rd

Tazzy

F, 2, Orange or tan

Red Tabby

Very affectionate & temperamental

See story in chapter 6: Feline Fetishes.

Bobby

M, 1, Orange & white

Manx

Mischievous & affectionate

We also have an orange and white, male, part Persian Manx, named Bobby, who is also very affectionate and has a very loving manner. He has a sound he makes when he greets you, that seems to mean "I love you", which resembles the sound you hear on Star Trek when they beam someone up to the ship. Therefore, every time he makes it, we all laugh and say "Beam Me Up Scotty".

FOREST CITY 28043

Melinda & Doug Martin, Rt 2 Box 139

Spooky

M, 20 dec, Black

Domestic shorthair

Highly affectionate, gentle, friendly, slept in bed with us.

Apparently abandoned, Spooky, 1-1/2, was fed by three families, including us. He chose us as his family by one day appearing on out third-floor apartment balcony -

a feat of great skill. Spooky would get on the railing of the landing between the second and third floor, leap six feet over, two feet up, through the air - three stories above the ground - landing on a narrow ledge, then weaving through the slats of the railing. He performed this feat hundreds of times.

Spooky was the sweetest, most loving, devoted lap cat ever, living to be almost 20. He was truly a special cat.

GREENSBORO 27407

Sheryl L Chubb, 1825 Halcyon St

Chloe

F, 1, Orange & white

DSH

Exhilarated live wire; comedienne

As a kitten, Chloe seemed to have catnip in her nostrils - she darts around the house as quickly as she can. She loves to dart past Chad, the dog, for him to chase her. She loves to play chase. You chase her . . . then she turns around to chase you. TRICKS: fetches paper wads and brings them back to you. Jumps vertically 3-1/2 feet in the air to catch wads. Hold out your arm and snap your fingers, and she will leap up and wrap all 4's around your arm. She sits on her scratching post and will catch toys when you toss them.

She heard the word "NO" so many times that now she can say "NO". She will sing the last word ("Do") to "Do Re Mi" after you sing the first part. Chloe loves people and loves to perform her tricks for everyone.

MORGANTON 28655

Lynda Garibaldi, 221 Cascade St

Nicholas

M, 1-2 yrs, Black w/ white trim

Medium hair stray

Confident, perky, unruffled

Nicholas arrived four days before Christmas, so my neighbor Rudell named him after St. Nicholas. How does Nicholas look? Black with white tips, with white up the side of his nose, much like the White House feline, Socks.

Unlike Sam (light grey stripe), who appeared in our basement and for months ran out the window when I went down there, Nicholas marched right into our house as though he owned it. After helping himself to food, he sprawled out on the living room couch, just as if he had lived here forever.

Great Gorgeous Morgan (longhair black & white) studied Nicholas for a week or two, really puzzled about just who this cat was and where he came from. Before long, though, Morgan started growling and charging at Nicholas.

Then one day, big, bold blonde Sugar, usually aloof and tolerant, stood on the porch with his tail high and his coat fluffed out and growling so fiercely that Nicholas cowered before him on the grass.

It's taken awhile, but as always with cats, they have adjusted to one another.

ROCKY MOUNT   27801
Sabrina, Ed, Joyce Webb, 120 S Linden Pl
Simon
M, 5, Black
Outgoing, much like that of a dog
Simon was a birthday present to Sabrina. He was an orphan from Mississippi. Sabrina was away from all of her family in Mississippi, so Simon became Sabrina's family.

Sabrina realized that Simon was a unique cat when she awoke one morning to have Simon nibbling on her nose. This nose nibbling later led to eye brow nibbling, lip nibbling, and in general face nibbling. This was Simon's loving way of saying he was hungry or wanted companionship. When Sabrina would get lonely and cry, Simon would stay right beside her and lick her eyes while she cried.

Simon later had to move to North Carolina and move in with his grandparents, Joyce and Ed. Simon continues with his face nibbling and took to his grandparents very well.

SELMA   27576
Nancy Gay, 642 New Creech Rd
Whiskers
M, 1.5, Orange and white
Tabby
Sweet, loving, finicky, and spoiled
Whiskers is my special kitty. Outside someone's home we found Whiskers, when he was just a little kitten. It was love at first sight - I had to have him. We traded a full

blooded pit bull puppy for him.

He's very smart. He plays fetch, just like a dog. I ball up foil and throw it or his fuzzy mouse and he brings it back to me. We also play chase; I chase him around the house and he turns around and chases me. He loves it!

When it comes to other people, forget it unless you have fresh chicken livers or turkey.

We really do have a special bond. He sleeps on a pillow above my head every night. He knows how much I love him and what happiness he brings me. And I know he loves me.

SKYLAND   28776
Carol Ward Cotter, PO Box 56
Stubby
M, 5, Grey/White Tabby
Manx
Intelligent, vocal, cautious, playful

Stubby transfers his love

Stubby, the Manx, loved only my husband, sleeping at his feet, playing "fetch", and sharing the morning paper in his lap -- until Ade's death. After weeks of lonely nights, I awoke to the occasional, gentle presence of Stubby on the foot of my bed; he's there every night now. He informs me of approaching visitors and tells me if someone came to the door or telephoned while I was away. I read the newspaper while he presses against my shoulder in our favorite chair. I provide for his daily needs. He senses my emotional need, and, as only he can, answers.

Lady
F, 15 dec, Chocolate point Siamese

Siamese

A refined lady, companion

As a pregnant stray, she carefully checked each home in our neighborhood over a one-week span before choosing us. Then she brought a single kitten, dropping it at our daughter's feet as she moved in with us. We gave her away once and "loaned" him while we were out of the states. She survived against all odds and forgave us. She even came to some acceptance of Stubby, the Manx, before her death in 1989. Along the way she mothered a Welch Springer Spaniel and a Rhodesian Ridgeback puppy in this crazy household she chose as home. She never seemed to regret having chosen us!

WINSTON SALEM   27106

Camilla Deyton, 2700 Reynolda Dr #302

Scarlet O'Hara Deyton

F, 6, White

Introverted, homebody

Devoted companion; she keeps order in her home. Affectionate with me alone; she hides under the bed at the least hint that someone else is coming in the house.

She sleeps under the covers, "talks" to me constantly, and gives "kisses" when asked - the best and most rewarding relationship I've ever had.

Her claim to fame is that she killed a snake that somehow got inside in 1988; then tried to convince me that there were more under the bed. We kept watch for 2 nights until we were sure the invasion was over.

Suzanne Sugarbaker Deyton

F, 2, Black & white

More like a chimpanzee than a cat.

Persistent, "carpe diem", happy cat

She answers to "Muffin".

An entertainer, she insists on grooming my hair right after I wash it. She sings when left alone and she plays pranks on Scarlet all the time.

She loves to watch the Discovery Channel on TV.

She knows she's cute - when told "NO", she looks at me, then continues to do whatever she's doing until I stand up. Then she stops, comes to me, and purrs. Of course, I just smile and love her back.

TENNESSEE

COLUMBIA   38401

Lindsay Pulley, 1402 Wilson Ct.

Buddy

F, 2.5, Orange-red stripe

Tabby

Loving, feisty, sensitive

Buddy was one stray of four. Some of the neighborhood kids had found them, so some people took turns feeding them. One day we had a yard sale and it was my turn to keep the kittens. Buddy was the biggest of the litter, but I had always been partial to the runts. With the help of one of my friends, we unsuccessfully tried to feed the kittens. Well, I was holding the runt, because it was my favorite. I left my friend with the three other kittens to feed, and she didn't like it. Then Buddy jumped into my lap and from that moment on I knew I was destined to have her. The kid across the street almost took her and I got scared. Fortunately, I got her and will always love her.

CORDOVA   38018

Nancy M Calvert, 605 Arbor Hollow Circle #101

Chapman

M, 7, Reo Tabby

Persian

Very loving, "athletic", full of energy & extremely intelligent!

Well, my name is Chapman and I was 7 years old on January 13, 1993. I am full of spunk and just love to have a great time. Nancy has to travel from time to time with her sales job, so while she is at home we make the best of it.

For example when Nancy is at home we enjoy watching TV together. I simply love to sit on the floor in front of the television. I don't sit like other cats, however; I choose to sit like humans. I sit with my back legs in front and with my front paws supporting me straight ahead. I often hear Nancy, her family and friends chuckle when I'm just "sittin" and being laid back and watching TV. Personally I still don't understand all the fuss, especially when she runs to get her camera and take pictures of me "sittin". When I'm in a playful mood, I love to leap in the air and catch ping pong balls Nancy throws to me. Nancy's brother was a college basketball player and just maybe I am following in his footsteps. For Christmas, Nancy places a handsome green bow tie around my neck and I actually do feel quite regal.

I think my tie makes me look quite regal

I am an extremely fortunate cat to have such a loving owner, but I adore her as much. She is always telling me how handsome I am and loves to comb me all the time. The treats I get from Pounce, etc. are always anxiously awaited. What more can a cat ask for? Well I must run along and hop on Nancy's bed before she awakes. She will be most excited to find out that I compiled this all by my catty self.

CORDOVA   38018

Jayme Fuhrer, 8425 Wind River Circle North

Mr. Pibb

M, 4, Black & white

Longhair ?

Intelligent, well mannered, loving!

Mr. Pibb has an upside down, heart-shaped spot on his nose and you'd wonder if it were put there to indicate how loving he is. Each morning when he sees my eyes open, he promptly climbs onto my chest and kisses my lips. Then, throughout the day he'll stand on his hind legs, with front paws resting on my legs, crying to be picked up and held. Truly he is the definition of lap cat!

HUMBOLDT   38343

Jack & Lisa Wirt, 65 McKnight Rd

Lucy

F, 1, Seal Point

Siamese

Innocent & lovable - curious to an extreme.

We call Lucy our little cat burglar because she likes to snatch and hide our jewelry when our backs are turned. Lucy quickly learned that I removed my wedding ring before my shower and slipped it into the middle of a roll of toilet paper on the bathroom shelf.

I spied her one night sneaking silently into the bathroom and headed straight for the roll of toilet paper. She slipped her paw into the middle of the roll, caught my ring in her tiny claw, slipped it out of the roll, put it in her mouth, then sprinted her treasure away to her secret stash where she keeps her play pretties.

She's always "checking" the insides of toilet paper rolls on the chance that there may be some shiny, sparklely "toy" hidden in there for her.

Lucy the Cat Burglar

Linus

M, 1-1/2, Blue Lynx Point

Siamese

Arrogant & bossy - aggressive

Linus the Lionhearted is not afraid of anything - not even our two gigantic dogs - a 120 pound malamute and a 70 pound husky. Linus does not meow, but makes a fussing, chattering, "barking" sound when he looks out the window at the dogs. In our crazy household it only makes sense that the cats should bark at the dogs!

KINGSPORT   37662
Karen & Russ Fig, PO Box 1561
"Kazz"
M, 10, Black
Persian

A loving person trapped in a cat's body.
We have been blessed to share our lives
with Kazz since he was a kitten. He has
always been full of life and surprises! For
the term "curiosity of a cat" . . . he rede-
fined it. He loves to lie on stereo speakers
and let music vibrate him. He watches
television and prefers cartoons - Pink Panther is his favorite. If the phone rings and
no one answers, Kazz will!! He also knows
dollar values. When presented with two
bills, he can pick the higher denomination
by rubbing against it. Some of his favorite
snacks are peas, mushrooms, raw potatoes,
and yes, watermelon!! Everyday Kazz
enriches our lives with love and warmth
and we are so thankful to have him in our
world.

"Fluffy"
F, 14, Blue
Persian

Lovable, mild-natured and faithful
Fluffy spends her life on a farm with horses and other cats. She likes the outdoor life
and sleeping in hay in the barn loft. She
always makes sure the farm animals are fed
by following loyally at your feet.

Her hospitality is expressed by running to
greet visitors as their vehicles approach the
farm driveway. She is very affectionate
with anyone she can steal attention from.
Through the years she has raised some
beautiful kittens and they have always had
her loving "purr-sonality". She is the attentive and gracious host of the farm!

MEMPHIS   38125
Lorie Smith, 7310 Winter Harbor Lane
Hannah
F, 5, Grey
Domestic long hair

Very sweet and friendly personality
From the first day I brought her home 5
years ago from our local shelter, Hannah
has been my personal shadow. I can't go
anywhere in the house where she won't be
far behind just talking away. She loves to
talk and if I'm not giving her much de-
served attention, she lets me know about it.

She is a very sweet natured cat and loves
everyone she meets - and I know the feelin-
g's mutual!

Bob
M, 2, Brown and beige
Tabby

Silly but sweet
Bob is one of a kind. He is a skinny, lanky
cat who likes to hang out by himself most
of the time. But when he gets silly, watch
out! He has this habit of running through
the house, jumps up on the door frame, and
slides down. If you tap the door frame,
he'll jump up and slide down again! Its
absolutely hysterical. He always keeps us
entertained and I wouldn't trade him for
any other cat in the world.

MURFREESBORO   37129-2065
Celinda B. Honig, 1502 White Blvd
Toppy
M, 6, White
Domestic short hair

Toppy – a symbol of enduring friendship

Outgoing and demanding little con artist
Fathers Day 1986 is memorable because a
precious dream came true; Toppy came into
our lives. A dear friend who lives on a
farm knew how I longed for a white, blue--
eyed kitten. Toppy symbolizes the bond of
enduring friendship. He also resembles the
beautiful white cat that gave me the happi-
est childhood memories. He is like a cuddly
security blanket when I feel sad. He enjoys
the role of social butterfly when guests visit
our home. He also seems to thrive on
"belly rubs" which my husband gladly
provides.

OAK RIDGE   37830
Karen L Curran, 215 Tusculum Dr

Tinker Bell

F, 5.5, White

Domestic shorthair

Loving with family, shy, independent

When we found Tinker she was about two weeks old and wandering the streets of Dallas, Texas. We moved to Tennessee shortly thereafter and for three weeks it was just Tinker and me in an empty house until our furniture arrived. I spent those long lonely hours training her with Pounce cat treats. She learned very quickly and can sit up and wave her paw high in the air. She rolls over on command and can say two short meows for "grandma" when she wants a treat. My father passed away in September 1992 and she has really helped fill the void and is a constant source of surprise and pleasure.

VIRGINIA

CULPEPER   22701
Debbie McCray, 406 E Spencer St Apt 4

Madonna "Missy"

F, 3, Black & white

Short-haired

Happy

Madonna likes to look in my mirror. Madonna meows and possibly thinks there's another cat around. She has been doing this since she was 4 months old. Madonna was abandoned by her first owner so I took her in. When she was declawed, she would push herself around and then afterwards she would run up the stairs.

FAIRFAX   22030
Karen & Ray Plewacki, 4107 Rust Rd

Freeport (Portie)

M, ?, Silver tabby

Maine Coon

Effervescent

Our Maine Coon, Freeport or Portie as we call him, provides us with a great deal of entertainment and companionship. From morning to night, Portie is our little shadow, following us from room to room, never letting us out of his sight. He loves to sit up on his hind legs and give us little kisses on our nose. When he's ready to play, Portie will drop his favorite toy at my feet and beckon me with his little voice to throw it for him. He will then fetch and return as well as any dog I've seen - and I didn't even have to teach him!

Come bedtime, Portie will race us upstairs. He will then jump into bed with us and curl up next to me right under my chin and purr himself to sleep. Everyday is an adventure with our "Mr. Personality".

Zack

M, 2.5, Black/grey/white

Domestic shorthair

Mr. Laid Back, easygoing

Zack is our grey and black tabby, and one of three cats in our family. Zack, like most cats, is crazy about birds. Even though he doesn't go outside, he loves to watch them from the kitchen window.

Every morning when my husband goes to work, he will go downstairs and pull up the blinds in the kitchen overlooking the front porch. If the birds are there, my husband will call to Zack, "Zack, the birds are down here. Hurry up!" Zack will come tearing down the stairs, jump up on the table and plaster himself to the window, his tail twitching wildly. Sometimes, he will sit there for several hours, hoping to catch a glimpse of his "birdies".

HERNDON   22071
Kathy & Danny Hertel, 3114 Nestlewood Dr

Missy

F, 1, Black & white

Domestic shorthair

Sweet & playful

We got her from a pet store. She was a Christmas present from my brother. She was very sick with worms and had to be medicated for a while when she was still a kitten.

We discovered that she loved to play with small paper balls made of newspaper. A trick she does is that she will return the paper ball & drop it at your feet so you can flick it again for her. She will do this several times until she or you tire of the game or the ball gets soggy.

Socks

F, 9 months, Gray & white

Domestic shorthair

Sweet, loving, independent, sly, playful

One reason my cat is special is because of her personality. I guess you could say she is kind of like the Dr. Jekyll and Mr. Hyde of cats. My cat is also very acrobatic. When you hold a toy such as a feather over her head, she will jump up and do a back flip. Another thing she does is stick her head in a drinking glass to drink water. She can also see two dimensional objects. At least I think she can because she enjoys watching the characters on T.V. She is also very mischievous. She will knock over the fish food, somehow get off the top and eat it. She is also very good at getting shut into places such as the bathroom, closets and drawers.

NORFOLK   23503

Ruth A. Hunt, 9268 Buckman Av

Twinkle Toes

M, 22 dec, Seal Point

Siamese

Was loved by everyone.

Twinkle Toes (King Tut) is a Seal Point. He was very aristocratic and loyal. Would warn me if anyone came near the apartment. Went everywhere with me (except to work) shopping, biking and etc. When flying, he would be wrapped in a baby blanket and held in my arms. Never a peep from him. Can't write enough about Twinkle. He would wake me up in the morning at six, and let me know when it was 10 pm by staring at me by sitting in front of me in the evening. Twinkle helps break the way for Siamese cats to be judged in their own class in the Household Pet Shows. For several years, I almost lost him but for a lot of TLC. Twinkle passed away at the age of 22 years. I still miss him, as he was my life.

Tigar

M, 26 dec, Seal Point

Siamese

Very good.

Tigar, a Seal Point Siamese passed away at age 26. A true Siamese with crooked tail, a bit slanted-eyes (cross-eye) which was constantly moving. A symbol of his ori-

gins. Like the others he will be missed. Tigar like Twinkle would watch out for the other kittens when brought home. Would step on their leash if they would go near the sidewalk. Love to play games that I make up.

RICHMOND   23228

Jane Reaves & Sarah Levy, 8404 Muldoon Ct #308

Samuel P. Katz

M, 2, Black and grey

Domestic short hair

Independent, playful, smart

"Sam" was adopted in 1992. He immediately displayed his disdain for cuddling, hugging, and affection. He did, however, show a great deal of interest in taking small items and depositing them into his food bowl or hiding them. I soon started to hide his favorite toys from him. It has developed into a great game. I hide his toy, he deposits it on my bed, and on and on.

He loves to play "fetch". He brings his color pick of the day (he has five balls to play with - all different colors). I throw the ball and he runs as fast as he can to bring it back. When he's tired of the game he brings back the ball, drops it at my feet, then sits on it!

RICHMOND   23235

Sue Roth, 1441 Elmart Lane

"Kitty" Roth

F, 7, Gray w/ black stripe and w/ cream shaded belly

Tabby

Kitty . . . phone home

Especially lovable, friendly to all, outgoing, loyal companion and loves to talk a lot.

THE CAT THAT LIKES TO TALK ON THE TELEPHONE

Several years ago Kitty started coming up to the telephone, pawing the cord and meowing up a storm as I was calling the weather each morning to check the forecast for that day. This was her way of getting my attention since she knew I'd be gone all day to work. Now whenever I make a call she will do this! With personal calls (most of those cat lovers), I will say "Kitty say hello" to that person and she will go up to the telephone and meow her "hello".

RICHMOND   23226

Loretta Statton, 1718 Rockwood Rd

Dylan

M, 3, Blue Point

Siamese

Very friendly, loved people, children and other animals

This is the story about my Little Buddy "Dylan". He was a stray kitten that I was going to find a home for, but when I saw his little face I knew I would never give him up.

I already had 2 cats, which adopted him and he took to them right away. He loved everyone, people, children, cats and dogs. He was the friendliest cat I ever had. I taught him to fetch one night with an aluminum foil ball. We would go outside and play fetch. Anyone who saw him do this was always amazed.

I taught him to come when I whistled. He would walk with me to get the mail and to

Dylan – the best cat I ever had

the dumpster to take the trash. He loved for me to take him for walks through the woods. If I went outside he would follow me everywhere. We would clean the car together. He didn't help of course, but he loved just being by my side. He was truly the best cat I ever had.

STAFFORD   22554

Sharon Riley, 38 Evans Lane

JR

M, 2, Yellow Tabby

Not real lovable, but loves to be with you.

JR doesn't put his toys away

JR likes to play chase around the house. When I stop and turn around to chase him, he jumps up for me to catch him. He will go get in the bath tub and meow in a tone that makes you look for him. When you get there he wants to drink water from the tub. If you ask him if he wants a treat, he will look at you and go put his nose on the can to show you where they are. He will only eat his treats from your hand. Our house looks like we have a small child. JR carries his toys around and they are all over the house.

STAUNTON   24401

Steve Hotz, 217 S Fayette St Apt C

Sandy

F, 8 months, Tan, red

Red tabby

She's a lot like another person and she's spoiled.

We bought Sandy at a pet shop for $5 and even though she belongs to me and my girlfriend, she won't have anything to do with her or anyone else. She sleeps just about anywhere, but likes the top of our TV set best. She jumps on my shoulder at different times of the day or night and stays there while I walk around and do things like housework and she nuzzles me a lot.

She also likes to have fresh water - she comes running in the kitchen every time I turn the water on. Recently I got a dog and since he's been here, we have to deal with him. But sandy and the dog play and have a great time - in fact they eat each others food . . . but Sandy also eats vegetables and hot sauce.

Tony
M, 1, Beige & white
Unknown
He's a little skittish.

Tony is a stray that wandered up to our door and we took him in. When he first came here he didn't like to go outside - even on good days. One time when he did go out he jumped off the second story porch (8 or 9 feet down to the ground), because we were trying to catch him.

Sandy, our other cat, bothered us whenever we eat supper, but Tony never did. He just sat and watched. He was really a strange cat. He started to spray and mess on things, so we just let him go now that the weather is warm. We haven't seen him much since, but we would like to see him and know he's OK.

VIRGINIA BEACH
Dawn Langworthy
Atila The Hun
F, 2, Mix of black, cream, red, yellow, white, orange
British tortoiseshell shorthair
Intelligent, dainty, affectionate, good-natured, stealthy, beautiful

Atila has one T instead of two T's in her name. She loves extra soft throw blankets to lay on. Eats a varied tavern style diet. Sits up like a prairie dog . . . self-taught. Loves to wear her collar and tags, but can still walk quietly. Begs better than most canines can. She loves to chew the covers on cat books. Is a ham when taking pictures and loves to pose. An expert exterminator - loves to watch nature, play in boxes and bags. Sleeps with stuffed creatures and is an Honorary Teddy Bear. A rare, devot-

ed and loyal breed and friend.

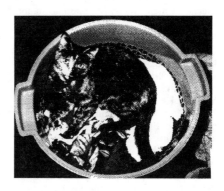

Honorary Teddy Bear

WEST VIRGINIA

MOATSVILLE   26405
Lisa Nine, RT 1 Box 88
Prancer
M, 1.5, Orange & white
Mixed
Smart, loving caring, playful, mischievous

My cat is special because he stays by my side when I'm sick. He protects me by growling when someone is outside before the dogs bark. He answers me when I ask a question by meowing back. He's better than a dog. He chases me around the house, he jumps and bites my legs. He answers the phone when it rings. He runs ahead of me and knocks it off the hook and meows. He loves other animals we bring into the house, even a hamster and birds. And he's so cute when he begs sweets off my mom and me. He loves to ride in the car. He is my best friend!

MORGANTOWN   26505
Trish Phillips, Rt 4 Box 174-B
Sterling Silver - alias: **The Penguin**
M, 1, Lilac color point - mitted w/blaze
IRCA Ragdoll

Sunny; child-like; thrives on love & attention; always underfoot Sterling Silver is special in many ways, but one uncommon feature, in particular, has earned him his nickname of The Penguin.

Often, throughout the day, Sterling Silver looks more like a penguin than a cat. He'll sit up on his hind legs with his back straight and his front feet hanging limp by his side. He often says "Me-up" instead of "Meow" when assuming The Penguin position so I'll be sure to notice him. He knows I think he's cute. Sometimes he even sounds like he's speaking English. If he wants something to eat, he'll go to the refrigerator and say "Me-up" as he sits by the door like The Penguin until I open it and give him a snack.

The Penguin does his thing

When I'm eating and he wants a piece too, he sits up like The Penguin. If I don't give him a taste, because I doubt he'll like it, he remains in The Penguin position and swivels his upper body up and down and from side to side, like Chubby Checker doing The Twist, until I give him a taste. And he usually surprises me by eating it!

PARKERSBURG   26104
Pam Lantz, 2305 45th St
Aspen
F, 10, Black w/white locket and one white foot
Longhair domestic
Shy, loner, selective of humans or cats
One year ago, after working the night before, I was sound asleep at 3:30 AM. Aspen, who hadn't slept in the bed since I acquired the 3rd and 4th cat, was pawing

me awake. Thinking she wanted to snuggle, I lifted the covers and petted Aspen. Her body was rigid and I thought maybe something was wrong with one of the other 3 cats. I jumped up with my bedside flashlight and followed her to the exercise room. The other 3 cats were there (usually they are in bed with me.) I heard a car start up at the side of the house. The next day I noticed the screen was off track on the sliding glass door. The incident prompted me to obtain a more secure door and Aspen received much praise at her intelligence.

Ajax
M, 10, Black
Domestic longhair
Aspens brother, loving, sociable
Several years ago I came home from work. My sister, who lived with me for a short time, was reading. Ajax followed me and paced back and forth with a strange expression on his face. I asked my sister if she noticed his strange behavior and she confessed she accidentally closed the refrigerator door on his tail earlier that day. I held him and gave soothing sympathetic sounds and he finally let me alone and rested - justice was served.

Chapter Thirteen

Who's Who in the Southeast

ALABAMA

BIRMINGHAM   35244
Jamie Brock, 4540 Lake Valley Dr
Sundance
M, 2, Blue Point
Himalayan
Easy going; affectionate; extremely intelligent
Sundance can do so many things that I never knew cats could do. He can spell the word "treat", goes to the door when the doorbell rings, gives kisses when properly asked, and loves to ride in the car. He has more personality than most humans. I've heard people say they wish their pets could talk . . . well, when Sundance looks at me with those huge blue eyes, he expresses himself perfectly and never says a word.

Cheyenne
F, 1, Golden Tabby
Persian
Perky & cute
Cheyenne is a perfect little girl, petite and feminine. However, she thinks she is a bunny since she never walks or runs. She hops. She also brings her toy rat to bed like a child with a favorite toy. She is very jealous of my other cats and will politely push them aside for my attention and affection.

BIRMINGHAM   35216
Denise Dowdey, 3228-C Westbrook Dr

Bits
F, 2, Black with 4 white paws
Just basic; has the sleek, silky coat like Burmese
Inquisitive, acrobatic
I knew Bits was special when I asked a group of caged cats and kittens, "Who wants to come home with me?", and a little paw came out through the bars. She made no sound. She just stared at me with big green eyes. So that's how she came to be with me and Mister, my older cat.
Bits and Mister love watching TV especially Catnip Video. Although Mister is my older cat, he has always deferred authority to Bits and watches her carefully to see what she does. It's clear they operate on two totally different wavelengths.
Bits most unusual talent has to do with her acrobatic abilities. She hangs upside down with her head down to look at you - it's one of her affectionate gestures. She can dead leap 5 feet easily. I'm filled with amazement, love and admiration.

Mister
M, 7, Yellow with 4 white paws & white chest
Longhair tabby
"Garfield"; priorities are eat, sleep & be petted.
Mister was a 2 year old abandoned "unfixed" male when I came across him. He KNEW I would rescue him; when I reached out to touch him, he immediately started purring loudly. At that time I had a dog. I'd never had a cat but I knew it was unusual for them to purr to a first-time stranger.
I read somewhere that animals are soul

companions. How comforting a warm, purring cat can be. His needs are simple. To be loved, fed and protected. He's too sophisticated to indulge in cat toys, though he will indulge in catnip on occasion and play chase with Bits.

Mister enjoys a favorite show

DORA   35062
James & Sandra Street, Rt 2 - Box 830
Casey
M, 8 months, Black/white
Mixed - medium hair
Very amusing & energetic.
My husband and I found Casey on the side of a lonely road near our country home. He was a tiny stray and very frightened. We took him home and he's been a joyful member of our family ever since. He has been so eager to please that he will fetch his toys and come trotting proudly back to us with his tail high in the air. At first we thought Casey was an accidental addition to our family. However, now we believe it wasn't an accident after all.

MOBILE
Colleen Gray
Honey Bun
M, 6, Beige/white
Shorthair mix
Sweet, easy going, determined
Honey Bun was a stray and adopted by a convent of sisters. He became the school and convent cat. It wasn't unusual to find Honey Bun asleep on the top of the pile of National Geographics in the library or snuggled in the bookshelf of a classroom. He was a comfort to both "stressed out" teachers and students.

When the school closed, Honey Bun became a celebrity. His photo was taken by a local paper and picked up by the AP which printed his photo throughout the U.S.

Honey Bun had offers for a new home. Fortunately, he stayed in the South. Now an apartment dweller in Mobile, he lives with a human and two parakeets. What a life!

Honey Bun – the Convent Cat

REFORM   35481-9802
Martha H Kilpatrick, Rt 2 Box 1 G
Morrisa
F, 9, Orange & white
Mixed (some Persian)
Affectionate, acute sense of hearing, lovable, nosey, understanding
Morrisa holds her white-tipped bushy tail up high, rolls on her back for a "tummy rub", rings bells on the back door on a string to go outside, goes around from back to front porch, to the rocking chair or swing, plays hide and seek when I am making up my bed - she crawls under the sheet. She sleeps on the foot of my bed at night, wakes me up with a kiss in the morning light. When I sit down to watch TV, read, relax, make a lap, she comes to cuddle close, curl up and take a nap.
See poem in chapter 8: Lap Cats Extraordinaire.

ARKANSAS

HARRISON   72601
Barbara Stewart, Rt 1 Box 190
Sassafras
F, 4, Chocolate spotted
Ocicat
Very friendly & people oriented
I work a night shift and every night when
I come home, Sassy greets me at the door.
She then runs around the living room once
or twice and leaps up on my shoulder and
gives me a hug.
Sometimes she almost knocks me down as
she weighs 12 pounds.

FLORIDA

BOCA RATON
Linda Sturdy
Savannah
M, 4, Ruddy
Abyssinian
Loving, friendly, and outgoing to people

Savannah loves the camera

Savannah loves to go out with me, ride in
the car, and be with people. We often go
shopping, to art shows, and on simple
errands and he loves it.
He was the official greeter of a national

Abyssinian cat show and was chosen as
"The Most Aby Abyssinian" by the Abyssinian Cat Club of America.
Most of all he loves to visit my first grade
classroom and spend the day with the children.
He will be featured in a locally produced
show about animals, which will soon go
into production. He loves it when I photograph him and usually he looks right at the
camera. He has met and been photographed
with Gunther Gebel-Williams, noted animal
trainer, James Galway, internationally
known flutist, and James Judd, Conductor
of the Florida Philharmonic Orchestra. He
has also met Dr. Louis E. Vine, well-kno-
wn veterinarian/author who will be writing
about Savannah in his next book "Kinky
Cats".
Jasmine
F, 4, Ruddy
Abyssinian
Sweet & loving
Whenever I come home, Jasmine is always
there to greet me with chirps, purrs, and
teeny little kitty love-bites. She loves to sit
and snuggle for hours on my lap, purring
all the while. She follows me around the
house and is always fascinated by whatever
I am doing. She is sweetness purr-sonified!
(Jasmine is Savannah's littermate.)

CLEARWATER   34619
Tarra McMillin, 360 Bayshore Blvd #107
Gidget
F, 1, Tortoisehell
Tabby
Loveable, comical, human
It was a cool, rainy March day. I was
working, thinking about the upcoming
weekend, when I got word of three kittens
found under a bush. Their mother was
nowhere around. I had to look. I already
had a four year old Himalayan. There she
was - a one pound adorable scared kitten.
The other two went quickly. She was the
last one left, it was quitting time, and they
were taking her to the Humane Society. I
wouldn't have forgiven myself - so home
she went.
It has been a whole year of joy and entertainment. She plays fetch - she taught
herself. I never taught her. You throw her
toy, she will run and get it and bring it

back and drop it in your lap! She also loves bread. One night I heard a noise at the foot of my bed. There she was with a brand new whole loaf of bread! . . . Eating it! She's a real talker and loves to sleep with me. Every night she goes into the bedroom by herself at 10:00 - bedtime!

One last thing . . . I think since she was taken so young from her mother and I had to bottle feed her for three weeks, she thinks I'm her mother. She will suck on my arm while kneading - just like she's milking! She's over a year old and I can't break her of this habit.

She's such a character - everyone always asks about her and asks what antics she's up to now. I could go on and on about the things she's done. Also her nickname is "Keepoo".

COCONUT CREEK
Mary-Ann Muchnick
Daisey
F, 11, White/black
Oriental mix
Friendly enough, but sometimes bites

She hisses, sometimes at us, usually at others. Daisey shakes hands and sits on command. She has cystitis, but likes to eat her prescription diet. But she sleeps a lot and runs under the bed if she hears load noises, such as a tea kettle. She scares easily. Sometimes she licks or kisses me on my hand. She loves treats and knows the word. When she wants a treat, she walks across the bureau to the cabinet and cries (meows) till I give her a treat. If I don't, she walks over to another part of the bureau and lays down. She also has good balance.

She also jumps up on things (furniture) and runs all around the house - and for an eleven-year old - that's something. I don't think she knows just how old she is.

DAYTONA BEACH   32118
Mary T Smith, 101 Seabreeze Blvd #314
Sarah
F, 15, Grey tabby
Outgoing, talkative and playful

Sarah was rescued from a neighbor who did not take very good care of her, and after a bout of ear mites and cystitis, she is now healthy and has lived with me 8 years. In January 1993, I had major surgery and was home in bed for 10 days. Sarah never left my side except for nature calls. When I was up and around, she was always at my side, helping to cook meals, supervising baths and greeting all visitors. She was an excellent care giver.

JACKSONVILLE
Tanya Gifford
Oliver
M, 9 months, Black, white & brown
Ordinary cat
Entertaining, loving, playful

I knew Oliver was the cat for me the day I walked into the shelter. He was in a cage all by himself. When I walked in, he put both paws outside the cage and let out a big meow. It was as if he said, "take me." So I did.

He's done many special things since then. I was sitting on the living room floor. All of a sudden Oliver jumped three feet high and grabbed a wasp that was flying toward my head. He wrestled it to the ground receiving a sting in the process. He was a little swollen, but was over it quickly. This story is special to me because I'm very allergic to wasps. I wouldn't have recovered nearly as fast. My little Oliver saved me from a lot of pain. He's my hero.

JACKSONVILLE   32225-3766
Sally Ann Hart, 3333 Monument Rd Apt 1609
Bugsy
M, 2, Orange and white
Tabby

Bugsy – a faithful walker

Arrogant, nosey, demanding but independent

Bugsy was the runt of the litter, so in turn he was the terror. He loves sliding across floors in plastic grocery bags. His meow comes in short, broken spurts, not the normal meow. His most unique characteristic is his love of going for walks with me. He follows along faithfully every night as we walk around the apartment complex. He sits and waits if I stop to pet another cat or talk to someone. If I'm not paying him attention, he'll run in front of me, throw himself on the ground and roll on his back until I scratch his stomach.

Chip [owner: Bonnie Hart - Bath, ME 04530

M, 7, Grey and white

Tabby

Aloof, arrogant, pest

Chip is a macho cat. He was found in a box of puppies. As a kitten, he terrorized the neighborhood by sneaking in and out of people's homes. One neighbor even took a hose to him to try to keep him away, but it did not faze Chip. He loves cantaloupe. He entertains at parties with his antics and expressions of disgust. He sneaks sips of people's drinks when they're not looking! His comical feature is his big ears placed to the side of his head which give him a funny look of disgust.

JACKSONVILLE

Christine Hunter

Shallimar

F, 4.5, Sealpoint

Balinese

Dignified, quiet, funny, loyal

When my daughter, Christine, comes home from work, Shallimar cannot contain her happiness. She jumps and dances with joy. If she is not in the mood to be petted by visitors, she hisses, but does not bite or scratch. Of course she never hisses at "the adored one". She follows her "person" everywhere. Sometimes, when Christine is reading or watching television, Shallimar brings one morsel of cat food from another room, puts it on the floor near her beloved, and eats it. Thus a human might bring in a cup of coffee to be companionable. A very special cat indeed!

JACKSONVILLE   32257

Major Gail E Marion, 3200 Hartley Rd Apt 70

Ray-Gun

M, 2, Silver tabby

Silver Tabby Domestic

Curious, independent, intelligent, loyal

Ray-Gun is an Attack Cat. One weekend a month, his owner, Major Gail E. Marion, reports to Army Reserve drill at West Palm Beach, FL. Private Ray-Gun is left charge of their quarters. A friend comes over to pet sit. Ray-Gun sees it as an invasion of the enemy. As soon as her car pulls up, he is in alert status and mobilizes for war. He attacks The Enemy - biting, grabbing her legs, hissing, and tearing her stockings. He cannot be bribed or misled from the mission with food or treats.

When The Enemy calls on the answering machine, Ray-Gun recognizes her voice and takes the receiver off the hook. When she calls on the phone, he bites the cord or steps on the buttons to disconnect. With his effective body language and vocabulary, Private Ray-Gun convinces The Enemy to retreat. He is dedicated and loyal to his owner; uniquely qualified as a Guard Cat and demonstrates courage.

Jacksonville

Marjorie

Sweet Pea

F, 9 dec, Gray, white, orange

Unknown

Loveable, independent and a thinker

A sophisticated cat

Sweet Pea was an unusual cat because: she had a special air of sophistication and a

mind of her own. She would let you know
when she was ready to eat, would nibble at
your ankles for a second helping. She
decided which door she wanted to be let
out, which bathroom face basin she wanted
you to turn on the water to get herself a
drink. She would put her paw on the grooming tools when she wanted special grooming.

The neighbors loved her and would talk to
her just as if she were another person. She
seemed to have understood. Sweet Pea met
an untimely death in November 1992. This
is in memory of the uncommon love we
had for her, an uncommon cat.

Jacksonville   32207
Grace Prescott, 1204 Peach Tree St
Lucy
F, 3, Multi
Calico Tabby
Princess-terrorist
Lucy was the runt, so I thought I was
getting a delicate princess, but what I got
was a 7 1/2 lb terrorist. Her first love is to
lurk in the tub, waiting to pounce out at
victims. We call her "Tub Shark". Next she
loves to sleep in the rain gutters, scaring
the neighbors by just leaving her feet sticking up. We do not say H A M aloud as she
loves it dearly and must have it! She hates
the ice cream truck and growls at its music.
She torments her older friend "Shah", who
is twice her size. I have enjoyed watching
her personality develop, but I'm glad we're
past the terrible two's!
Shah
M, 11, Brown Tabby
Domestic Shorthair
Senatorial/pompous
Shah was born in a closet at the office and
is my husband's first cat. We raised him on
my father's diet of chicken livers and
whole milk to "build a big cat." He's 16
1/2 lbs. His favorite food is fried chicken
and he will steal it anywhere he finds it. He
is known for walking on the highest surface
available - indoors or out. He loves Albert
and sits in his lap every night. He stocks
the dining room with lizards and pulls them
out when he's bored. He also sorts through
my kitchen cabinets.

JACKSONVILLE   32257

Barbara Wells, 4150 Castlebay Dr
Tiger
M, 5, Orange
American domestic shorthair
Loving, obedient and curious.
Tiger was the smallest cat from a large
litter, rescued at about six weeks. He has
the most loving heart of any cat I have ever
met. He seems to sense when I am unhappy
and does his very best to comfort me by
cleaning my face and rubbing his head on
my chin. His love is unswerving and unending, especially when he deposits his
fifteen pounds in the middle of my chest
and proceeds to purr louder than the television or stereo. He comes when he is called
and goes to his room at bedtime without
any argument. He is truly remarkable.
Skrapper
M, 4, Orange & white
American domestic shorthair.
Playful, curious, a bit standoff
When found on the third floor of a hospital
parking garage, Skrapper was covered with
fleas, dirty and starving, but he had capti-
vating blue eyes. He has learned to drink
from a bowl without drowning. He has
taught us all, even visitors, how to play
"fetch" with him. He brings milk bottle
rings for one to toss and he "fetches" and
returns for another toss until he has had
enough. He doesn't cuddle much, but he
shares his love in his own remarkable way.

LAKELAND   33809
Tillie Carlson, 941 O'Doniel Dr
Hoby
M, 6, White
Mixed shorthair
Hyper, very friendly, fast moving
My uncommon cat, Hoby, does something
unusual that I've never heard of another cat
doing. Almost daily he (all 18 pounds)
leads me to the bedroom and gives me a
great massage on the back of my neck
using his declawed paws, standing there
kneading about 10 minutes. Uncommon,
also are the different ways of communicating with his two live-in boarders - my
husband and me. Although he's my cat - he
sits on my hubby's lap, plays and eats with
him (never with me); but I get to wait on
him hand and foot. Hoby just has to -
whistle - oops - MEOW!

Hoby gives a great massage

LUTZ
Michele Meehan
Toby
F, 17.5 dec, Shiny black, white dot on chest, white "underwear"
Domestic
Loyal, humanlike, best friend & companion
Toby was large but firm, agile and athletic as a kitten for 17 years. 25 years and more than 25 cats later - still none compare. She raced down the corridor jumping up in time to turn the light switch. From day one she'd call out to me when lonely, especially at bedtime. Sleeping against my pillow, she'd knead my hair. We played hide-n-seek, peek-a-boo, and tag, taking turns. When brushing my hair, she's stand behind me, moving her front paws high in the air for minutes, in imitation, until I finished. Her spirit lives on.
Mr. Wheedles
M, 7, Chocolate swirls, white underside & paws
Tabby
One of a kind, indescribable
I found a box of 6 orphans, 2 weeks old. After weaning them, Mr. Wheedles took over. Just one year old himself, he taught them to be cats: grooming, hunting, wrestling, loving. Cookie and Mittens, "made out of love", picked me to be their mommy. But Mr. Wheedles is their daddy.
Despite his soprano meow and small size, he has an 8-cylinder purr and can hunt in his sleep. He has jumped out of his sleep, spun around, and leapt at a spider on the wall.

I feel loved and protected by him. Twice he was lost; I prayed until I found him.

MIAMI   33183
Lynn Vernon, 8700 SW 133 Ave Rd, Apt 208 Bdg 8
Angel
F, 1.5, All white
Mixed
Loving, protective, jealous, can be a brat.
People are cruel. I found my Angel stuffed in a dumpster. She was all white with sky blue eyes that melted my heart. She acts like a child because she loves to be held like a baby and is very protective of her "momma". Whenever I take a shower, Angel sits on the sink and mimics "momma" washing her face. She also does this to get attention whenever company comes over and she wants to show off. She is a breath of fresh air and she will always be by my side.

Angel . . . like a child

T.J. (Tiny Junior)
M, 3, White & brown
Mix - Lynx Point Siamese & brown Tabby
Nurturing, strong, loving, can be a bully.
My cat T.J. is special to me because of his nurturing personality. He is the patriarch of all my cats. He loves anything little. When I brought a kitten home that I found in a dumpster, he suddenly became surrogate daddy. He groomed her and kept her warm. He must have done too good of a job because she thought he was momma and tried to nurse on him! He also is very vocal and "talks" constantly.

MIMS   32754-5264

Trish Freeman, 3838 Billie Pl.

Sylvester "Sly" Freeman

M, 2, Black/white

Mixed

Outgoing, friendly, loving

Sly had a pretty rough start in life. When he was a mere 3 months old, he somehow managed to slither up into the motor of my '84 Camaro, of course unbeknownst to me. Imagine how bad I felt when I started that car! But, through hard work and a lot of love (not to mention $300), Sylvester survived with only a small scar on his nose to remind us of the tragedy. It took him awhile to start filling out after his shock, but now he's my "big ole' Sly Guy"! I never thought he would forgive me, but I think he realizes I couldn't help it. In fact, every time he comes in through his cat window, he insists on sauntering over to me on the couch and giving me a grateful "high five" with his big paw suspended in the air and a hearty meow in his throat. This is why my Sylvester James is a very special friend and companion to me. I'll never forget what we went through together. There's no other like him!

NAPLES   33999

Erin Stubbe, 4997 17th Pl SW

Bernie

F, 1, Black

Mixed

Affectionate, loving, playful

She has a keen sense of survival and devotion to her family. Three months after she was so ill, my 12 year old daughter got very ill and missed 3-1/2 months of school. The entire time she was sick and at home, Bernie never left her side. Wherever she was lying, Bernie was cuddled as close to her as possible. When she started feeling better, Bernie started paying attention to the rest of us. It was like she knew Erin was out of danger so it was safe to start being with someone else.

See story in chapter 3: The Good Samaritans.

Buddy

M, 8 months, Grey tiger

Mixed

Very playful but loving

He sometimes thinks he is a dog and comes running when you call. He also loves to play fetch. He always follows his sister to the litter box, but very patiently waits outside the door until she's done - then goes in and takes his turn.

NORTH FORT MEYERS   33917

Pat Roberts, 11721 Foxhill Rd

Cirrus

M, 1-1/4, Cream

Persian

Stuck-up - lovable to known family members

A meow for all reasons

Cirrus is special in all ways. He has a different meow for things - to go outside (on leash) - his favorite toy - a treat - a critter from outside. For a tummy rub he has a silent meow then he does a somersault and rolls on his back for his rub.

He likes to play hide & seek and chase. I say to him "I'm gonna get you" and he'll go and hide. I'll look for him and he jumps out at me. He doesn't like to be held - but once or twice a week. He'll come and stand at my feet and meow and ask to be held. This may last for 15 minutes of hearing him purr and be lovable - then it's over.

ORLANDO   32854-1037

Brenda Reyes, PO Box 541037

Cream Puff

F, 6, White w/ cream & gray

Longhair of Maine Coon descent

Gentle & affectionate - IF you're allowed near.

"Love Puff, adore Puff, couldn't live without Puff." "The ugliest of the litter," she was to be euthanised when the family moved. So David brought her home to me.

Cream Puff is the most beautiful cat in the world. A meow so dainty and soft it's reminiscent of Marilyn Monroe's whisper. She's my baby girl. When Puff wants to be carried, she says so, then raises her arms to encircle my neck as I lean down to reach her.

Puff is generally very wary of strangers. On rare occasion someone is allowed to pet her on first meeting. Some are NEVER allowed near. To be "Puff-approved" is truly an honor. She purrs so hard she "rattles". Put the vase in the bathtub, please. Puff will overturn it to make her bed in the flowers.

Tubby

M, 6, Brown/black Mackerel Tabby

Domestic shorthair

"Professional Pest", with love

On one Sunday I made my usual trip to Albertsons for cat food. Instead I got a cat! Tubby had been left atop a large trash can outside the store, where two young stock boys found him. They accosted me before I got into the store. "NO! The last thing I need is ANOTHER cat!"

"Meow!" "Meow!" "Meow!!" He looked like a miniature of one already in residence. As my old VW bug had a huge hole in the floor, "Mini" and I waited outside while the boys found a sturdy, ventilated box in which to take him home.

"Meow!" "Meow!!" I could at least keep him until I found a good home. Later that day I returned for the cat food.

Six years later, at 12 lbs, with a waistline approaching the size of my own, "Mini" has been changed to a more fitting "Tubby." He still retains that loud, squeaky "Meow!" As affectionate as he is big, he makes a great lap rug (he insists!) as often as he can. PURRR!!

PALMETTO

Kim Atrosh

Secret

M, dec, Looked like British blue

Mixed

Loving, cuddly, intelligent

I had a very special bond with my cat Secret. Secret seemed able to read my mind. He responded to my thoughts in an almost human-like way. He made me feel protected and comforted. We had gone

through a lot together, and during it all he never left my side. If I were in a chair, he was in my lap. I always fell asleep with my face buried in Secret's warm tummy as he cradled my head in his arms.

This is my tribute to Secret. He died two years ago of kidney failure. I miss him everyday.

Punkin

M, 2, Cream with a hint of orange

Mixed

Loving, mischievous

Punkin was a creamy, orange colored kitten that came to us in the fall of the year. Soon after we had him, we realized Dennis the Menace would have been a better name.

Punkin is two years old now, but still acts like the mischievous kitten he once was. He is curious and gets into everything. He purrs like a steam engine and tries to eat anything he can get his paws on - from the rug on the floor to the knob on the fridge. The best thing about Punkin is his kisses. He loves to give kisses and I love to receive them.

PENSACOLA   32514-6444

Mary Curtis, 4051 E Olive Rd #231

Tip

M, dec, Orange

Persian

Pleasant, easy-going, smart

Tip was my favorite cat. He lap-sat for hours without squirming. He was steady, agreeable, smart, relaxed and a perfect gentleman. He was not a finicky eater and loved his milk, cat chow, water and special treats - vanilla ice cream and sour cream.

He lunched with me, sitting in a chair at the table, his arms resting on the table. He had beautiful table manners and looked so pretty as he daintily licked his ice cream with his rose-petal tongue. He was a joy to behold.

Rorschach

M, dec, Black

Domestic shorthair

Faithful & devoted

Rorschach was so beautiful, assuming all sorts of positions. Hence his name - for each pose resembled an ink blot.

He loved to sleep with us late on weekends, stretching out between myself and my husband. At noon on Saturdays and Sundays, he wanted brunch and gently pushed us out of bed! Like all our many cats, he loved our great fuchsia azaleas and camellias and sniffed them with pleasure!

SEBRING　　　　　　　　　　　　33872
Patricia Lloyd, 3215 Grand Prix Dr
Okeechobee Red
M, 9, Orange & white
Tabby
Loving & easy going
Okee is a very loving cat. He'll let anyone do anything to him. He comes when you call his name or whistle. He likes to play in the rain, play with dogs, go for car rides and cuddle with you on the couch watching TV. He goes out on a leash, fetches and retrieves balloons and likes to comb your hair with his paws. In 1987 I had cancer. During the time I spent on crutches, Okee developed a limp. We found that the only time he limped was when I was in the room. Otherwise he was fine . . . Is that cat comedy or cat sympathy?

Muskogee Gray
F, 7, 2-tone gray & white
Siamese mix
Sassy & independent
Musky is very choosy about who is allowed to touch her. She is very independent and lets you know what she wants - not only by body language - but also from her very clear speaking.

She comes when you call her name or whistle. She goes out on a leash and likes to take walks. She likes to play hide-n-seek and loves to chase lizards (only to bite off their tails and let them go.) She likes to go for car rides also . . . but only if you listen to her choice of music.

Some people call her mean, but she'll always be mama's little girl.

STUART　　　　　　　　　　　　34997
Sharon Hodges, 4506 SE Windsor Ct
Misty
F, born 8/92, Blue, cream & white
Calico-Tabby
Excessive curiosity, agility & tenderness
Misty was adopted after hurricane Andrew.

She's strictly an indoor cat but would love to explore outside. She has to know where my husband and I are each second, or she will meow nervously as if we've abandoned her.

Misty carries her Frisbee

Each morning I pick her up and she climbs on my shoulders and stays perched as a bird might. She plays "fetch" (when she feels like it). She enjoys carrying her stuffed puppy in her mouth, even running with it or other toys. Her keen eyesight zeroes in on the most minute bug or hapless lizard. She'll alert me to her prize before fatally pouncing. The best part of my day is returning home finding Misty waiting for me on the couch with a kiss & purr!

SUNRISE　　　　　　　　　　　　33351
Victoria Link-grimes, 8623 NW 36th St #201
Bosco
M, 9, Cream Point
Himalayan
Totally loving, easy going & curious
Bosco came into my life just prior to my divorce and then accompanied me through 8 years of employment relocation throughout the country. Bosco made the car trip from Missouri to California two days after major surgery . . . stitches and all without a complaint. He has flown so much he has frequent flyer miles! And he only travels in the cabin - NEVER with the luggage!

Bosco has been through his share of my "relationships". He always had good judgement in the men I dated - I learned to watch his reactions and then decide on future dates! I've recently remarried after 8 years and Bosco has totally accepted my new husband and vice versa.

Bosco has warmed the hearts of everyone he's ever met, even if they don't like cats. He has touched my life in so many wonderful and loving ways and will always be a very special part of me.

WEST PALM BEACH   33405-3903
Barbara J Russo-Avrett, 705 Colonial Rd
Smoochie
F, 5 ?, Solid gray
Domestic (stray)
Loveable
My cat Smoochie adopted me when I was sitting on my front porch. She was a mess - fleas, ear mites and thin as a rail. I've always had a weakness for gray cats, and as messy as she was, she was still beautiful.

All I did was say "Hi Kitty" when she walked in front of me and she came right over. I petted her and gave her some food and sat with her till she finished. When she was done she crawled into my lap for more petting. She then started pawing (no claws) at my face, as if to motion me to bring my face toward her. As I did I asked her "what do you want, kisses?" With that she stood up in my lap and started licking my nose like crazy.

She will not do this for my husband or any of my friends, but now all I have to do is ask for "kisses" and she comes right over, jumps in my lap and licks my nose like crazy.

Knee-ca-nu
M, 2, Solid gray
Domestic (Smoochie's son)
"Mr. Mellow"
Knee-ca-nu is a huge cat (almost 23 pounds) and his claim to fame is his "Belly Show."

While petting him, if you want to rub his belly, that's fine with him. Just tell him to "plop and show me the bell." Upon request - he drops from all fours to his back and spreads out so you can rub his belly - and don't quit too soon or you'll get a very dirty look!

WEST PALM BEACH   33415
Susan Levine, 930 Woodland Ave

Jingles
M, 5 months, White & black
Very loving and well behaved
Jingles has an elf like quality. He is mostly white but has a black tail with a tiny white tip and black spot under his mouth. Every night around midnight he likes to wake us up with a kiss - on the mouth.

He likes to play with cat toys and baby toys. One day I gave him a ball to play with on my bed. He decided to run in the living room with the ball in his mouth and exchange it for another toy, which he brought back to bed.

E.T.
F, 10, White, brown, red, black
Short haired calico-tabby
Loving to family, reserved to strangers
E.T. looks like a chipmunk, with long stripes down her back. She has beautiful expressive eyes, lined with black. Her favorite activities are eating (every two hours) and standing over her favorite ball and meowing. She purrs like an alarm clock when you pet her.

GEORGIA

ACWORTH   30102
Sheila Ratliff, 1136 Norfolk Dr
Ariella
F, 1, Shaded silver
Persian
Very friendly, loves people
I know cat owners aren't supposed to use the "D" word, but Ariella's resemblance to a dog is uncanny. The person we adopted her from had 25 cats and kittens up for adoption. Ariella, looking like a purebred Persian, was definitely the friendliest of the bunch. Since day one, Ariella comes when called. She would rather sit on my lap for a tummy rub than any other activity in the world. Ariella rolls over, begs and gives kisses. Are you ready for this one? Ariella even plays fetch with a catnip mouse. Honest, we never trained her to do any of these things!

ALPHARETTA   30201
Daisy Hoyle, 194 Cold Creek Dr
Fremont
M, 4, Orange tabby
Domestic shorthair
Sweet & gentle

So who needs a litter box ???

Fremont is a very special cat. He lives with his twin brother Frisco and two buddies Zeke and Batman - all males and neutered - and they get along together very well. One morning he was investigating the bathroom and hopped up on the john - and got the urge to go. So now he uses it every time he's in the house. He doesn't understand why everyone gets so excited and takes his picture.

ATLANTA   30311-2220
V. Carolyn Harvey, 3224 West Manor Ln SW

Sphinx is pure poetry

Sphinx
M, 5, Tan - white (blue eyes)
Flame Point Siamese
Affectionate, obedient, energetic, loving, playful. Loves to cuddle, rollover & give kisses.

Sphinx was abandoned and homeless,
  we took him in,
And all our love he began to win;
  this kitty was there to claim it all;
Frolicking, playing, and having a ball!
Sphinx wakes me with his paw and a kiss,
  because his breakfast he's afraid he'll miss.
He beats my husband to his favorite chair;
  just to make sure he doesn't sit there!
Sphinx baby-sits and to stop baby's crying,
  he tosses his bell and tricks he keeps trying!
After work he meets me at the door,
  when I call his name, he meows for more!

ATLANTA   30319
Gene Rubin, 1106 Gables Drive
Boy
M, 1, Black & white
American shorthair
Extremely inquisitive and alert

I'm having too much fun to sleep now!

If New York is "the city that never sleeps", I have the cat that never, ever slumbers. He's awake at least 16-18 hours a day, intensely staring and deeply "thinking".
Boy is incessantly active, carrying his toys to me regardless if I'm sitting on the couch or sleeping in bed. If I throw them away, he instantly retrieves them. If he doesn't like a toy sitting in the upper perch of the scratching post, he'll climb it, remove the

toy and "bury" it under the bathroom throw rug. He's an amazing high-jumper, ascending 4 feet plus and descending heights as great as 7 feet. His "Prairie dog" imitation is outstanding, as he sits up on his hind legs, checking out unfamiliar sounds.

Tuna

M, dec, Gray/white

American shorthair

Gentle/loving

I traded 12 ice cream bars for a box containing a 6 week old kitten. He slept on my pillow, around the top of my head, for the next 19 years, then ran away from home one September day. Tuna loved cantaloupe, and always helped sooth my hurting moments with "head-butts" and purrs.

BAINBRIDGE

S. Kay Keller

Pookie

M, 3, Dark with white toes and throat, green eyes

Mixed

Very laid back; wise and all-knowing; big-brother type

Pookie was born in a kettle in my barn with 5 brothers and sisters. He was the darkest and smallest of the litter, and I picked him up and called him "Pookie" and the name stuck. I took him outside everyday and when he learned to walk he would come and stand on my foot when I wore my blue tennis shoes. As he got older, he would play around my horse, and look out for his siblings. When my mother sat outside holding her persian cat, and he would get down and run off, Pookie would help her "round him up" - he always could find the persian if he hid. All she had to do was say "Pookie, get Kirby" and off Pookie would go. Pookie likes to play on a window perch and watch the birds. He sleeps on the bed with me at night, and looks at the clock pointedly when bedtime rolls around. He enjoys looking at "Star Trek" on TV. Pookie is a real big brother - he looks after the house and keeps Tory in line.

Tory

M, 8 months, Beige and brown, blue eyes

Chocolate Lynxpoint Siamese

Very energetic; very loving

Tory was abandoned when he was 2 months old. He had been abused and was very thin. He became very dependent on me and didn't want me to leave him. Every morning he gets up on the vanity and watches me put on my make-up - he steals my powder puff if he can. He goes with me to the door when I leave for work, and then runs to the window perch to watch me drive away. He is very talkative and lets you know that he is cute and precious, and that he wants a treat. He plays with his adopted brother Pookie and they sleep together in their favorite chair. He and Pookie fight over who will sit in my lap - sometimes both do. Tory watches figure skaters on TV - he stands up and puts his paw on them. When the alarm clock goes off, Tory jumps on the bed and meows. Tory puts all his toys in the water dish, and watches to see if they'll float.

CAIRO

Joyce I Keller

Karlie Summer

F, 9 months, Gold & beige

Tabby Persian

A little debutante who's occasionally rambunctious.

Karlie is my companion and friend. At bedtime she curls up close with her back to me to be petted, where she purrs until she goes to sleep. Karlie is an avid mouse watcher - at night mice come to eat from the windowsill bird feeder, and keep her entertained. By day, Karlie keeps an eye on the feeder and hurries to frighten away the birds who, she thinks, come to eat the mice's food. Karlie hates to be brushed, even though her long hair gets tangles. When I try to comb her, she pops my face with a furry paw. Karlie tries to nap on the enclosed porch in the afternoons in a big yellow plastic tub in a rocking chair, and soak up the sun. She also likes to sit on top of her indoor cat tree and drop her toys for me to pick up and hand back to her. Karlie waits until I am reading to decide she wants to sit in my lap. When I am eating, she comes over to investigate and perhaps beg a little tidbit with her tiny, soft-spoken meow.

CARTERSVILLE   30120

Craig & Brenda Shaw, PO Box 1191

Snow Princess

F, 2, White

Turkish Angora

Feisty, sweet, lovable, perfect

Princess was picked (or should I say she adopted me), at the Bartow County Animal Shelter.

She is so sweet, she sits at the desk with me as I'm typing my husbands manuscripts. She has to be EVERYWHERE. She has learned to pull the indoor clothes line down as I hang up clothes. When she sees the dog do tricks (sit-up, roll over), she does them too. When we go anywhere we tell her when we will be back. When we get home we have our greetings.

Her favorite pastime is sleeping on Mom's coat to let everyone know who's boss. She doesn't like other cats and she wants to be the center of attention. Princess is also unique, because she likes to have her toes tickled, and does cat aerobics - when she has an audience that tells her "she is such a pretty baby". Whatever she does, you can't help but love her.

My love for her is very special - she is God's gift to me.

CLAYTON   30525-0381

Nell D Crisp, PO Box 381

Yellow Boy

M, 12.5 dec, Yellow

Domestic shorthair

Friendly, affectionate, charming, magnetic, superior intelligence My cat, Yellow Boy overtly expressed appreciation for his food. From a young cat I observed that every time I bent over to place his plate of food on the floor, Yellow Boy would stand upright on his back legs straining to reach my face with his mouth. I discovered he was wanting to kiss me. This became a daily ritual. He would not eat a bite until he kissed me on the mouth. He would then proceed with his meal. When I was hospitalized and a friend came to my home to feed my cats, he reported that Yellow Boy would not eat until he gave her a big kiss. [Yellow Boy died in August 1992.]

DOUGLASVILLE   30135

Michelle Posten, 6266 Dorsett Shoals Rd Lt#309

Melanie

F, 2, Black and white

Mix (but she looks like she's Siamese)

Funny, very affectionate with me

I was outside doing my yard work, when I met Melanie - my uncommon cat. I heard a cat meowing. I looked up and there was a kitten running to me. She looked up at me, and the next thing I knew there was a kitten climbing up my pants leg and into my arms. She fell instantly to sleep.

She slept for 4 hours in my arms. When she awoke, she didn't even seem curious to know where she was. She just started playing like she had always lived here. And that's so odd, because she is a very cautious and curious cat. She will not let another living soul touch her. When I think back to the day we met, I know now what she knew then - that we were meant to be together.

NORCROSS   30092

Ruth Ketron, 2821 Ashley Club Circle

Sugar

M, 3.5, Frost

Siamese mix, Frost Point

A "people" cat - avoids our other cats

Sugar loves to play with a furry, grey mouse, not a white one. We throw it and he'll retrieve it. We instruct him to "find your mouse" or "go look for your mouse". He'll search until he finds it and then bring it to us to be thrown after a reward of a tummy rub! If ignored, he jumps into our laps and paws our faces, then returns to the floor to sit for us to throw the mouse. He does this until he tires, or until another cat "steals" his mouse. He then crawls into our laps and sleeps.

Zorro

M, 10, Black and white

Domestic Shorthair

Prefers being involved with me

Zorro is a bad poker player, as he gives away his hand by

"chattering" when he's into something he's been told is a "NO". Just thinking of doing a "NO" starts him "chirping" loudly. It's so comical. When directed to go to his bed, he does so and stays until he can come out, if not too long! He'll also obey if told not to go through a door.

NORCROSS   30071

Jim And Lu Ann Ruhoff, 5151 Running Fox Trail

Elvis

M, 2.5, Black

Sweet, friendly

Elvis came to us in a strange way. One day while my husband was loading the trunk of his car going from his home office to the car several times, he found a black kitty about six months old laying amid the various computer cables and such. He put him down in the driveway and went on his way. This friendly little kitty was undaunted, however, and wouldn't go away. Soon we were feeding it and, after a week, he had joined our cat family. He has become the sweetest, most loving cat we own. We call him Elvis because of his loud voice.

Lil Bit

M, 3, All gray

Very long hair

Sweet

Lil Bit is what we call a kissy face. It's my fault. We raised him from about 3 weeks old. Someone dumped him by our back fence. I had to wrap him in a towel to feed him his bottle, and of course, would kiss him like a baby. As he grew to trust us, he soon took to licking our neck, ears, chin, and nose. Only, however, when HE wants to kiss, not necessarily when we want to. But to this day, he is like a baby to us.

RIVERDALE   30274

Shanna & Zach Perry, 582 Roberts Dr #6

Bilbo

M, 1.5, Gray, black

Tabby shorthair

Very human, smart & sweet

Bilbo is one of the smartest cats I've ever known. First of all, Bilbo found us when he was a kitten - he followed us home. That day he followed us for 3/4 of a mile. We got home and he made himself comfy.

Bilbo has a knack for opening drawers and cabinets. He unplugs: lights, fans and alarm clocks. If he doesn't like the way it sounds, he'll unplug it. He also sleeps with his head and front paws out of the covers and on the pillow. I think Bilbo is a human stuck in a cat's body. Oh, he also says, "Ma Ma", when he wants food.

I thought I left my toothbrush in here?
Bilbo

Kaz-A-Rooney

M, 1.5, Orange & white

Tabby medium hair

Very sketchy

Well Kaz is a cat 100%. He's totally different from Bilbo. Kaz does some cute things. He'll give you a kiss on the mouth, if you stick your lips out.

He also answers the telephone if you let it ring more than two times. He pushes it off the hook and then meows. Quite unique. Kaz and Bilbo share our home with Gandalf. He's a 6 month old male, gray & white tabby that is half human - half cat. He turns off light switches and is as clumsy as a dog.

```
LOUISIANA
```

BATON ROUGE   70808

Raina Weldon, 537 E Boyd

Micro

F, 7, Gray tabby on white

Mixed

Demanding, but lovable

Micro was so named as the runt of the litter, but she has since outgrown her name and is now often referred to as "Macro" as she is lovingly teased about her slight weight problem.

She considers all visitors to be her property and immediately gives them a thorough sniffing over before settling into their laps and demanding petting. She uses the toilet rather than the litter box, she loves to eat peas, although she turns her nose up at most people food, and she is a constant inspiration to me as I study to be a veterinarian.

Junior

M, 1, Light orange tabby

Mixed

Relaxed & lovable

Junior was a stray who won our hearts with his lovableness. He waited on our doorstep and rolled over on his back to be petted whenever he saw us, and he happily shared the food we put out for him with any animal that showed up on our porch.

As my birthday present, my boyfriend had Junior neutered and vaccinated, and he is now a very happy indoor cat. He's content to watch birds through the window and "hunt" cat toys, and he doesn't let Micro's occasional hissing deter him from trying to befriend her. He's a real sweetheart!

MANDEVILLE

Raina & Grama

Biscuits

F, 8 months, Calico

Very affectionate, smart, playful!

Biscuits was a stray kitten who needed someone to love. After much patience on the part of Raina, the kitten became trusting, slowly allowed petting, began to eat with someone around, and came into the house.

Biscuits was really easy to potty train. When she got her check-up before being neutered, the feline leukemia test was positive. Since 5 year old Micro was already living with Raina; Biscuits moved into the laundry room and didn't seem to mind. Lonely Grama asked Biscuits to share her home, explore lots of space and have a full time playmate!

NATCHITOCHES   71457

Priscilla R Rachal, 1426 Grace Ave

Blackie

M, 13 months, Black

Mixed shorthair

He starts purring the second I come near

Blackie is one of a family of 16 cats that reside at my address. He was one of the third litter of cats that were born in my house. He is the friendliest of the group and is always in a good mood. He makes me feel good because he purrs all the time I am near him. I brush him almost everyday and we enjoy playing with his toys. He has one that he especially likes and he will bring it to me if we do not put the other toys aside and play with that one.

Janet

F, 2, White, black & orange

Calico mixed shorthair

Makes things happen

Janet is the cat that has nine lives. She is the lone survivor of the first litter of kittens her mother bore. I enjoy watching her tease the other cats, stalk birds, and most of all chase her own tail.

Janet disappeared one evening after we fed her. After about a month I wrote an emotional plea to our local newspaper. A lady 5 miles away had seen Janet and called me after reading my article. After that incident I do not allow her outside at night!! With 2 lives gone, I plan to spread the other 7 over the next 20 years.

MISSISSIPPI

FRIARS POINT   38631

Norma Marinelli, PO Box 132

Muffins

M, 3, Dark gray

Alley

Loving, devoted

See story in chapter 3: *The Good Samaritans.*

SOUTH CAROLINA

COLUMBIA   29223-2406

Sharon H. Perloff, 7400 Hunt Club Rd Apt 303

Cee Cee

F, 3, Black, gray, brown, white

Tabby

Affectionate, talkative, persistent, extremely playful, more like a dog than a cat

Her favorite meal is pressed ham and boiled squash. Her favorite game is chase. Cee Cee lived the first 5 months of her life with a cockatoo that would chase her around the yard. To let me know when she wants to play, Cee Cee arches her back and tip-toes sideways. She drinks water only two ways and neither of them is out of a bowl: out of a juice glass (which I have to hold for her) or from the bathroom sink. When she wants the water turned on, she pulls at the drain stopper with her claw until the noise gets my attention. She does many tricks; with a piece of squash as a reward she, on command, sits, begs on her hind legs, and while sitting will give me a "high five." When family comes to visit, Cee Cee will have nothing to do with them, but my friends are always welcomed in HER apartment and are greeted immediately and warmly.

SIMPSONVILLE

Renee Howard

Schnoop

F, 10, Gray & white

Half Persian, half alley cat

Strange

Schnoop is a 18 lb cat that we have had since she was first-born. She has been an inside cat most of her life so when she goes outside, everything is strange and unusual. There was a memorable evening when she climbed a tree and couldn't figure out how to get down. When we finally coaxed her down, she came down head first. Her back end kept flipping over her front end because of her size. She would stop, turn around head-first again and start over. Finally when she was about 6 feet from the ground, she fell out of the tree. After we determined she was not hurt, we laughed at the whole scene.

The trait that people request to see most often is her expression when the base of her tail is scratched. She turns her head from side to side in perfect rhythm to how her tail is being scratched. When the scratching reaches the optimum level, she sticks her tongue out and it moves with the rhythm as well. This is pretty strange looking but she enjoys the attention.

Delilah [owner: Judy Simpson]

F, 1, Mostly black with a few white tips

Your average alley cat

A trickster with innocent eyes

Delilah is different from most cats that have owned me. She knows how to do tricks that are normally taught to dogs! One of her favorite tricks is fetch. She has a white plastic whiffle ball with holes in it that is great for throwing and retrieving. Whenever the ball is thrown, she chases it, picks it up in her mouth and brings it back for another turn. She has even caught it in mid-air a few times. Most of the time, my throwing arm gets worn out before she gets tired of the game.

She also sits, rolls over, and will occasionally beg - although I believe begging is basically beneath her dignity. She still has the wild kitten aspects to her personality which means hiding under the bed and attacking toes, pouncing on invisible enemies, and generally never sitting still until she is completely worn out. Whether she is digging in the potted plants or asleep, she constantly wears the expression of innocence that says she could not be guilty of anything!

Chapter Fourteen

Who's Who in the Great Lakes

ARLINGTON HEIGHTS
Penny & David Ripley
Oscar
M, 1, Grey
Grey Tiger
Very curious, very playful
Oscar adjusted instantly, and we knew he was special when he started playing with his toys. His favorite trick was to catch sponge balls and carry them away in his mouth. When Oscar wasn't playing with the balls, he was dragging a shoestring; he always had something in his mouth.

He sleeps more now, and grunts, groans and snores during his naps. He is territorial and will chase anyone out of "his" bean-bag. He thinks he is tough, but runs away when anything takes him by surprise.

Oscar's latest game is to bat his dry food across the floor, and attack it like an intruding enemy.

Felix
M, 15, Orange
Tiger
Lazy, laid back, uptight to the dog
Felix really doesn't do any tricks, unlike his cartoon friend. But whenever you talk to him, he always talks back. You can talk to him for five minutes straight - and he will keep talking. He is a lap cat and he always makes sure he rubs you back. But when you scratch a certain place on his back - he licks you continuously and won't quit until you do. We call this the "licky spot".

He is very loving. When I moved, I was afraid he would not be excited when I visited . . . but he does get as excited as a 15 year old cat can. And Felix, although very territorial, does not even care that I smell like another cat. By the way, he weighs 15 pounds and sleeps on my head when I visit.

CHICAGO
Feisty
M, 2, Black/gray/white
Tiger
Lives up to his name
Feisty was exclusively my husband's pet from the day we adopted him from Adopt-A-Pet. I was allowed only to feed him and clean his litter box. (This was Feisty's decision.)

When my husband died one year later, Feisty lovingly transferred all his affection to me! This included sleeping next to me, kissing me, curling up in my lap (even when it isn't convenient) and doing his best to cheer me up when my spirits are down. Feisty was - and still is - a great help in getting me through bad times.

I firmly believe all animals can sense and respond to people's needs and emotions just as Feisty has.

DE KALB 60115
Nathan Luman, 224 Lexington
Chessie
F, 1, Black & white
Common domestic shorthair
Loveable & active

A fetching feline

From an early age Chessie would fetch foil balls, with no training, and bring them back to you. She then drops them in shoes and tries to get them out.

ELGIN   60123
Katherine C. Waltz, 390 S Commonwealth Av
Cashmere
F, 6, Tan and white
Tabby
Moody, spoiled

This is my favorite resting place

Cashmere is a spoiled rotten cat. She was very ill when I got her; the vet and I nursed her back to health, and she has been pampered ever since. She hates all men with one exception - my father. I think her earlier days caused this attitude. When my fiance (Brent) tries to climb into bed, my feline friend bats and hisses at him for stealing "her" side of the bed. Brent has

tried to gain her friendship. He has taught her to play fetch out of nylon balls in order to somewhat satisfy his need for a dog that he will probably never own (my cat would not allow it!) It must be nice to be a spoiled rotten brat...I mean cat.

GENEVA   60134
Vicki Hlavaty, 1020 Manchester Course
Sam
M, 3.5, Black
Mixed breed
He is "completely wonderful", treats his human very well

I just love to chase crumpled paper

There are many reasons why my cat is special to me. I couldn't possibly name them all. One very special thing that Sam can do, which I have never known any other cat to do, is retrieve paper. I was so amazed the first time I saw him do it.

One day my boyfriend Andrew crumpled up a piece of paper and threw it across the room to watch Sammy chase it. Well to our surprise, he not only chased the paper, but he brought it back! I remember saying how I wished we had a camcorder to record the event because I was sure it was pure coincidence. We threw the paper again, he brought it back! Time after time after time. I think that this is just the most fascinating thing I have ever seen a cat do. Sam loves to play "Retrieve the paper!" I can't crumple a paper without him going into the garbage can to get it and play. He knows - canines have nothing on him. He's the greatest! I brag about him and show others how intelligent he is.

LAGRANGE PARK   60525
Kathleen A Kaspar, 1120 Alima Terr
Missy
F, 7, Smoke gray & white; green eyes
Domestic shorthair
Very smart, she opens cabinets, drawers, etc.
Missy was found under the floor of a building in a crawl space where the mother kept her kittens. Four out of eight from the litter died. It was fortunate that I did what the vet told me to do, and we brought her through. I raised Missy from about 4 weeks old - feeding her pablum and baby food. She didn't know how to drink water. Lucky, my black male, took over with her cleaning and drinking water. Now she's healthy and my special character. She has come up to me, wrapped her front paws around my neck when I was in tears and snuggled her head under my chin with her motor boat purring. She used to sit in our back hall watching our dog Trix pull her door open to go outside. One day she decided to do the same thing and has been doing it ever since.

She is definitely my cat and so is Lucky – they both sleep with me.
Lucky
M, 8, Black; gold eyes
Domestic shorthair
Lucky is very small for a male. He's a very loving cat also. I love both Lucky and Missy very much.

MELROSE PARK   60160
Crystal A. Nauyokas, 4501 Westlake Terr
Dorry
F, 3, Gray, beige, white, cream, reddish-brown
Tortie
Lovable, weird, playful, spoiled
Dorry was found by a little boy when she was barely two weeks old. As soon as my best friend, MJ, brought her to me, I knew God meant me to be her mama. I had to bottle feed her, teach her how to eliminate before box training her, and she used to even use my lip to teethe on (until she got teeth!) One day, when she was only a few months old, I threw a toy for her, she got it and brought it back repeatedly. Thus she taught herself to play fetch.

Every morning, between one and three AM, she loves to come and stretch out on me to sleep. If I tell her to wake me up at five, you can bet she's back meowing or making noise at five o'clock. I've yet to figure out how she tells time! She also knows how to kiss if I ask for one - when she wants, of course; though sometimes to her a kiss means to nibble Mom's lip.

NILES   60714
Dan O'Connor, 9018 N Chamberland Ave
Blue
F, 2, Lynx point & white
Siamese mix
Outgoing, very curious, talkative, assertive, protective, extremely friendly
My cat Blue is a "Retriever". If I throw anything that she can fit in her mouth, she'll bring it right to my feet, drop it, sit and face me waiting for me to throw it again. She'll continue to do this until she tires.

Also if I'm cooking or busy around the kitchen and she's in my way, I'll say, "Get!", and she'll go to her favorite chair. Then I'll say, "Lay down!", and she does. She also talks back every time I say "Get!" She meows once. I say it again - she meows again (and also goes to her chair).

She also likes to go outside for walks (on a leash). P.S. We're not allowed dogs in our building . . . so I guess Blue is my dog!

PLAINFIELD
Charlene Lysek
Kitty
F, 10 months, Charcoal gray w/ silver
Unknown
Loving, playful, loves to climb trees right to the top
Kitty came to me one day in my backyard. As I was planting flowers, I felt something rub up against me and meow. She was so skinny. She was about 6 weeks old. I gave her milk. After that she would always run to me when I came outside. So we decided to keep her.

At 6 months I had her spayed and she had her shots. She sleeps in my indoor porch on a soft bed I made for her. I let her out at 9 A.M. I tap on my kitchen window which is about 3 feet off the ground. She sees me and comes running and climbs on the ladder lying under the window. She puts her paws on the window sill and looks at me and meows. She is so cute.

I never thought about having a cat and didn't really want one. But I am so glad someone put Kitty out by my house and she came to me. We are so glad. We spoil her and love her a lot. She is a beautiful charcoal gray color with silver tips. She has brown eyes. I named her Fancy, but we call her Kitty.

A Fancy Kitty

SKOKIE   60077
Cherie Gaiser, 5244 W Mulford
Nickie
F, 6, Black & gray tabby
Domestic shorthair
Affectionate to me; aggressive to others
I wonder about the relationship between Nickie and me: mother and child? And is it animal and human?

She will retrieve any object I toss down the basement stairs, again and again. When another person attempts joining our game, she sits down and just stares at him. When I turn on our treadmill (slowly), Nickie will jump onto it and walk for awhile. When it's nail trimming time, she will hiss and bite any living being insight - except me the nail trimmer!

At night she sleeps under the covers besides me and purrs herself to sleep. Nickie's favorite foods are tomatoes, asparagus, and Granny Smith apples!

Murphy
M, 8, Light gray tabby

Domestic shorthair
Affectionate; dislikes strangers
Murphy is a real oddball. An attention-getter, he will jump onto our backs and shoulders, then purr loudly and bite us - a nasty show of affection. He slaps and intimidates the dog, although she is 3 times his size. The strangest thing he does is watch us through a reflection. He jumps on the mantel and looks at us through a big mirror, and if the T.V. is off, he sits in front of it and watches everything going on behind him. Murphy goes out of his way to knock over any glass, full or not, so we are well-trained to put all glasses away!

SLEEPY HOLLOW   60118
Cynthia & Joe Barber, 748 Sycamore
Noel
M, 2, All black
Domestic shorthair
Happy, loving, outgoing
I opened the cage door at the shelter, but instead of running out, the 4 month old kitten dragged himself out - his two back legs useless. But what a sweetheart; he licked my face and hand and purred. I feel in love, we adopted him and named him Noel because we expected a miracle by Christmas.

We took him to a cats-only vet; he had a deformed spine, back legs and tail; also a collapsed lung, pneumonia and nutritional secondary hyperparathyroidism (no calcium in his bones). He needed much medication and nursing and he stayed tiny because of his problems.

He can now run and walk, though wobbly, but can't jump. He is friendly to people and animals and is very happy and loving despite what he's been through and doesn't let his handicap bother him.

Jason
M, 16, Black & white
Domestic shorthair
A lap cat with us, shy with strangers.
He started out as a trapped feral cat that no one wanted and hid in our basement the first two years we had him. By the fifth year he was a friendly, loving lap cat.

He had PU surgery at six years of age for stones and at eleven, had 12 inches of intestine removed because of cancer, but he still purrs when the vet examines him. The love in his heart overcame the fear.

ST CHARLES   60174
Debbie Derrick, 313 South 11ᵗʰ Ave
EEE
M, 10, Yellow
Tabby
Very cuddly & loving; never short tempered
EEE enjoys brushing his face with a brush. If you put a brush on the floor, he will hold it with his front paws and brush his face for long periods of time. Every night when I sleep on my stomach, he sleeps on my butt!! When the alarm goes off in the morning, he gets in my face and meows until I get up. Then he is content to fall back to sleep again!!!

He loves to play with helium balloons with long ribbons attached to them. He will pull the balloon all around the house. He is good-natured and likes everyone except white people with dreadlock style hair (mop head look). He lays back his ears and hisses at them and eventually attacks full force!!! He also enjoys sitting in my lap and watching TV - especially Catnip Video!!!

ST CHARLES   60175
Jim & Donna Hinton & Family, 7N680 Cloverdale Circle
Coonsboro's Mario "Indy" Coondretti
M, 2.5, Brown classic tabby with white
Maine Coon
Affectionate, curious & very laid back
See story in chapter 7: Wild & Wacky

WEST DUNDEE
Chris Koenig
Rambo
M, 2, Gray tabby
Domestic Shorthair
Mama's boy
Rambo is special because he says "bless you" whenever someone sneezes. Rambo will chatter (as if to say "bless you"!) He will continue to chatter until you stop sneezing - even if it takes ten sneezes - and say "thank you, Rambo."

WILLOWBROOK   60521
Roberta Dee, 607 68ᵗʰ St

Cecil
M, 2, Solid white
Tabby (odd-eyed)
Friendly, outgoing, curious, mischievous, talkative
Cecil "talks" to me often. If I call him, he'll come running to me. He enjoys people and is quite "the ham". Cecil will follow me all around from room to room quite often. He's extremely loving and affectionate and will sit on my tummy when I'm laying down. He always sleeps with me. He loves playing on and in the sheets when I make the bed - no matter how many times I take him off, he'll jump back on. He also loves jumping in the clothes hamper when I'm taking out my clothes to wash.

Cecil & Basil – a ham and a scaredy cat

Basil
M, 2, Tiger-like Tabby
Short-haired Tabby
Loyal, shy with others, talkative with those he knows
Basil voices his opinions about everything! When I got him from the Humane Society they had to keep him in a special room because he cried so often and so loud! He is the epitome of "the scaredy cat". He is extremely loving and loyal. He follows me all over (except when I have company). Then he will hide under the bed. He's extremely well-behaved and only needs to be told once not to do something! He adores his brother Cecil.

INDIANA

BOONVILLE 47601-9567
Helen K Tomino, 344 S Center Rd
Tigger
M, 10, Red and white
Domestic
Mostly laid back and loving

The refrigerator cat

When Tigger was young we started finding our refrigerator door standing open. My first reaction was to blame my sons! Then one day I watched Tigger stick his leg under the door, working it back and forth until the seal released and he could get his nose and rather large head in to push it the rest of the way. Next he did the same with the freezer above by sitting on the stove! I was able to easily teach him to sit and "shake hands" for treats. He loves to eat and has weighed up to eighteen pounds.

CLARKSVILLE 47129
Lori Lowery, 56 Pinehurst Dr
Binky
F, 3, White
Domestic shorthair
Lovable, friendly & outgoing
My cat Binky does some strange things, but one of the oddest is that she plays fetch like a dog. She brings me the ball, a small Nerf-like ball, and drops it in my hand or in front of me. I throw it into the other room and she brings it right back and she's ready to go again. What's even more odd is that we have a vase on our coffee table and sometimes she drops it in the vase, like she's playing basketball. She will also get the ball and drop it in shoes and open purses.

EVANSVILLE 47715
Lori & Steven Black, 6317 Bristol Ct
Miss Kitty
F, 8, Seal point w/ white feet
Snowshoe Siamese
Miss Kitty is very special to my son and to myself. She helped us through a very stressful separation and divorce. A dog was too much to handle, but not having a pet wouldn't do . . . so we got Miss Kitty. She helped reduce the stress a lot.
Kitty was four years old when we got her. She is now eight. She is very gentle and affectionate, and she talks to us all the time. She doesn't claw the furniture or get on the counters. Kitty is not a lap cat, but she shows her love in other ways. She will be with us forever.

Sissy
F, 7 months, White, cream, brown
Snowshoe Siamese
Our cat Sissy is special because she is almost identical in looks to her mother, Miss Kitty. They are different in personality, though.
Kitty is not a lap cat - Sissy is. Kitty doesn't care for games - Sissy does. Kitty is lazy - Sissy is super-frisky! Sissy loves to play hide-n-seek with my son, Steven. He taught her a trick. We put a magnet on the back of a toy, and she has jumped as high as six feet to get it off the door. Now she has taught the trick to our new cat . . . Misty Blue!
Misty Blue Dawn is a 1-year old, Russian Blue female. When I saw her at a breeder's home, I fell in love the second the woman put her in my arms. She is the softest cat I had ever felt! The woman didn't want to sell her, so we left. I couldn't stop thinking about her. I kept calling this lady until we made a trade, and a week later Misty Blue was in our home. Lucky us! Misty is super affectionate and a beautiful cat. I highly recommend anyone who loves cats to get a Russian Blue. They're great!

FORT WAYNE   46835
M/M Tibor Bierbaum, 6809 Thamesford Dr
Casper
M, 12, Grey
Blue shorthair
Very loving to family and visitors - rules the household by the clock.

Casper – the artist

Casper is a blue American shorthair cat companion who, not only rules our home, but teaches art classes to local 4-H members. He is allowed to choose a "walk-on", "sit-on" or "lie upon" so his canvas touches acrylic paint (on a rimmed cookie sheet). Under pressure points a masterpiece is created. As soon as we put a fresh canvas over the colors, he makes his move and delights on-lookers with his talent.

His works have recognizable figures to them such as flowers; others resemble speckled inkblots with lots of color and style.

The beauty is that there is no mess.

Shadow
F, 2, Black w/few white chest hairs
American
Loves family - no strangers

When we prepare packages for mailing, Shadow supervises the popcorn machine for packing material. She loves to help fill the boxes with "things" and pat them down securely. I just hope we never mail her, too!

INDIANAPOLIS   46220
Julia & David Hughes, 6125 Indianola Ave
Mikey (Mikie)

M, 10, Yellow Tabby
Lap sitter, loving, loves to be talked to, brushed etc.

Mikey is an uncommonly friendly cat. He's special because his personality is such that he can turn cat-haters into "reasonable" people! He appeals to dog-people because he's similar to a dog. He comes to you when you call him (every time), he fetches his toys, he plays, loves attention and to be brushed, and tolerates the indignity of lying on his back to get his nails clipped! At Christmas he carefully selects a "toy" from the tree branches, plucks one off and considers it the toy du jour. At spring cleaning time, I'll find ornaments under all sorts of furniture and in boxes in the basement!

Anna
F, 13, Black, tan & white
Maine Coon
Mild, loving, friendly, playful!

Anna senses when I'm down emotionally or not feeling well physically. A year ago I miscarried; the surgery and emotional aftermath were difficult. Anna was there for me every minute. She even missed meals to be with me. She purred very loudly while lying on my chest; she gave me an occasional lick and "head-butted" me to let me know she was there. I knew she knew - I was sad and not feeling well. She was there for me when my husband was away. She helped me get through a very difficult time in my life. Now she's intrigued with our new daughter!

INDIANAPOLIS   46256
Jennifer & Todd Kolber, 8529 Whipporwill Dr #E
Shadow
M, 2, Black & white
Unknown
A juvenile delinquent - a monster!

Shadow is one of the freshest cats around. When we first got shadow he was only 12 weeks old and even then he loved to beat up my mom's 4 older cats! Shadow loves to play and one of the things he's best at is jumping way off the floor to get a piece of string. Shadow is able to jump so high that we nick-named him "Air Kitty". He's got such a nasty disposition that we also call him the IMP. But for all his rottenness, he still loves to cuddle with his mommy at night, and I think he is the cutest cat in the whole wide world!

Limerick
F, 3, Grey with white marks
Unknown
Sweet but knows her own mind.
Limerick is a one-of-a-kind. She adores her daddy and loves to be with him. She likes people but hates other animals except Shadow. Limerick's favorite game is chasing balls down the hallway. She also likes to run out the front door when someone comes in! We got Limerick at our local Humane Society and we are so happy to have her in our lives to love! We call her our "Princess".

LA PORTE   46350
Gloria Freshour, 910 Scott St
Todd Mikel Freshour
M, 12, Black & white
Great disposition; loved by all
June 1980 Toddy Mikel showed up at my back door - a kitten of 8 or 9 months.
November 28, 1980, Dr. Busse amputated Todd's right leg at the shoulder - circulation shut off by a rubber band wrapped tightly around the leg. Todd Mikel adapted well to three legs.
1990 Todd was diagnosed having F.U.S.
August 10, 1991 diagnosed having leukemia and aids.
January 6, 1992, diagnosed a diabetic.
Dr. Heinold calls him the "Wonder Cat". Wonder he's still alive with all these ailments. He's very much so. All due to a lot of T.L.C. That is why Todd is an Uncommon Cat.

MERRILLVILLE   46410
Natalie Madej, 5461 Mary Anne Ln
Opie
M, 4.5, Orange and white
Mixed with long hair
Sweet yet mischievous
The first time I saw Opie, my neighbors had just saved him from a group of boys who were torturing him. He ran up to me and started purring, and I fell in love. When he was hit by a car two years later, I nursed him back to health. He had a

broken jaw and one eye was sewn shut. One eye was eventually removed. Although completely blind, he is fully recovered and acts like any other cat. He catches shrews, chases squirrels up trees, investigates the aquarium and hamster, loves to run with me up and down the lawn, and comes running when the refrigerator is opened, swatting with his paw until he receives a turkey slice. When guests come for dinner, he jumps up on a chair and looks as though to say, "Where's my plate?".

Opie comes through

MISHAWAKA   46545
Mrs Marilyn J Stoll, 54763 Merrifield Dr
Myah Stoll
F, almost 1, Brown tabby
Devon Rex
Part cat, part dog, part monkey, & all witch
I always imagined that when I reached sixty, I should like a facelift. But since we have had our Devon Rex, I really want a tail transplant.
Her exquisite tail tapers into infinity, and has a complete life of its own. It can drag, spin, slither, and convolute.
Politically viable, it expresses movements both democratic and dictatorial. It is capable of serenity, anger, discernment, and delight, and likes to be scratched at its base, and caressingly kissed upon its tip. Manipulating, uncompromising, sensuous and loyal, it follows me from room to room, rashly risking mutilation and downright extermination from car doors, trash can

lids, scissors, and suction.
Its [the tail's] owner's name is Myah, and she is loved.

Emmy Stoll

F, 20 dec, Black & white
Longhair mix
Loving, fearful, & apologetic
She was found in a field; a pathetic, abandoned little ball of knotted, filthy fur. Her eyes were glued shut with dirt and pus, and her bony rear was infested with maggots - but she still lived. She survived repeated vet visits, and 3 months in the garage until our vet declared her worm and infection free, and ready to live in the house with our other two cats.

She was afraid of all people except our family. Throughout her surprisingly long life, Emmy never learned to play or hunt. Her joy was to lay on our bed or in our laps, and be loved. She died as she lived . . . quietly, without making any fuss.

SYRACUSE 46567

Kelly Warrick, 200 E Harrison Ct
Tippy
F, 1.5, Gray tiger w/orange "tippy" tail
?
Playful, ornery, comical, but shy with new people, loving.
Tippy is quite a character - she love to play with milk jug rings. We keep them in a drawer, and she knows exactly where! She'll sit there pawing at it until we give her one. If you toss it, she chases it down, pounces on it and brings it back to you to toss again. Sometimes she just likes to throw it around by herself.

We have a "Kitty Tower" (carpet covered cat tower) that she likes to "conquer" and take a break on top of after a long day of play. She is also a very nosey cat - she pokes her head through the miniblinds on the windows whenever a car goes by.

Tommy
F, 6 months, Brown/black tiger
?
Very loving and loyal. Playful, sneaky, talkative.
Tommy is special because she has quite an attitude. One minute she is a loving, gentle, purring kitten sitting in my lap. The next

she's pouncing on one of her brothers or sister "just because".

She likes to "ride around" on my shoulders like a parrot. If we leave all of the cats in the house while we're away from home, Tommy sits on the chair nearest the door when she hears us coming and "talks" to us until we say hello and pick her up. When I let her sleep with me at night, she curls up next to my face and purrs me to sleep.

Tippy and Tommy share our home with three other cats. Teddy is "the milk kitty" because he loves milk. Timmy is the "frady-cat" of the family even though he's the biggest. And Missy is a real tease but loves to sit in your lap and purr, purr, purr. I think all five are "uncommon cats"!

MICHIGAN

DEERFIELD 49238

Debra L Cooper, 20928 Deerfield Rd
Stimpy
M, 6 months, Snow leopard, white, grey ears and tail, light brown body spots Bengal
Extremely playful - talkative - keeps his humans laughing
Stimpy and I have a very close bond. He was the last born of five kittens; I delivered him. His mother was so young that the vet helped deliver two kittens and I the rest. He was the only snow leopard, white - with light brown spots - blue eyes.

At two months he started fetching cat toys, and once I threw his toy 35 times, until he was worn out. I take off my watch before I shower and put it on the sink. Well, I forgot to put it back on and Stimpy brought it to me. Once he brought my bra from the bathroom to me (Ha-ha!). He also drinks from the faucet.

P.S. I love him very much and he obviously loves me too!

DETROIT 48232

C K McConnohie, PO Box 32059
Lady "Scamp"
F, 2+, Grey-white

Unknown
Friendly, loyal & defensive
Arjuns I
M, 11 dec, Solid grey w/ white chest
Household cat
Gentle, loyal
Won two C.F.A. ribbons: 1 level, 3 place ribbons - which was the first. Saved my life once by awakening me.

FARMINGTON HILLS   48335
Julie Crago, 38928 Polo Club Dr 14-203
Buckeye
F, 6 months, Tortoise/black
Independent & adventuresome
   DOUBLE TROUBLE
My husband, Dan, and I adopted Sparty and Buckeye from the Humane Society on our way home from our honeymoon last October. The date they were brought to the Humane Society was the day we were married, 09/26/92, so we knew they were meant for us. They were sisters from an unwanted litter and as soon as we opened the cage, they were all over us.

Dan and I love animals and knew we could provide a good home. I have always been a dog lover but ever since Sparty and Buckeye came to live with us, they have won over my heart.

Sparty is black with white fuzz on her belly and Buckeye is black and tortoise. They both have green eyes and purr constantly. They love to open drawers and sleep in them. They love to jump in the shower and they only drink water from a glass on the bathroom counter. Buckeye sleeps on top of the bathroom door and Sparty sleeps on the towel racks.

How did they get their names? Dan went to Ohio State and I went to Michigan State!

Sparty
F, 6 months, Black
Laid-back, lovable
[see above]

GRAND RAPIDS   49508
Lori & John Teichman, 853 68th St, SE #4
Willie
M, 6 months, Black, gray, tan, white
Brown Tabby
Happy, smart, and sometimes very mischie-

vous; he loves attention.
Willie is very unusual; he was taught how to fetch his little white teddy-bear that he has had since he was 8 weeks old. His basic routine for fetching is that we play with him for a minute with the teddy-bear and throw it; he will run, grab it, do a somersault and bring the teddy-bear back to us. Ever since he was a kitten he has done somersaults when he is playing with a toy. It is so cute!

We have a nickname for him, Frogman, the reason being is he sits like a frog, swims with his legs. His back legs and feet lay flat so he reminds us of a frog. I think he associates his tricks by the tone of our voices. He is very intelligent. People are amazed by Willie and how smart he is. People who are not cat lovers fall in love with him.

He travels with us when it is possible. Another thing that seems to amaze Willie is showers, and when I do dishes he loves to watch, also when I cook. We love him!

LAKE CITY   49651-0485
Tina Renae Simpkins, PO Box 485 (124 Northview)
KiKi
F, 1 yr 4 mo, Black/gray/white tiger stripe
Tabby
Independent, affectionate
We have a carpeted ladder going up to our loft, and KiKi loves to do gymnastics on it. It started when we were watching the 1992 Winter Olympics. She was watching ladies gymnastics with us and she started doing loops and jumps and being crazy.

KiKi also comes when you whistle. I was on vacation and my boyfriend came home from work. He said he was playing his guitar and whistling (since he cannot sing). He freaked-out when KiKi came running down stairs and jumped on his lap. Now she comes running whenever we whistle.

TJ (Taz Jr.)
M, 1, Cream, yellow & white tiger stripe
Tabby
Very independent / a REBEL
TJ purrs like he's got a Harley engine inside himself. He could be upstairs and you'll be downstairs, and you'd think he was right next to you.

When my sister-in-law comes over for the

weekend, TJ swats at her when she's sleeping (because she snores). Also if my boyfriend Mel doesn't give TJ attention in the middle of the night, he grabs hold of Mel's beard and jerks it.

MT PLEASANT
Liz White
Katie
F, 4, Black & white
Domestic short hair
Bossy; protective; independent; shy.
As a pregnant stray who was chased and kicked by thoughtless children, Katie came to live with me in June, 1991. On August 13, 1991, she delivered five healthy male kittens. A friend adopted two, I kept three. Katie and "the boys" have been with me ever since. Because of her trauma, sudden moves make Katie nervous and she withdraws. She is content to spend her time sleeping on my bed while I'm at work, but enjoys playtime in the evening. Katie doesn't have a particular talent nor do any tricks. She simply loves me. Isn't that what it's all about?
Socks
M, 1, White and grey Tabby
Domestic short hair

Socks loves his aqua-bar

Shy, playful
Socks is the average 15 lb neutered cat: fat, lazy and happy! One of his hobbies includes sitting at the "aqua-bar" (my aquarium) on a carefully placed stool. Another of his hobbies includes jumping on my shoulders. Occasionally his mother, Katie, will have to put him in his place if he gets out

of line with her or his two brothers, Teddy and Hoppy. As it is with many cat owners, I think mine are the sweetest, cutest and best cats one could ask for. Of course I'm slightly biased!

OAK PARK
Mary Kay Beyer
Samantha Van Dyke
F, 11, Black w/magnificent brown sheen & white whiskers
Mixed
Cautious, wary of strangers, very expressive and loving when secure.
Samantha picked me as her human by appearing out of nowhere and stationing herself on my picnic table. After several days of interviewing me from a distance, she decided my offerings of food and respect suited her, and she cautiously came inside to continue the evaluation process. Eventually she claimed my home as hers, and now, 7 years later, her purr-motor turns on instantly upon my touch, or my voice sweet-talking her.

When waking from a nap, she jumps to the sofa arm for a l-o-n-g, full stretch and yawn, yet holds back her claws because ONCE she was told "NO!" She saves her "furious" raking for her Cat Claws corrugated cardboard!

And finally, Samantha is so very special because she makes ME feel special!

ST CLAIR SHORES   48080
Virginia Kunce, 23049 Gary Lane
Grizabella
F, 1 dec, Grey
Russian Blue
Warm, loving, devoted
I never owned a cat until Grizabella, a Russian Blue, came into my life. I was totally captivated by this warm and loving friend. Her favorite resting place was curled around my shoulder as "Grizzy" meowed her day's experiences and I shared mine.

Then Grizabella looked tired and the vet's workup found her very ill. On her last visit to the vet, Grizzy never came home; she died two days before her first birthday. I planned a party to celebrate her life but instead cried because it ended. Her time with me was short, but I cherish our total, loving commitment. This biography is my memorial to her presence.

ST CLAIR SHORES   48082
Jessica Schultz, 22425 Raymond
Smokey
F, 7, Gray & white
Mixed
Independent, easy going, loving
Smokey was found very much afraid and hiding in our bushes when she was 8 weeks old and she immediately became my pet. She sleeps with me, tucks me in bed every night and sits at the front door waiting for me to come home every day. She lives with three dogs and likes to play hide and seek with them. She also plays ball and attacks our toes when we wiggle them.

Smokey the writer

However her most unusual talent is typing. When I leave my typewriter unattended, she starts hitting the keys. She is a very special pet and I can't imagine life without her.

TROY   48083
Pati Lubinecky, 2432 Hinge Dr
Cisco
M, 5, Tan
Siamese
Good sense of humor, loyal, loving
Born in Cairo - Egypt, April 1, 1988. Transfered to Detroit in 1990.
Cisco has fetched after toys, paper balls and anything else you throw since he was 6 months old. He likes to play and hide my hair bands, earrings and ball pens. Once a

month I clean out his hiding places, normally under the couch or behind the bookcase.

Cisco enjoys the finer things

Cisco also likes the finer foods in life; he loves to eat smoked ham and liver pate. When up-set he will let you know by leaving "packages" behind in cupboards. This is very up-setting to me. However, he loves to cuddle up next to me every night, he wakes me with his purring in the morning and he comforts me when I'm ill. Cisco and I are best friends. Life wouldn't be the same without him.

OHIO

AKRON   44312
Terri Prosise, 2913 Albrecht Ave
Mystery
M, 9, Black & white w/ moustache
Mix
Intelligent, affectionate, self-confident, loves attention
Mystery is a unique cat. Rescued from a pound as a kitten, he constantly amazes everyone he meets. I began teaching him tricks when he was less than a year old, and after 8 years his extensive repertoire includes rolling over, jumping through hoops, waving, "talking", and playing his electric keyboard. He enjoys traveling and

performing in front of audiences, and has entertained and astounded many.

A Mystery that amazes

Mystery's still as curious as a kitten, and continues to learn new behaviors. I believe that his intellect has been sharpened because of the things he's learned and the experiences he's had. Mystery's bond with me is very strong, especially because of how we work together. At times I feel as though we can tell what the other is thinking. He's truly a remarkable cat.

BARBERTON 44203
Marsha Cross, 3535 E. State St
Siam
M, 7, seal-point
Siamese
S (sensitive, stately) I (intelligent, interesting) A (attentive, admirable) M (memorable, my friend)
Siam - our purrfect friend! One of the cutest things he does is roll on the rug and put his chin up to be petted, talked to and made a fuss over. He is very loving and sleeps with his arms around my neck. His blue eyes seem to talk to us. He plays hide and seek and meows loudly when I talk on the phone. It makes our day when we come home and he runs to greet us. Siam is our V.I.C. - Very Important Cat!!! Our lives have been made richer and more fun by the times we have shared with Siam. He is our purrfect friend!!!
See story in chapter 8: Lap Cats Extraordinaire.

BARBERTON 44203
Ocona Lloyd, 110 Sylvester St

Feisty
F, 5, Black and orange
Mixed
Loving to me
Feisty has many interesting habits. Her Christmas habit is the place to start. Each Christmas Eve I show her where her gifts are under the tree and I give her the first gift. Then she knows it's time. So then when I walk towards the front room after that, she runs toward where her presents are and waits for me, watching me, not taking her eyes off me until I go over and give her another gift. If I don't, sometimes she will come over and tap me with her paw and meow, looking at me with big yellow eyes. How could I say no to that? She also plays ball; she gets her little round spider and when I throw it she will go get it and bring it back to me to throw it again. I'm now going to tell you about how I know if she wants a treat. I keep them on the microwave and Feisty will jump on the counter and stare at me until I come and give her some. If I don't see her sitting there, she will get on the microwave and take her paw and tap the box, or punch to try and get the treat out herself.

She likes Tender Vittles for a treat. When I go over to give her a treat, she will not eat it out of a bowl. So I pick them both up and put them down toward her and she puts her paw on the one she wants or when I pick up the one she wants, she will come to the counter. If I trip and fall, she hears me. She knows by the sound most of the time, and if she sees me, she will run to me and kiss me by putting her nose on my nose. This may sound strenuous, but it is honestly the truth. I'm very pleased with her; she is my friend.

CIRCLEVILLE
Carolyn & Bob Clemons
Toupee
F, 3, White with black
"Barn cat"
Perky, lively
Toupee (pronounced two-pee) is so named because her markings look like she wears a toupee. She descended from a long line of barn cats on a farm. One day when she was a small kitten, I threw a small wad of paper. She retrieved it and brought it back to me. Since that time she has been a

champion retriever.

She likes the balls to bounce high so she can catch them in her paws. Toupee will bring her paper ball to us when she wants to play. She "chirps" to tell you to play if you don't happen to see it or are not coming to play fast enough. Visitors are fascinated and most people state that they have never had a cat retrieve. She especially likes to bring the ball to play a few times just at bedtime. She also likes to deposit the ball in something. I frequently find one in my shoe or in her dry food bowl.

Tinker

F, 15, Black with white

Housecat

Calm & beautiful

Tinker is special because she is so loving. She will crawl into my lap any time I am sitting down and purr away. When I have to get up I will put her down on the chair. She stays there until I return and pick her up again to put her back in my lap. She will do this for hours. I think she would stay in my lap all day if I was able to sit there the entire time. She just loves to be petted, hugged and loved in return. Tinker is very chatty. We talk to each other a lot.

CLEVELAND 44111

Dara Hanners, 11505 St Mark Ave

Slick Hanners

M, 12 dec, Black

Domestic shorthair

Intelligent, psychic, opinionated, loyal, "cool"

Born under a friend's porch, he started domesticated life as "DINKY" -- it soon became apparent this was NOT his name as he disdained answering to it! Growing into a handsome, debonair "cool" teenager, a really slick character, I finally discovered his SECRET name!

Slick demonstrated uncanny ability to tell time and kept his various curfews to the EXACT minute he was told to be home! He stalked bugs, "helped" with the gardening and treated his favorite toys very humanely -- seeing to it that they had a dip in the food bowl, water bowl, and a "litter pan break" daily!

Until his death from cancer, he was the loyalist friend, best listener and SMARTEST cat I've been blessed to know.

Buddy Hanners

M, 8 months, Grey/silver tabby

Domestic shorthair

Playful, affectionate, sociable

Although he is still a youngster, Buddy already exhibits the qualities of a leader. He is tireless in his play, indifferent to food -- stopping to eat only when he can find nothing else to occupy his attention! He'd rather have a fast romp through the house than a kitty snack any day!

Although you rarely see him sitting still, when he DOES, he is a warm, loving little guy who loves to nip at my nose when I'm trying to sleep.

CLEVELAND

Margie White

Rascal

M, 21 dec, Gray tabby

American shorthair

One-person cat who only tolerated the rest of the world.

My loving companion of 21 years died recently. A sickly five-week old with a badly abscessed infection, he was brought to my door by a neighbor. I almost refused to keep him as I had just lost a cat.

Now I am forever thankful for having him be a part of my life - even the hard times. His favorite spot was my lap whenever and wherever I was sitting. Many comforting hours were spent like that - just the two of us.

He will be mourned and greatly missed. This is my memorial to a faithful and loving friend.

COLUMBUS 43224

Janet Overmyer, 1260 Oakland Park Av

Dana

M, 10, Sable

Burmese

Loving, mischievous

Dana is my first and only boy cat in a family of four. As a kitten, he had medical problems, including a lump on his shoulder which I treated with a warm piece of cotton for 5 minutes thrice daily. He squirmed so much that at times I quit at 3 minutes. He carries off pencils, watches, anything small, and hides them or drops them down the floor register.

As a kitten he climbed floor curtains; as an adult he still does. He chews all electrical and telephone cords. He knocked over my former floor lamp and little by little dismembered its shade. He ran between my legs when I climbed stairs.

Once, he popped out a strip of plexiglass at the top of my room air conditioner and landed outside (my cats are indoor cats.) But he also lies on my chest purring and licking my face. He has perfected the two-pawed bottle cap catch, swatting down thrown bottle caps and returning them to be thrown again.

A few years ago, while hanging curtains, I was thrown to the floor when the chair leg buckled and sprained my wrist. Dana put his face up to mine, mewing: "Can I help you?"

Caitlin

F, 9, Mink

Tonkinese

Sweet

Caitlin is love personified. The only cat I allow in my study, she is crawling all over me and the typewriter as I type this. She goes to everybody who comes over, purring and rubbing and licking and explaining just how wonderful we all are. I look down at my lap when I am reading and she is curled up, love on four paws, sound asleep and happy.

COLUMBUS   43211

Kelly Witt, 2683 Joyce Ave

Cody Witt

M, 3, Strawberry blonde/red-orange

Loving, understanding, gentle

Cody is very loving and gentle; he is also very expressive with his face and his emotions he relates with people better. I really do think that he thinks he's human. He understands and is very gentle with his surroundings even with our bird. He's my son and I'm his mother and that's how our relationship looks to others. Cody is a good listener and very intelligent. He loves to be held at any given time and loves to hug people around their necks like a child. You just can't help not to love him because he gives so much love in return.

CORTLAND   44410

Lori Barta, 3201 Bradley-Brownlee Rd

Kiki

F, 2-1/2, Gray w/pale orange marks

DSH

Friendly, quiet, unassuming

Kiki was the first of my half-a-dozen cats. We adopted each other while I was working at our local shelter. She was shy, quiet, and unpretentious, and always being over-looked by prospective cat-adopters. After having been in the shelter for quite some time, I decided to take her home.

Kiki was not what you would call friendly, at first, but she had an unbelievable personality change. Now she is very loving and reigns over the house as mother of all the other cats and therefore has been named "Queen Kiki".

Dylan

M, 1, Cream

Angora X

Sweet, friendly, lovable

Dylan is the joker and Romeo of my cat family. He came into my life at about four months old, when I brought him home from our local shelter.

Dylan's most outstanding feature is his beautiful amber eyes. Just a glance into those eyes and one can't help but fall in love, even if you're not a cat lover. He is always eager to cuddle and loves to play leap-cat with my other cats. He is soft and cuddly and has become my favorite snuggle-bunny , or should I say "snuggle-kitty"?

COSHOCTON   43812

Brandy Hughes, 1801 Glendale Drive

Bitsy

F, 1.5, white, black, gold, and tan

Calico

Friendly, but a bit aloof. When mad, sounds dangerous, but she's all bluff.

My cat Bitsy has two ways to get attention. The first way is to do a somersault on the bottom rung of a kitchen chair and thump the rung with her back feet until someone notices her. Bitsy will also give a loud indignant snort to get attention or when she wants food. Sometimes she even combines the two, flipping and thumping, and if that doesn't work, she'll snort. There is a running strip of weather information that moves across the bottom of a news channel on the television which Bitsy loves to chase, pawing at it and chasing it as it moves. She thinks it should be coming out of the side of the television set and sometimes looks on the side, trying to find it. We've taught her to sit up and beg, to yawn when someone winks at her, to sit up and wave, to shake hands, and to "box" with someone.

EASTLAKE   44095-1107
Marlene Pedder, 191 E. Overlook Dr
"Trapper" John, M.D.
M, 16.5, Gray white mix
Maine Coon mix
Happy, loving, playful
"Trapper" is special because he went from being an abused, abandoned and unwanted cat with a desolate start to a wonderful companion.
See story in Chapter 3: Against All Odds.
"Minua"
M, 8,
Bombay mix
"Minua" is a warrior cat. He starts trouble by his war whoopee sounds. "Minua" is also my wake-up cat. When its time to get up, he makes sure that you are up - about 2 minutes before the clock rings. That is why he is special. I have not been late in the years he has allowed me to live with him.

FAIRBORN   45324
Nona Brothers, 88 Circle Drive
Marvin
M, 3, Brown / tan / black
Sealpoint Siamese
Untypical Siamese - friendly & quiet
Although Marvin looks like a typical Siamese, he has the most unsiamese personality. Marvin greets everyone who enters his home with demands for a head scratch. He grabs your hand and pulls you to him. If the requested scratch does not follow, he just goes on his way . . . no meowing . . . no fuss. Marvin's human used to sleep with her feet sticking out from under the cover. Not anymore! Imagine her surprise when she woke up one night and couldn't move because her feet were tied. Marvin wraps any exposed feet with whatever strings or scraps he can retrieve. Marvin's most unusual attribute is his fetching ability. He retrieves anything you toss his way, usually by mouth, but pushes those larger items.

FAIRBORN   45324
Elizabeth A Keates, 249 W Dayton-Yellow Rd #249
Squirt
F, 2, Tan and black
Tabby
Intelligent
Squirt was a 5-week-old stray when I found her a week after Christmas. This is weird, but she got her name by having an accident on the carpet. I had fed her but forgot about providing a litter box. Oops! I am proud that she gives "special cuddles" only to me. She sits on my shoulder, snuggles her face to my neck, and purrs. She won't sit on anyone else's shoulder. Sometimes she sits very still with a faraway look in her eyes. My husband says she is an alien communicating with the Mother Ship. Very intense.

Bam Bam
F, 1.5, Black and white
American shorthair
Lovable scamp
Bam Bam is a feline alarm clock. Monday through Friday she meows me awake 5 minutes before the alarm goes off. On weekends, though, we both sleep in. She doesn't have the holidays down pat yet. She'll still wake me up in the morning if the holiday falls on a weekday. At night she jumps onto the bed and kneads my stomach. Then she sleeps in the crook of my arm. She looks like a big "puddle of fur"! Bam Bam is just plain nosey. She's always where the action is. She's usually part of the action.

GOSHEN   45122
Teresa Stahl, 3131 Park Rd
Crackers
M, 3, Black & white
Mixed
Friendly - outgoing
Crackers is a very friendly and outgoing gentleman. He was born on my birthday, July 4th. The only kitten his mother, Rose Marie had. He resembles the White House cat "Socks".

Being raised around a stable he loves to sit on my horse "Sis". He is also very protective of "his" yard. He chases all strange cats out and growls at the dogs. His favorite spot to sleep after all his rowdy games . . . is the bedroom where he was born.

Boogies

F, 1, Tortie

Manx

Very lively

She has earned her nickname "Cat from Hell". It seems she is everywhere at once. She has a knack for climbing the wall to the ceiling. She also likes to go into my bathroom sink whenever I run the water. I can hardly brush my teeth! She likes to try to chase the water down the drain. After all this, her favorite place to nap is on my lap.

JACKSON   45640

Mary Jane Humphrets, 65 Vaugh St

Baby Bear

M, 4.5, Blue point Siamese

Siamese / Himalayan mix

He loves to be loved & he is crazy.

Baby is the family clown. He is full of life and lives it to its fullest, with his two girls Priscilla and Majic. Baby came into our lives unexpectedly soon becoming our monster in the closet. Growling and hissing, and refusing to come out even to eat. After a slow start and a little patience, he accepted our love. A year later he is king of the house and loved very much by his family. His crazy antics and painted Siamese face remind me of a circus clown.

Priscilla

F, 1, White & gray

Domestic longhair

Fun loving and very flighty

Sillie is very special to us. She is an all around weird cat. She is a vegetarian. She loves fresh veggies, especially cauliflower, lettuce, cabbage and mushrooms. She also enjoys an occasional bite of spicy salsa and sour cream, green olives, and sauerkraut. Sillie likes to chase her snack food and play with it before she will eat. She also likes to play with the flashlight beam. She runs all over the room and tries to catch it. She cries when Mr. Light takes a nap. Her favorite game with the flashlight is to climb to the top of an old door curtain and play with it on the wall. Even though Sillie is crazy, we love her a lot.

JACKSON   45640

Sarah Humphreys, 17 West St

Mistey

F, 2.5, Black & white

Domestic shorthair

Sweet but feisty

Mistey is my li'l acrobat. When she was small we had an older dog in the house. Anjellica would get after the kitten whenever she would get in the dog food or water. Mistey was feisty and would jump on Jelly and try to entice her to play. After too many growls and snaps Mistey became a furniture cat. She would jump around the bed rooms on the beds, chests, etc. as her means of transportation. She never got down on the floor. Our dog is gone now, but as an adult Mistey still jumps on the furniture. I still love her anyway. Her greatest acrobatic feat is jumping 8 feet across from my stereo to the bed.

LAKEWOOD   44107

Jenny Jorgenson, 1639 Parkwood

Bear Jorgenson

M, 1 dec, Solid black

Mixed

Spunky, lively, playful, unusual, loveable, missed

I believe that my cat Bear Jorgenson was very unusual. Since he was born I've taught him tricks. Two that I think are unusual:

1. If you asked him to give you a kiss - he would. And if you asked him to speak - he'd meow.

2. When he was outside and wanted in, he'd stand on his back legs and look in the door.

He was a great cat.

Griz Jorgenson

M, 6 months, Solid black w/ white spot

Mixed

Smart, spunky, playful, loveable

My cat Griz Jorgenson is unusual. He is six months old and loves to play fetch. If he hears you crumple up paper, he'll come running. And when you throw it, he'll go get it - pick it up in his teeth - and bring it back and drop it in your lap.

He plays till he drops. He's great!

LIMA   45806

Penny & Tanya Turner, 2100 W Hume Rd

Baby

M, 2, Orange

Tabby

Loving & shy to strangers

He gets lonely and starts to talk. He can say "I love you" and "mom". He thinks he's a person or one of the kids. He howlers "mom" when the poodle starts to pick on him. Just like the kids do. When he wants mom to show him love, he says "I love you".

Sweeters

F, 3, Multi-Calico

Calico

Prissy

If she gets mad at you, she sticks her tongue out. If she is lying behind you and she wants something, she will tap you on the ear very easily.

NEW ALBANY   43054

Eileen Hull, 4172 Avis Rd

April

F, 1, Buff (light tan)

?? Part Tabby

Nosey, curious, elusive & pesty-smart

April in Winter

April is a petite little lady. She was a stray 4 month old kitten when I found her hiding under a car in the parking lot of my office - hungry, meowing, with grease on her head on a cold and rainy day. I put her in my car (provided her with a chicken sandwich from a vending machine) to take her home later and clean her up.

The date was April 1st. Named her April and I was the fool.

April's claim to fame is that she fetches. If you throw a sponge ball or rolled-up paper - she'll fetch it and drop it at your feet. If your shoes are off, she puts it in your shoe. If you toss something in the trash, you'll see her walking with it in her mouth . . . could be an envelope or a bottle cap. She also has a stuffed toy kitty about her size that she carries from room to room. At time she's very motherly to it - other times she attacks it and wrestles it around the room and has been video-taped in action.

NEWARK   43055

Sue E Boughton, 709 Karen Parkway

Kitty

F, 8, Gray

Tabby

She's a lover - not a fighter

A friend asked me if I would take a one-year old male stray she found in the snow. I agreed sight unseen. It was pretty obvious to me that he was really a she. After which the vet determined Kitty to be approximately eight years old.

Kitty loves people, but she only comes for loving when she wants it. She'll knead my stomach and then curl up on me, beside me, or on the furniture in back of me. She's a cozy cat.

NEWARK   43055-5945

Robert W Taylor, 584 Prior Ave

Missy

F, 4.5, Black, gray, white

1/2 Maine Coon Cat - 1/2 Blue Persian

Talkative, roughhouser, - doesn't get on laps

She is strictly a house cat. She can learn tricks in a matter of days. Bells are hung on a door knob (inside or out) to an enclosed porch - she states her wishes by hitting the bells. Current tricks, by voice command or hand signals, are:

1) Sits up.

2) Rolls over.

3) Shakes hands.

4) Jumps through 2 or 4 hoops.

5) Walks the tight rope [1" square wood rod].

A real trickster

6) Weighs herself on the platform kitchen scales.

7) I whistle for her to come to bed [like calling a dog].

8) Goes to scratching post - scratches - with no front claws.

There is more!

TOLEDO 43614
Brett & Diane Varner, 1871 Cherrylawn Dr
Bucky
M, 3.5, Orange & white
Domestic shorthair

Affectionately cuddly, Bucky loves people. He's a very happy cat who loves to play the feather game with his brother and sister Bubba & Bonnie.

Bucky – Morris Award Winner

Bucky is an extraordinary boy whom we adopted 3-1/2 years ago from the Toledo

Humane Society.

Just a kitten, Bucky made an impressive public debut by twice capturing the Morris Best Household Kitten Award, at Dayton and Toledo cat shows. He's appeared in the 1992 and 1993 *365 Cats Calendar* sold nationwide, and is featured in a print advertisement for National City Bank. Most recently, Bucky won grand prize in a national Ralston Purina / Fuji Corporation photo contest!

Yes, the camera certainly loves Bucky. But we love Bucky for just being himself. He never tires of greeting us with a gurglely purr and a warm nudge of affection, or of contentedly nesting by our sides after paw--pawing the bed quilt. Bucky means the world to us; life wouldn't be the same without him!

WARREN 44483
Veronica & George Allen, 3518 Lafayette St NE
Harry
M, 3, Dove gray / blue point
Ragdoll / Birman

Lovable fur ball monster.

Harry is long, thick boned & medium haired, with white mittens front & back and a fluffy white chest ruff. Blue points and eyes round out this 14 pound loving tank. When someone he knows comes to visit, Harry flops over on his side and rubs his face with a curled front paw. He then wiggles on his back when petted. Harry's favorite toy is a black & silver Raiders shoe lace that he drags around like a security blanket. He drags it with him to look out the window, to eat, and even to use "the box". We're hoping to have Harry (and his shoe lace) featured on "Funniest Home Videos" doing a spoof we created called "Bungee Troll and the Giant Cave Bear." Watch for him!

Leo (Moose)
M, 16, Orange / tan
Domestic shorthair / tabby

Loud demanding old-man.

Moose was my first cat and he's lived through all my others. He's been beaten up, chewed up, hit by cars, and neutered. He's done it all, and at 16 - the only thing that's wrong is that he's losing his hearing. Everything you pick up - Moose thinks it's for him. Since he's losing his hearing, he doesn't meow anymore - he YELLS!

Moose lives with my Mom & Dad and basically runs their lives. He's got them trained very well. They buy him tuna in a can because he won't eat cat food. Even though he's picky, loud and grouchy - he was the first and I'll always love him.

WARREN   44483

Marguerite Logan, 5208 Copeland Ave

Molly

F, 2, Tortise-shell

She wants to be with us and is a quiet cat.
Molly came from the Animal Welfare League. She weighed 2-1/2 pounds - she is 12 pounds now. When her supper is ready, I kneel down and say, "Look what I've got." She then gets up on her hind feet and rubs her nose against my cheek - she is then fed. When our company leaves, she follows them to the door, which opens part way. She sticks her head out until they go. She plays with a small ball and brings it to our feet; if we ignore it, she puts her paw on your foot. When it is bounced to her, she jumps up in mid-air and catches it. These tricks she does on her own. We did not train her.

She is very clean and loves to be combed. Her fur is long and very soft.

WESTERVILLE   43081

Ann Davis, 3434 Saigon Dr

Snowball "Cat"

M, 14, White

Domestic shorthair

Loving, a people cat

When I'm feeling down, I can always count on him for a purr to make me feel better. He's so loving and giving. He's my best friend and the most special and wonderful cat in the world. If he wants to catch your attention, he gently pats your hand.

Calico

F, 6, Calico

Domestic shorthair

A real charmer

Calico is such a cutie! She curls her head under a paw and makes a sound like "murk" when you enter the room. She is polite, too - she'll "ask" permission to sit next to you on the couch.

WISCONSIN

BROWNTOWN   53522

Deborah Hazeltine, Box 135 115 E South St

BJ

F, 12, Grey & white

Mixed

Friendly and very loveable / she thinks I'm her mother

BJ is all personality

I raised "BJ" by hand after her mother left her and four others at two weeks of age. She became my house cat after being severely injured when she was hit by a car. Her front leg was full of steel pins and was wired together. BJ is more than just a pet to me. She is a loving constant companion who is always cuddling and giving me hugs especially when she knows I don't feel good or have had a bad day. What my dear "BJ" lacks in pedigree, she more than makes up for in her personality.

CHIPPEWA FALLS   54729

Marvin & Edith Nauman, 17932 W Edgewater Dr

Sinbad

M, 3, Brown, white & black

Seal Point Rag Doll Mitted

Patient, greets visitors believed to have sense of humor.

He was adopted from the Eau Calire Animal Shelter. He was about 10 months and picked up as a stray. We have a wood sliding door in our enclosed entrance and basement. Sinbad lays on his side with his hind feet digging into the carpet and pushes on the door with his front feet until it moves. He doesn't care how long it takes. The other three house cats wait and watch. As soon as the door opens, they follow him into the hall and wait for him to open the basement sliding door. This time, he sits on his haunches and again pushes with his front feet until the door moves. Down the steps the four cats bounce with tails waving high . . . into my husband's toy train collection. In and out of the train tunnel they run and play their games of hide and seek. When tired they climb the shelves of trains and find a place to sleep.

We didn't know what he really was until we entered him in a household cat show and a judge told us that he was a Seal Point Mitted Rag Doll.

GREEN BAY   54304-2503
Helen Harrington & Rebekah [daughter], 855 15th Av
"Puff"
M, 12 dec, Brown & white
Tiger striped domestic shorthair
Intelligent - affectionate - showoff (world class)
Puff was rescued from the local Humane Society. (Their room for cats was very small at the time.)

Puff sleeps like a doll

My daughter was five and old enough to have her own cat. I decided to surprise her when she came home from kindergarten. I faced cage after cage of sad-eyed cats, all seeming to be apathetic about their death sentence. All but "Puff" that is. Sensing a possible stay of execution, he cried out, "Take me," all the time reaching through the bars with his paws to make personal contact with me. When I approached his cage he purred loudly to seal the bargain. I took "Puff" home and gave him to my

daughter. What else could a five year old name her very own cat?

Never did a cat try so hard to please a little girl. Although he was aggressive enough to run a stray dog off the property, for her, he was a pussy cat.

Under her tutelage he learned to: jump through a hoop, over a stick, from chair to chair, eat while sitting in a high chair, take a bottle while laying in a doll bed, play Barbie dolls and ride a stroller. Other children delighted in watching "Puff" go through his paces.

Once he even made the ten block, traffic filled route to school with Rebekah pushing his stroller. As he clung to the bars with both feet, eyes fixed straight ahead. After doing his act for the second grade class, he and I made the trip home alone, down the back streets, with the stroller folded and "Puff" under my arm. "Puff" died at nearly 13 years of age with cancer of the jaw. He could no longer eat when the vet "put him to sleep." I think he also knew Rebekah would soon be moving on in her life.

JANESVILLE   53545
Sheryl Isenhart, 423 Center Ave
Peach Tootie
F, 1, Gray, sleek
Not known
Loving & playful
Our gray common housecat is a darling, loving kitten. We brought her home at 7 weeks. Her intelligence became evident at once. She attached herself to each of us and loved to play with mom's canvas ornaments. As the Christmas tree went up so did Peach Tootie. She was 2 lbs and able to climb up the inside of our artificial tree. She chose her favorite ornament and down she raced to bring it and drop it at our feet. We played a game of 'fetch' with her. True to a cat's nature, she fetches when she wants to.

Our old house has a bricked-up fireplace in the front room. We placed a chair below the mantel and Peach Tootie climbs up on the mantel. Our daughter received a Round Striker dart board with soft tipped darts from Gma and Gpa. We nailed it up over the mantle. As we throw the soft tip darts, Peach climbs up on the mantel and waits for us to finish the game. Then she cleverly reaches up with her paws and pulls the darts to her mouth, jumps down onto the chair, from there to the floor, races over to us and drops the dart at our feet.

We praise her, and she vocally answers and repeats the process until the darts are retrieved. After a rousing game of darts she heads for mom's lap and takes a catnap. She is four months old now and still 'fetching'.

MANITOWOC   54220
John & Judith Lango, 2128 Hunters Ridge Ct
Pastie
F, 6, White & orange
Domestic shorthair
Precocious but precious
We found Pastie, an orphaned stray kitten, at our summer cottage in 1986. Pastie is the smartest cat we have ever known. Pastie's favorite pastime is darts. At our summer cottage, when someone new came in, she would "meow" at them, then run over and sit under the dart board, as if to say, "come play darts with me." She had her special stool she would sit on. When someone played darts she hoped the darts would fall off the dart board and she would chase after the fallen darts. Pastie was also smart enough to know if someone wasn't very good at darts, she would sit off to the side and not directly under the dart board. She never got hit by a dart.

PHELPS   54554
Diane Biederman, PO Box 108
Tippy
M, 5, Black & white
1/2-Siamese & 1/2- ?
Curious, friendly, affectionate
From the time we got Tippy, he was different from other cats. He would talk back to us and get into the craziest things. Any cupboard or drawer that could be opened - would be. We were never surprised to find our drawers rearranged or the kitchen cupboards reorganized.
When he was 2 yrs. old, I was attending college, and had to leave very early. My husband worked nights, so went to bed as I was leaving for school. We heated with wood at the time. Tippy was very noisy one morning and kept howling in the basement and running up and down the stairs. Before I left, I went down to the basement to scold him for being so noisy and discovered he was howling about a chimney fire. Had I left for school, the house would have burned and everyone would have been killed.
Tippy's current projects are to open the roll-top bread box (he has a plastic bag

fetish) and to get the refrigerator door to open.
Smokey
M, 6, Blackish brown (sable)
1/2-Burmese & 1/2-Gray Persian
Friendly & affectionate
He seems to know when someone is not feeling well or is sad. He climbs on your back & puts his paws around your neck and literally hugs you. Sometimes he grooms your head, as if trying to comfort you. He's the "Mother" of the house. Everyone gets mothered by him regardless of who they are.
I never set my alarm clock. He wakes me up every morning at the same time by first peering in my face (tickling with whiskers), then nudging me and finally getting behind my pillow and pulling my hair with his teeth. Then when I yelp, he purrs and licks my nose as if to say "Sorry".

RICHLAND CENTER   53581
Laci Ann Keller, Rt 4 Box 172
Thumper
F, 1, Calico
Barnyard Run
Funny & caring
When Thumper was a baby she didn't move like her litter mates. She would pull herself around with her front feet when the others were running around. I helped teach her to walk by coaxing her to come and get her feed. Thumper's hind leg is twice as long as the rest and is deformed. But that doesn't stop her from playing like a normal cat.
She likes to jump in the bath tub and chew on the bath mat, crawl under the covers when it's bed time and turn my light off and on. She gets very crabby when she doesn't get her afternoon nap. She can also purr and hiss at the same time.

Chapter Fifteen

Who's Who in the Heartland

```
┌─────────────────────────┐
│                         │
│         IOWA            │
│                         │
└─────────────────────────┘
```

CEDAR RAPIDS   52401
Sue Gaulke, 1201 15 St SE Apt 110
John
M, dec, Orange Tiger
Domesticated shorthair
Affectionate
John's Ma abandoned him when he was two days old since he had distemper. I wiped his nose and eyes and kept John warm. It took almost two days before he caught on to lapping milk. John grew up fast. When he was almost two years old, he weighed 35 pounds. John showed how much he loved me. He would rub his head on my legs, or if he was on my lap, John would rub his head on my chin. What I thought was so unusual was: every night John would lie across my neck and P-u-r-r [his way of singing to me] real loud, until I fell asleep. Then, never failing, exactly at 6:00 A.M., John would wake me up by licking my face.

she was quite ill but recovered and came to grace my household. This gorgeous calico (black, orange and white) is the sweetest cat I have had in my half century of living. She comforts me when I am sad, she makes me laugh with her antics, and she is always there for me.
Throughout all this hustle and bustle she has remained my loyal companion. I want to thank God for sending her to me.
"Livvy" (Olivia Newton-John)
F, 8, Chocolate point
Siamese (traditional)
Shy, lovable, very vocal at times
When my Siamese died I was devastated, so I began my search for another. I was referred to a breeder that I found was running a horrible cattery. I was shown this tiny, last of the litter kitten, who huddled in the corner and appeared very frightened. I couldn't leave her there, so I bought her.
To this day she is scared of the world, hides all the time; but when we are alone she shows me love despite her fears. I will always love her and protect her, for she returns love in her own way and is a good companion.

CLINTON   52732
Paula Kany, 323 4ᵗʰ Ave N
Groovy
F, 8, Black, orange, white
Domestic shorthair
Mellow, playful & adjusts to all situations. Is a Quad Supreme household pet in ACFA.
Groovy is her name, cat shows became her game, and that's how she rose to fame.
When rescued as an orphan in Cool, Texas,

CLINTON   52732
Betty J Larkin, 202 N Bluff Blvd #102
Rusty
M, 3, Red mackerel tabby
Domestic shorthair
Feisty, loving, overly curious, foxy, very smart
If there ever was a cat true to the "9 lives" theory - this is the cat.
His name from the shelter was "Lucky",

but I changed it to "Rusty". First off, he choked on the cat food and my daughter successfully performed the Heimlich method. Two weeks later he ate fresh tulip petals and needed a shot to save his life. He was sneaky in getting those petals - he ate only the black ones so we didn't know what his problem was until we moved the tulips. He now has 7 lives and seems to know it - is very good - and exceptionally lovable.

Rusty (front) & Frieda – ready for bed

Frieda

F, 3, Blue mackerel tabby

Domestic shorthair

Lovable, laid back, nosey, touch only when she wants touching

When her 3 kittens were killed by cars, she came to my daughter's house crying. She became very ill and was sick for weeks, costing a small fortune to cure. As she began to get better, my daughter talked me into taking her. She fit right in with my other cat Rusty and they became buddies. She has emerged a very lovable, caring and fat cat. She made up for lost time on eating and is chunky now.

When people visit me she makes herself quite comfortable on their laps and demands petting and all their attention. We feel it was and is worth every penny it cost saving this sweet cat.

MANCHESTER   52057

Ron & Jan Mummert, 541 Prospect St

Twinkles

F, 2, Calico

Shorthair

A little cutie who has a sweet disposition to match.

Twinkles and her brother Tarzan came to our home straight from the farm. When we picked them out, Twinkles was the prettiest calico we had ever seen. Twinkles was named for her twinkling green eyes. She is very curious and loves to sniff things over. Her nose crinkles and starts twitching as she takes in all the different smells.

Twinkles is a people-pleasing cat. She has the occasional "wild streak" when she and her brother pretend to be jungle cats. When she relaxes, Twink will roll over and wiggle to let us know it's tummy rubbing time. Twinkles brings peace and joy to our lives.

Tarzan

M, 2, Orange & white

Shorthair

He loves attention and will do anything to get some.

When we went to the farm to pick out our cats, Tarzan came right up to us as if to say, "When do we go home?" He made himself comfortable from day one.

Tarzan is a very unique cat. He thinks he's a pretty tough cat one moment . . . and the next moment he's an affectionate, overgrown kitten. Tarzan loves attention. He will "chirp" and bug us until we give him some.

He also keeps us entertained with his antics. Tarzan loves to pounce on invisible mice under the covers and unroll the toilet paper when no one's looking. One of his favorite things to do is wrestle with his sister, Twinkles. Tarzan can be a troublemaker, but we love him just the same.

OELWEIN   50662

Cathy Gilson, 1115 West Charles

Ashley

F, 10 months, Black and white

Common - adopted from animal shelter (Humane Society)

Sweet, feisty, spunky, independent

My cat, Ashley, is unique in many ways. She loves to play ball. She brings a foam ball and drops it at my feet. I'll then throw it and she races after it. She catches it and carries it back in her teeth where she places it to be thrown again. If she drops it out of reach she bats it with her paw to get it close enough to reach. Ashley also loves water. She plays in her water bowl and whenever the faucet is turned on she comes running. She can't be in the bathroom when you're taking a bath because she will jump in. Even on my worst days she can make me laugh. She is truly a wonderful cat.

"Let's play ball!" Ashley

KANSAS

HAYS   67601
Connie Ernst, 1320 Douglas
Shadow
M, 2, Seal point
Siamese
Playful, affectionate
Shadow plays catch with us! Whenever we throw a ball, Shadow jumps up, catches the ball in his front paws, and drops to the floor with it. He must, however, stalk the ball from behind something! If nothing is laying on the floor, he comes from behind the couch or under the piano bench to "attack" his prey. Almost any cover will do - he's hidden behind a sandal and even crouched behind a rag! He's wonderfully vocal and even "chirps" at the ball as he jumps. We love him!

HUMBOLDT   66748
Kaella Huse, 1301 Central
Shadow
M, 2.5, Black
Manx
Shy of strangers, loving towards family
Shadow was very outgoing when he was a

kitten. I raised him like he was a human baby and he took to it real well. Now he has to be carried on my hip like a baby. He has a sister and won't go anywhere without her. He meets me at the door every evening. If my alarm clock doesn't go off he's waking me up. He loves to sleep flat on his back.

Patches
F, 2.5, Orange, black, white
Dark Calico
Very outgoing
I found Patches on a farm. She was wild. She spent her first days at home living under the couch. Now I can't keep her down. She's very energetic. She does all sorts of acrobats. She loves to tease the dog and kids. She also loves to sit on top of the refrigerator and "look down at the world." She is completely different from her brother.

LAWRENCE   66049
John & Debbie Buckley, 2500 W 6th St Apt #119
Kiger Buckley
M, 1.5, Black & white
Shorthair Tabby
Mischievous, clever as a fox
When my husband returns home from work, Kiger will greet him at the door with a ten minute hello. He's very stuck on himself; he will stare into mirrors for minutes on end.
He's always playing either hide and seek or tag with us, never letting our lives get boring. One day we were amazed to find out that he had awoken our neighbor from his bed. He also loves to watch T.V., nature shows being his favorite. He loves to go on walks with us and follows behind us like a dog. Kiger is one special cat.
Spoon Buckley
M, 1, Black & white
Longhaired Tabby
Loveable, bashful & compassionate
Spoon is many things but the thing he is most is loveable. When the alarm rings in the morning, he stands on my chest and gives me morning kisses. And when I turn away he will stretch his arm out and lightly put his paw on my cheek and turn my head toward him. He also shares my addiction to ice. Whenever he hears me getting ice, he

will come sliding into the kitchen and sit by the refrigerator until I toss him a piece of ice. Spoon is truly special.

NEW CAMBRIA   67470
Nancy Lightner, 8005 E Mariposa Rd
Baby Girl
F, 6, White
Caretaker
Baby Girl was the only survivor of a litter of 5 kittens. When she was 2 years old she became so sick she had to be hospitalized. After 10 days with no improvement our vet sent her home to die. At the end of a month with our love and care she started putting on weight and was totally well.

Shortly after that my husband was diagnosed with colon cancer. When he was released from the hospital Baby Girl became his caretaker seeing him through all his chemo and radiation therapy. She never left his side when he was home. Baby Girl deserves a lot of the credit for his recovery. He has now been cancer-free for 3 years and Baby has only an occasional sneeze to remind her of her brush with death.

OSAWATOMEE   66064
Glenda Y Newell, 144 Pacific - Apt C
"Marcel"
M, 5, Black/white
Not known
Independent, talkative, demanding at times of my attention
He came to me on New Year's Eve 1988 as a scrawny, flea-bitten kitten and quickly grew into a large, beautiful cat whose independence was apparent from day one.

Marcel was a roamer, especially around the holidays. He would leave and be gone for 2-3 days, even 5, almost as if he had someplace/someone else that needed him more. The most memorable "walk-about" for for 30 days - from December 14 to January 14. Thinking, after 7 days, he was gone for good, I acquired another cat (I already had one before Marcel); so when he showed up like nothing unusual had occurred, he was greeted by the three of us instead of two. We have adjusted well.

OSAWATOMIE   66064
A T Mosimann, 126 15th Street

Pinkie
F, 2, Jet black
Alley
Independent & tolerant
Pinkie, a stray, was brought home by me when a half-starved, skinny kitten. Was spayed, inoculated, and licensed at age 6 months. For me, she is the model for proper living - a survivor who appreciates God's gift of life and so lives her life. Eats, sleeps, enjoys, and accepts, in gratitude, her blessings.

OVERLAND PARK   66212
Maureen Kramanak, 9408 Hadley
Cameron II.
M, 2, Black & white
A cat with a sense of humor.

Cameron II – the perfect match

When my "tuxedo cat" Cameron I. passed away during a routine veterinary procedure, I decided that another cat should be given a chance to live. As a result, I went to every animal shelter in town to adopt a black & white male "tuxedo" cat with green eyes. I found "Cameron II." after much searching. As I was signing him out, I discovered that he was found between 10:30 and 11:00 a.m., the exact time Cameron I. died. Cameron II. went on to be the American Cat Fancier's Association's Pet of the Year for 1992. During our year "on the road", Cameron II. learned to flush the toilet, order X-rated movies, and escape from his airline carrier. Cameron II. and I have a very special relationship, and I love him very much.

TOPEKA   66604-3317
Ms Joy Niehoff & Cathy Shymanski, 2044
SW Bowman Ct

Margo

F, 14, Tortiseshell

Domestic shorthair

Aloof but caring, no sense of humor, very serious type

I opened my eyes one morning to find that Margo had used the pillow in front of my nose as a litter box. I didn't get mad; it immediately occurred to me that no one had told her that my room-mate who had left abruptly for the hospital was not gone forever. I explained to Margo that Cathy had gone to the "Vet" and would be home soon.

Upon arising the next morning I discovered that Margo had brought me a peace offering while I slept, a now flat mouse. I thanked her graciously and disposed of it.

Again the following morning I awoke to the offering of a second dead mouse in my bed. I thanked her again and secreted it out to the trash. This time she understood that all was forgiven and life continued as normal.

Solo (Briarson Baby Boomer)

F, 7, Silver patched tabby

Scottish Fold

People-oriented, quiet

Solo is very good at understanding English. When I told her once to take her 4 week old kitten back to her nest, I said "take her to bed." Solo did! She took her to my bed and insisted that she and the kitten sleep in bed with me ever since!

On another occasion, I awoke one morning to a loud, repeated noise. Then my ear felt moist. Yes, Solo was sucking on my earlobe!

Solo is probably special most of all because she is the queen that is the foundation of our Scottish & Highland Fold breeding program. Thanks, Solo!

MINNESOTA

ANDOVER   55304

Ann Henry, 4217 149th Av NW

Jim

M, 4, Black with one white whisker

Very hyper

I found my cat in a very special way. As I was walking down the driveway to meet a friend, Molly Nystrom, I heard a faint meowing. I looked around to see what it was and I saw a tiny black kitten. As I lifted the cat in my arms, I realized I had to find its owner. My heart sank. I put an ad in the paper and when the owner called she said I could keep the cat because the mom cat was abusing it. That's how I got my special cat.

Angel

F, 8, White

Very lovable

My cat is special because I got her right after my other cat died. She was a real comfort to me. After the years, I loved her as much as the cat I had lost.

GLYNDON   56547-0082
Myrtle S Hanson, 106 Partridge Ave SE

Keetszer

M, 4, Beige - black & gray

1/2 Siamese - 1/2 Tabby

Very loving

First of all I feel he protects us - as he hears whenever a car drives in our driveway, so we are aware of someone outside by the way he raises his ears and looks at the door.

My work has been sewing drapery in my shop and Keetszer always is near, laying in his basket while I sew until it gets to be 5:00, he comes to me and lays on the fabric - if that doesn't work he starts to bite at me, like he can tell what time it is. Then he wants to play ball. We throw a sponge and he'll go fetch it in his mouth and bring it back to us to throw again till he's tired.

MILACA   56353
Rose Webster, 11074 210th St

Stitches

F, 14 dec, Calico (orange-black-white)

Very affectionate

Stitches was a very affectionate cat. When I went to bed she came to cuddle. This was our special time together. Many a night I fell asleep listening to her purr. Stitches could talk. She would tell me when she wanted me out for a walk on her leash. She loved moonlight strolls. Stitches passed away on my birthday Dec 3, 1992, of a stomach tumor. She is deeply missed by her brother Buffin, adopted sister Taska and myself. The love we shared together is eternal.

Taska

F, 2, Calico (orange-black-white)

A survivor

Taska had a very bad start in life, but has survived. Taska has grown to a very beautiful and intelligent kitty. Taska was abandoned at birth. I found her, warmed her, fed her and when she was strong enough another momma cat adopted her. At the age of 4 weeks she came to live with Stitches, Buffin and me. Buffin became her godfather. We live in a motor home. Taska loves to travel. Taska's special talent: she loves to retrieve crumpled-up paper or foil.

MINNEAPOLIS   55403-4073

Virginia Howell, 330 Oak Grove St #703

"Sia"

F, 7, A blending of gray, tan, & white

Siamese and Tabby mix

Best described as "sweet". Also - playful, mischievous, extremely curious - and very affectionate and loving

"Sia" is special in many more ways than I could describe here. She's truly the joy of my life! She gives me unconditional love, and allows me to love her with all my heart.

Just a tiny 7 week old kitten when I got her, she is now 7 years old - a longhaired, blue-eyed beauty - with 4 white-tipped paws. "Sia" has a cute personality - but will only display her "charms" for a select few. She's very shy - and runs away from strangers. With me, however, "Sia" is extremely affectionate - always rubbing her face against me - and following me around like a shadow. She sleeps with me every night - and often purrs us both to sleep!

> # MISSOURI

GRANBY   64844

Connie Simpson, R#1 Box 1143T

Miss Connie Chung (Miss C.C.)

F, 1.5, Calico colors

Unknown

A bundle of love, gives me love without penalties

My little CC is always waiting in the window for my return at night. When I'm home she is my right arm. Everywhere I go, she goes. At night before I go to sleep, she lays on her back in my arms, takes a baby bottle full of milk, and then lays on my arm all night. Life without CC would be terrible. I really believe she knows my inner soul.

Garfield Odie Weatherspoon III

F, 3, Calico

She thinks she is the Queen of all my cats

Garfield has given me a lot: she gives love, unlike the others. She shows me warmth and sensitivity. She is Queen of all my cats.

HARDIN   64035

Ann Shumaker, 507 Parkway

Maudie

F, 14, Black

Crossbreed

"Mother Superior" of her domain

Maudie enjoys her bike rides

Maudie, my black crossbreed, has used three of her nine lives. One - sure death by abandonment, two - severely injured in a car engine mishap, three - locked in a neighbor's shed for thirteen days without food or water.

Maudie found sleeping in the bike handle-bar basket very enjoyable. As the bike moved out on trips around town she just stayed onboard. Now she dearly loves her rides! With head high and wind blowing through her whiskers - or snuggled down on her rug - she never wants the outing to end.

My uncommon, bicycle-riding, Maudie, draws many surprised and amazed looks.

KAISER   65047
Nancy Hoffman, PO Box 334

Menace
M, 4,
Himalayan

A precocious extravert

Menace does his morning thing

Menace is a holy terror, living up to his name. He loves to watch me get ready for work in the morning. I stand at the bathroom sink putting on my make-up; he is walking back and forth across the sink knocking things on the floor. So one day I picked him up and put him in the sink; now that's where he stays to watch me. He loves people and having constant attention.

Molly
F, 5, Black
Himalayan

Introvert

She is very shy around other people; but at home with just me, she is her normal inquisitive, mischievous self. She is a very special cat to me.

KANSAS CITY   64151
John & Barb Noble, 8238 NW Birch Ln

Rascal
M, 11, Silver
Mixed Persian

Our most uncommon, common cat seems to have been caught up in the fitness craze - he joins me in stretching exercises after a brisk walk.

But first some background about this fellow.

Three years ago we adopted Rastamon, a large handsome silver gentleman of mixed Persian ancestry. He had been mistreated, and ran from any man. For the first month, he hid in our dark basement. Slowly, this grand fellow made his way upstairs. But always he looked down and away.

After our second month together, he turned his face up to ours. Thus began a rewarding love affair between our regal friend and my wife and me, a bond of trust, accented by soft purring. A common cat, uncommonly wonderful.

We had thought that cats, in their independence, were unfeeling. Not true, we learned. Our new friend, gradually showing us his feelings, was very sensitive.

When we returned from trips, or a day at the office, he was overjoyed. Romping and playing, he showed his happiness. Or eating his breakfast, untouched during our absence. And always, he stayed close to us.

In our time together we also have learned how much he is like us, and we like him. Like people, he doesn't want to eat alone. Later, he began to ambush and tease us, and he got a new name ... Rascal. One of his great joys is to hide and gallop.

Most days, he follows us from room to room in our house, a quiet companion. At night, he snuggles in our bed. We think that Rascal is very handsome, and when we visit his doctor, other pet owners say the same. Although gorgeous, he is unspoiled, a reminder to us of his painful past. Perhaps he is smarter than we.

One day as I stretched arms and legs on the living room floor, I looked over to see him lay on his side, extending and withdrawing his front paws in a certain rhythm. Of course he needs no aerobics, possessed of blazing speed and incredible agility. These he combines with unerring sight, hearing and smell.

We love him - the child we never had.

KANSAS CITY   64119

Debra Beavers Sutton & The Beavers Family, 5017 NE Sherwood Ct

Stubby

M, 17 dec, Red,cream

Red tabby (domestic shorthair)

Affectionate, loving

Stubby, a week-old red tabby kitten, was found abandoned in my grandmother's barn. He was bleeding from a jagged wound where his right hind leg had once been. After the veterinarian expressed doubts about the little orphan's chance of survival, our mother cat accepted Stubby into her new litter and relentlessly bathed his wound with her abrasive tongue, draining it of infection. Stubby slowly gained strength. The wound healed over and fur covered the stub. Stubby adjusted to life on three legs, eventually learning how to walk and even to run. He lived with us for seventeen pampered years.

Stubby with his Xmas mouse

OSAGE BEACH   65065

Wendy L. Habermehl, PO Box 264

Rascal

M, 7, Black/white

One of America's dumped and homeless

Very affectionate

My husband always hated cats until Rascal was dumped off at our house. He was barely weaned, and scared to death. But with lots of coaxing with some ham, I won him over. He's been here ever since. One day, he pushed his way through a small hole in our screened porch and disappeared into the woods. He was gone 4 days. My husband and I were leaving for a short

vacation and Rascal still wasn't home. I was really worried because he knew nothing of the outside world. Well I finally found him, about 40 feet up a tree. He was so scared, his hair was falling out and he'd eaten a lot of bark off the tree. We had to cut the tree down to get him out. Needless to say, he never left the porch again.

Rascal (left) & Muffy are a matched pair

Muffy

F, 8, Calico

Mixed

Loveable

She came to us so thin, she could hardly walk. She had worms so bad, she was coughing. Well 9 visits to the vet and 4 different worm medicines later, she's one healthy fat kitty. Now she resembles the poster of "Fat Cat". My vet "Doc Jim Wilsman" says she's a "basketball with a head" and we love her.

SENECA   64865

Sarah Beetem, 711 Osage

Garfield

M, 5, Orange and White

Just a tom-cat

Very playful, wild, and happy

Garfield came into my life a month and a half after my mother died. He was given to me from a co-worker. He reminded me a lot of my mom's cat who had died the year before. As a matter of fact, he looks exactly like my mom's cat except he has a shorter tail. Through his love and playfulness he has slowly helped me cope with her death. Every time he lays on my lap and purrs, I can look at him and pet him and know the joy and companionship that my mom's cat gave her. He is more than a pet, he is my friend.

Alexander Michelob

M, 4, Blue

British shorthair

Quiet, reserved, snobbish

Alex is my first pedigreed cat. He is very beautiful. I have always loved cats and my favorite color is blue. I was thrilled to learn that there were blue breeds of cats. He is a Neuter Triple Champion!! He is not real sociable but he is very special to me.

ST LOUIS   63108

Dorothy H Claybourne, 40 N Kingshighway -11F

Evie

F, 12, Gold & white

American shorthair

"The sweetest cat in the world"

Evie in one of her places

Evie is my own sweet-natured foundling. We have shared a happy companionship since she first attracted my attention - she was in a campus rose garden and started mewing when she heard me. She was hot (97° and muggy), lonely, hungry, thirsty, and needed to use the litter. My co-workers and I met her needs and she came home to live with my beloved Adam and me.

She is beautiful, playful, comical, affectionate, loving, intelligent, 95% well-behaved, and a wee bit timid. She has a tendency to "Mother" both Seth and me!

Seth

M, 8, Black, tan with white trim

American shorthair

Sweet & mischievous

Seth was given to me by a friend when I lost Adam. Unfortunately taken from mother-cat three to four weeks too soon. He's sadly underdeveloped socially - with both Evie and me - but mutual love has overcome most of this. I was told he was the runt, to explain his size! He gets carried away with play and starts World War III! During his kitten year he woke me nightly between two and four to play. His major trick - setting the electric can opener buzzing (with his chin) when I'm late with meals or he dislikes what he's fed!

ST LOUIS   63121

Lawrence & Patricia Ducharme, 4343 Normandy Trace Dr

Smokey Sue

F, 5, Black, grey, white

Domestic house cat

Gentle, playful, loves to eat, sleep and "fish"

We adopted Smokey Sue from the Humane Society when she was 3 years old. She had been awaiting a home there for 10 days, and my husband and I could tell that the barking dogs were making her a nervous wreck. There were many cats to choose from, but when my husband approached Smokey Sue's cage and looked inside, she quietly let out a small "meow" which seemed to plead, "Please get me out of here!" My husband said, "I want that one." She has been the joy of our lives ever since.

Her favorite activities include bird watching from the windowsills, playing with her cat toy fishing pole with her Daddy, watching the bathtub fill with water, running through the house after visiting the litter box, and sleeping in a warm human lap.

ST LOUIS   63139-1708

Bob & Cecily Westermann, 3275 Jasper Pk

Bernie

M, 14, Grey - black stripes

American short hair

Calm, curious, competent

Back in 1979, when Bernie was a 6-week old stray kitten, he wandered into a housing project -- where a "disturbed" teenager doused him with barbecue fluid and set him on fire. The veterinarians at the humane society where I work usually have to kill animals in this condition to prevent them from suffering more. But there was something different about this kitten, and he didn't have problems breathing. They amputated his charred ear tips and asked if I would try to give him a chance for a normal life in our multi-cat household. From the beginning, Bernie has been uncommon. When he wanted the dog or the other cats to move, he would just look at them and they would move. When he wants to eat, he just looks at one of us and we feed him. He has been the only cat at dog show presentations - but the dogs don't seem upset. Bernie was the October 9, 1991 *Workman Cat-a-day Calendar* entry and was one of the few cats to ever be pictured in *American Survival Guide Magazine* (7/92).

He faces photographers with the same courageous calm he faces everything else. Bernie is about 14 now, and even though he's an indoor cat, he'll be exchanging his body soon. Wherever he transits to, I'm sure it won't be hell. He's already been there.

Unknown

?, ?, multi (usually American short hair)

All

13,447 cats had to be killed at only five St. Louis area animal shelters during 1991. Although a few of these cats were old or ill, and put down at the request of caring owners -- most either did not have homes, or had owners who didn't care enough to claim them. These cats, too, were uncommon. Each was special and each should be remembered.

NEBRASKA

ELWOOD   68937

Kathy Weismann, PO Box 114

Riley

F, 7, Black striped

Very independent; very perceptive & curious; sympathetic

She's my best friend & a good companion. She loves to eat, ride in our Bronco, but only around town. She does not like the country. She's a city girl! She howls when you leave town! She's been known to switch off lights. She knows lots of words like: bye bye birdie, she will look toward a window, Tuffy, my mom's cat, potty, etc. When you tell her to do her trick, she sits up! She needs no hand motions. She really eyeballs our visitors and decides if they are fit company! We love her and likewise her big brother, Snowball & little brother, Joey. Her favorite toy is a candle she carefully removed from the Xmas tree.

NORTH LOUP

Alan Mars

Samson

M, 1.5, Gray, tiger stripped

Everyday "alley cat"

Very loving and active

After a cold and rainy fall, Samson came into our lives as a kitten with a case of pneumonia. In the time since, he has developed a talent of his own. You can be standing by the bed or such, in the middle of the floor or just bending over, and the next thing you know he's on your shoulder. Sometimes, you don't even know he's around until its too late. Afterwards, he'll either ride on your shoulder or reach around to your face and love you up. All this and he can land without using his claws (not declawed).

OMAHA   68106

Tina Wilwerding, 6454 Pierce

Fawn

F, 5, Chocolate point

Siamese

Loving, craves attention

I bought Fawn from a vet, a connoisseur in the Siamese breed. I wanted Fawn to be shown but he did not feel Fawn had quite the makings for a "show" cat. Well despite his disagreement with me, he showed Fawn for me. With only a few shows under her belt, Fawn Grand Championed. His response to me was, "The judges loved her." Now that Fawn has retired from the show ring, and become a mother of five beautiful kittens, she now follows me around the house, sleeps under the covers with me every night, and gives me kisses every morning.

Asia

F, 1, Seal point
Siamese
Mouthy & mischievous!

Asia is only a year old and already knows a few tricks. She knows roll over, shake and beg. I think the beg came instinctively though. Her favorite pastime is to play with Fawn, our other Siamese, and hide in the ceiling in the basement. This will scare the life out of you if you're not used to it. Asia certainly has made our life a little more exciting. She loves to cuddle and give kisses which I think she picked up from Fawn but it makes it all the more enjoyable.

OMAHA   68134

Scott K Zehr, 3101 Maplewood Blvd

Tribble

F, 11.5, Grey striped
Tabby
Very, very loving

Tribble is a very loving cat, and a very spoiled one also. When I am at home, she spends 95% of her time close to me. If I am sitting in my Lazy-Boy reading the newspaper, she will push her way under the paper to get my attention. If I'm sitting anywhere she has to be in my lap.

The only time she isn't with me is to eat or to spread her dozens of toys around the apartment from her toy pit.

She looks forward to visits from my parents, so she can sit in their laps, play, and sleep with them.

cat would make a good pet. He told me Benjermen had ½ hour to live. I took him out of the cage and fell in love. I called him grouchy at first because he hissed when anyone would come near him and he hid. Slowly we gained his trust and now he is the king of the house. He decides when my desk needs to be cleaned by knocking stuff on the floor. He picks on the dog and he plays fetch - something he taught me. I know my life would be empty without him.

Rosemary

F, 3, White and gray
Tabby
Patient and loving

Rosemary loves to watch the fish. She stands next to the tank batting at the glass most of the time, chasing a reflection. Another favorite hobby of hers is shredding paper into small pieces and playing with them. She has taught the family dog this skill of shredding paper. She sleeps on top of the heater vent in the winter and in the tub in the summer. She likes to play and cuddle.

NORTH DAKOTA

DICKINSON   58601

Theresa Nelson, 1100 3rd Ave W #12

Benjermen

M, 5, Cream and orange
Beramisees (Long Hair)
Not a people cat, very independent

Benjermen was at the pound. I was looking for a kitten. I asked the guy working which

Chapter Sixteen

Who's Who in the Southwest

ARIZONA

FLAGSTAFF   86003
Shorty & June King, PO Box 2566
Catnip
F, 3, Black
Unknown
"Talkative", intelligent, inquisitive, independent
On the night we met her, she was a pair of frightened gold-marble eyes hiding in the marigolds. A starved, half-grown black female, shivering in the rain, she was entirely out of ideas that cold September night.

Two years later, sleek and spayed, with a beautiful silk-satin coat, she is "family", our close friend and companion - our constant reminder that life is interesting and exciting, full of things to investigate.

Tiger
M, 3, Tawny orange & white
Unknown
Sensitive, loving, affectionate, "purry"
I wanted to adopt ALL the cats at the Humane Society that spring afternoon. Tiger was "Mr. Macho", pacing, indignant to be caged, flapping his gorgeous striped tail-'flag' in distress. When I opened the cage to get acquainted, he leaped out to my shoulder and began licking my face, adopting me on the spot!

A beautiful 13-lb. orange tabby with a white star on his face, Tiger often climbs up to snuggle and touch my face with one big soft paw in a profound expression of affection.

GLENDALE   85302
Miss Elizabeth Llewellyn, 4913 W Diana Av
Beethoven
M, 3, Black
Unknown
Quiet, very dignified
Beethoven is a beautiful, immensely dignified black shorthair. As I look into his intelligent green eyes, it is difficult for me to remember the terrified feral cat that he was two years ago. Beethoven was so fearful that I had to use a humane cat trap to capture him. He was so afraid of me that he couldn't even bring himself to look at me. He took swift sideways glances. I actually had to force society upon him.

Although he became very tense whenever I held him, he never made a single combative move. He fit in almost immediately with my three other cats and now the foursome are close friends. It seems wonderfully ironic that the cat who couldn't bring himself to look at me now enjoys sitting in front of me and fixing me with an intense stare, and I look at my loving wonderful friend.

KINGMAN   86401
Brenda Orr, 3509 Milky Way Rd
Squirrel
M, 1, Gray & white
Tabby
Sweet
Squirrel is one of the most unusual cats I've ever known. He has a very human-like

personality. He understands when someone is in a bad mood, and comforts them. He can always make me laugh with his crazy activities. He loves being with people and always wants attention.

He acquired his name because he has a kink in the base of his tail, so when he's happy, his tail runs up his back towards his head.

Squirrel has learned to open doors, and we are trying to get him to shut the door after he comes in. He has made all of our lives happier and more interesting.

MESA   85204
Shirley Harding, 1804 E 2nd Av

Lady Tuppence

F, 1, Classic brown tabby

Scottish fold

Prissy - I could see her presiding over an elegant dinner party, bedecked in fine jewels.

What makes my Tuppy, as I sometimes refer to her, special? She has a purr that could melt anyone's heart. She loves to crawl on my chest at 2:00 A.M. and rub her face against mine, all the while purring. That's her way of telling me she always wants her ears and chin scratched. Then she throws herself on her side trusting that I will catch her before she slides off me and onto the floor or bed - depending on which way she decides to throw herself. Needless to say, I can't get angry with her for waking me up. She's my Tuppy and my joy.

MESA   85204
Molly McGuire, 1804 E 2nd Av

Mercedes

F, 2, Black & white

I have five cats and it is hard to choose one which is special enough to write about. But . . . Mercedes is my "BOO-BOO". She's always there to greet me after a long day. She's always near by and seems to always know when I need a hug or a head butt. She's a little mother. Always taking care of the other kitties. When I'm sad, she comes to cuddle me. When I'm sick, she just sits with me and licks my hand. When I'm busy, she just sits where I can see her and winks at me. She loves me unconditionally and is always close by to let me know she's

there for me.

PHOENIX   85015
Karen Catalioto, 4730 N 19th Ave #229

Cleo

F, 8, Black/white

Domestic shorthair mix

Inquisitive, independent, agile, affective

Cleo has been somewhat of a "savior" to me, assisting with my hearing impairment. Ranging from hearing out door-knocking (by moving her ears, then jumping on a stool) to saving my place from an embarrassing flood (by staring toward the sink from a distance), her "chosen" instincts have never missed a cue. Cleo posed as a local model and is featured in the 1992 edition of *Who's Who of Animals*; she even has her own keepsake and photo album! Cleo enjoys being a life-long indoor friend and also lives with a new Shih Tzu pup-pal, Beau!

PHOENIX   85028
Jeanne Elcock, 3109 E Desert Cove

Wiggles

F, 3, Tabby

Sweet natured and very wiggly

When my mother cat died, I wanted to get a new cat. We went to the Emergency Animal Clinic who will fix harmed cats that are found. There we found Wiggles. Wiggles' right eye was bulging and had blue goo on it. They told us she had glaucoma. She was so sweet and lovable, we had to adopt her anyway.

The veterinarians sewed a fake eye into the eye socket and then they sewed the eye shut. About 2 years later, this eye was enlarged and she was in pain. When we took her to the veterinarian, they said that she was having an allergic reaction to the prosthesis (fake eye) and they removed it and sewed her eye shut again. Wiggles is uncommon because she only has one eye.

Sniffles

F, 2, Orange, black, white

Calico

Shy, sweet-natured

When Sniffles went to a local pet show, she broke out of her break-away collar. (It was our first pet show and we didn't realize we should use a harness.) She raced up the tree four feet away. My mother had to climb up the tree waving a hot dog. When Sniffles came down close to the hot dog, my mother grabbed her. For the rest of the afternoon, the judges called her the Tree Kitty. Sniffles was born with a broken tail. Her tail starts out normally and then ends in a knot, with an itty-bitty tip that she waves when she's happy. Her tail won her first place for most unusual cat.

I had another female cat named Mouse. She was a gray longhair that was a sweet-natured airhead and is now deceased. Mouse was special because she liked to sit in her litter box for hours at a time. She would sing in the litter box. She had a very pretty singing voice. While she was singing in the litter box, our other four cats would be waiting in line to use the litter box. We finally had to get another litter box.

PHOENIX   85011

Pamela S Gardner, PO Box 16492

Blanca Negra

F, 11, White/black spots

Domestic shorthair

Affectionate & loyal

Blanca Negra (aka "Snoody") is the most dependent cat I know. She hates to be left alone. When I am home she is always in my lap or on the back of the couch next to me. She comes when she's called - of course she likes me to wiggle my fingers as she comes. At night she sleeps on my chest and puffs her paws.

I have 6 other cats - 5 of which she cleans and plays with. When she is left alone or I am gone, she goes into seclusion, but as soon as I walk in the door, she's there at my feet, dying for me to pick her up or to just pet her.

I got Blanca when she was 2 months old from an emergency animal clinic where I was doing my clinicals to become a vet assistant. She had a bad case of Coccidia (a protozoan parasite) and ringworm. I treated and babied her to death. When she was 6 months old I had her spayed and declawed. She played that up to the max. For 2 months I carried her to her litter box and to her food and water dish. And then I placed her back on her perch in the middle of my bed. Who owns who?

She has grown to depend on me always. Only once did she become independent -

she ran outside when the door was open. I chased her, but she was too quick, and I lost her trail. Panic set in. I searched and searched, tears rolling down my cheeks. I decided to go through my hedges and look into my neighbors yard. There she was - lying in the only patch of sun to be found - just cleaning and grooming herself. When I shouted her name, she just looked at me, "meowed", got up, stretched and walked over to me. I was so relieved to find her that I forgot how angry I was.

To me Blanca is the most perfect cat ever. She never does anything wrong, and it's not that I'm prejudiced, because I love my other 6 cats as much. But they are far from being perfect. I do believe that Blanca is the only living thing in my life that comforts and consoles me and also relieves my stress. I'd be lost without her.

PHOENIX   85076

Mindy Machanic & Brad Shearer, PO Box 51777

Sweets

M, 19, Gray & white tiger

Tabby (domestic shorthair)

Intelligent, funny, friendly, mellow

Sweets adopted me late in 1979. He was a scruffy adult stray who appeared on my doorstep and wouldn't go away. I finally let him in after a month or two. In 1984 he brought home a white Angora (now known as Honeycat) and asked if we could keep him. He raised a neighbor's kitten, and when we got a new kitten (Huggybear) in 1992, Sweets immediately adopted him and taught him how to be a cat. They are now best of friends.

Sweets has lived in Los Angeles, North Carolina, the Washington D.C. area, and Phoenix. At his peak he was 18 pounds of speed and muscle; in his old age, he's still handsome and healthy.

Huggybear

M, 1, White with red & black patches and a black tail with stripes

Domestic longhair (Turkish Van coloring)

Feisty, intelligent, funny, loving, talkative

Huggy was only 6 weeks old when we got him - all fur and strut. He liked to suck . . . our chins, a rag . . . always wetly and noisily. He still sits on our shoulders and sucks our necks in bed when he is happy.

At 7 weeks old he figured out how to use the cat door just by watching Sweets and Honeycat use it.

He demands attention and when we are in the backyard, he yells at us until we pick him up and carry him around. He's fascinated by water, and puts his paws in puddles, the water coming from the tap, his water bowl, and plant pots when we water them. He regularly catches lizards and crickets and literally levitates 4 feet up to pluck moths and butterflies from the air. He's good friends with the two children next door, and talks to them from atop the fence.

PHOENIX   85043
Bob, Sandi, Peter, Yvette Wilson, 6512 W Van Buren Space 25
Leo
M, 5 or 6, Shades of yellow
Mellow and easy going
Leo belonged to someone else but liked our home better. It was like he adopted us and ran off all the other cats that hung around our home.

What makes Leo so special is his way of coming and going. He knocks on the door with his paws, to come in or go out. He is one of the best cats we have owned. All our cats were strays that adopted us.

PRESCOTT   86301
Gloria Mar, 824 W Gurley St #111
Daughter Cat
F, 18, Calico
Sensitive
Daughter Cat, at 3 weeks, was found on a doorstep in L.A. and delivered to my office to be given away. Nobody wanted a girl kitten so I took her home. Her favorite trick is to take my brassiere out of the dressing room while I am dressing and deliver it to my company waiting in the living room.
Sunny Cat
M, 4, White
Shorthair
Ornery
Sunny Cat, an 8 month old tom cat, became stranded in a snow storm, so he went door to door crying for food. No one would take him in so I threw out a box and

placed food in it. He survived several months before returning home to discover his family moved. He thanks me for adopting him each time he places a mouse on my doorstep.

WINSLOW   86047
Suzi Warwick, PO Box 404
Buster
M, 9 mos, Black
Domestic shorthair
Not afraid of anything, energetic
One night my fiancé left some wood too close to our stove and it caught on fire. My kitten, Buster, and I rushed downstairs to put out the flames.

I was pouring water on the burning wood and tossing it into a separate pile. Buster would then circle the wood making sure it was totally out. If it wasn't, he would look at me then at the wood to let me know I had missed a spot.

We successfully put out the fire with no damage to the house. I never thought a 4 month old kitten could be a firefighter - until Buster came along.
Unique
F, 7, Black
Domestic shorthair
Motherly, talkative
I was given Unique when my mother and I stopped at a country store seven years ago. She managed to have one litter of kittens before I got her spayed. Unfortunately she didn't know how to care for them and they died.

Ever since, she has had a very motherly attitude. She treats me like I'm her overgrown kitten half the time. And she would rather be with me than with anyone. Unique may not look like a one of a kind to anyone else, but she's a one of a kind to me.

I have been blessed with six other cats. Natty Gann was ladylike and independent. Almost human (but better).

Munchkin is shy, loveable and very sweet in spite of her nerve damaged leg. She was a cat I was "only going to hold for a minute."

Babe came from a farm and is gentle, innocent and excitable. He has a special gift to be so kind to wildlife.

Finny is a cat unto herself. She is conceited yet friendly. A beautiful cat who is a Queen in her own right.

Kattie was playful, comforting and a best friend. She was a beautiful companion and I'm thankful for every moment we had together.

Noel loved all people - but hated animals. She got her name by arriving on my doorstep Christmas morning.

NEW MEXICO

ALBUQUERQUE   87120
Beverly McCracken, 6128 Bent Tree Dr NW
Pooki
F, 3.5, Tortoise shell (black/gold)
Manx
Extremely affectionate, antic-oriented

Pooki loves shoestrings

Pooki is extremely social, well-mannered, intelligent, and fun. She follows me from room to room until I sit down so she can curl up in my lap and purr contentedly. She never meets a stranger, and welcomes friends by jumping up in their lap. Her favorite toy is a shoestring. She can jump as high as 3 feet to catch the end. She "fetches" her rubber ball by turning a forward somersault after securing it in her mouth. Pooki knows the words "no" and "get down" and stays off kitchen counters, tables, and couches. Pooki is MY PURR-FECT PAL!

ALBUQUERQUE   87104
Betty J Skelly, 2037 Old Town Rd NW
Scruffy
M, 20, Gray & white
Maine Coon ?
Friendly, independent, dependable, faithful

Old Town Greeter

Feline version of Sinatra's "My Way", very much a "people person". Spent his days visiting shops in the Old Town tourist area. Attracted business in the shops he visited. Seemed to feel he had a job to do, and he did it every day up to a week before he died. Lived on the streets until I adopted him. Personality plus. Very tolerant of children - if he didn't like the way they petted him, he would just walk away. Photographed by people from all over the world. Greatly missed by all of Old Town.

OKLAHOMA

BARTLESVILLE   74003
Rush & Lisa Giffin, 1668 South Oak Ave
Joe
M, 2.5, Seal point
Himalayan
Silly comedian with heart of gold!
Our cat Joe (after Joe Montana) loves cartoons and the Discovery Channel. He likes to jump on our back and sniff our ears. He also can't stand for us to sleep late. If we're not up when he decides, he jumps on our headboard and stares us

awake. Ever since we got Joe he took control of our household immediately. As a cat lover my whole life, I can only say "I love cats because I enjoy my home; and little by little, they become its visible soul."
- Jean Cocteau

Joe is early to rise

OKLAHOMA CITY   73132-2232
Gretchen Kifer, 6412 Urschel Ct
Stonewall
M, 7, Cream colored with gray points
Lilac Point Siamese
Quiet, serious, and not very active
Stonewall can be in a room alone for any length of time, sitting down with his face two inches from the wall, and just stare at it. He'll also sit in front of a mirror and stare at himself.

Stonewall will sit in my lap, sitting like a normal person with his feet sticking straight up, and he'll put his paws on his feet, holding them. When Stonewall's cold, he'll go over to a heating vent and sit there right by it, as it blows warm air on him with a look of great contentment on his face.

Quincy
M, dec, Orange and white
Orange tabby
Talkative and very lovable
As Quincy stood on his hind legs with his paws on the rim of our two-foot swimming pool, peering in, the pressure caused the side of the pool to fall in, and the water poured out, splashing all over him.

STILLWATER   74075
Abby Lehman, 4902 N Britton Dr

Spunkey
F, 4, Black & white
Part Siamese
Sweet, "spunkey"
I got her when she was very small; they had already given the mother away. She thinks she is a person. She sits on the couch the way a person would and watches T.V. When we are called for meals, she is the first one at the table. She sleeps cuddled up to me, with her paw around me. She is one of a kind. Once at the vet they had to take her pulse because she was purring so loud they couldn't hear her heart beat.

WELLSTON   74881
Liz & Vernon Janway, Route 2 Box 33-E
Ahab
M, 4, Yellow tabby
Crossbreed (domestic shorthair)
Dislikes anyone who doesn't live in "his" house!
Ahab loves to travel. If asked "Do you want to go?', he lets out a distinct "meow", races to the door and stands there wailing until we leave. I've even taken him riding on my ATV four-wheeler, but he prefers the car where he can sleep! Our veterinarian refers to Ahab as the "Cat From Hell" due to his not-so-affectionate disposition when he visits her. He has never been congenial. Instead, he growls and hisses from the moment he enters the doctor's office until allowed to leave! Ahab is an alarm clock, a "mouser" and sometimes demanding, but always there when I need him.

TEXAS

CORPUS CHRISTI   78412
Claudia T Maxwell, 1005 Clare St
Chrissie
F, 7, Black/white
American shorthair
Extremely alert, very affectionate; talks a lot!
Chrissie was "rescued" from the Humane Society mainly because she seemed to have claustrophobia in the cage, screaming

endlessly. She is rewarding us with continuous love and devotion. She is attuned to my moods as some of these examples will demonstrate:

Chrissie the Mood Reader

1. I used to get anxiety attacks while in the shower. One day I got the claustrophobic feeling again and had to step out, full of soap, and ran with a towel around me into the living room. I was miserable and almost crying. Chrissie saw me since she was sitting on the couch. Suddenly she emitted three loud "meows", quickly in succession. The "meows" sounded highly urgent but to me they said: Mom, calm down, that's alright - calm down! - I calmed down immediately and went back to finish my shower.

2. One day I had a very bad cold flu. I coughed all night, but Chrissie stayed with me on my bed. In the morning, I sat up with another cough attack. Chrissie was sitting on my bed in front of me. Suddenly Chrissie made a coughing sound! She had imitated me! She never did that sound again!

DUBLIN   76446
Carol Kunz, Rt 5 Box 258
Chimey-Ling
M, 14-1/2, Tan w/ dark brown points
Seal point Siamese
Happy
As a kitten, Chimey earned his name because every time I called him, his meow sounded like a chime. He would also roll over in my arms. Now 14-½ years later, when I say "Chimey wana roll?", this huge

Siamese cat swings his head back and forth because he doesn't know which way he wants to roll.

HOUSTON   77092
Ellen Watkins, 5603 Chantilly Lane
Itty
F, 9 months, Black/brown/white
Ocicat - alley cat
Spitfire, very loving & energetic
My sister convinced me to take Itty for a trial run, even though I wasn't sure my three spoiled cats would accept her. Sure enough the three giants immediately descended on the tiny kitten. Her black spotted coat over a creamy white underbelly made her look more like an ocelot than an ordinary house cat. Her temper was also more like that of her wild ancestors. She let the three giants know immediately that she did not like their attitude with hisses and low growls.

Besides cowing the cats, she captured my heart with her spunkiness. We haven't had a kitten in the house for years and her boundless energy takes some getting used to. But her purrs and loving ways have made her a home here - our little wildcat.

KERRVILLE   78028
Donna Shomette, 573 Johnson Dr
Merlynn
F, 1.5, Brown/grey tabby
DSH
Merlynn is a very affectionate cat who loves to perform many magical tricks!!!
See story in chapter 7: Wild & Wacky.

LUBBOCK   79414
Trixie Austin, 5005 36ᵗʰ St
Missy
F, 13, Gray, tan/white tabby
Domestic shorthair
Quiet, loving, good natured, intelligent
She has a heart shaped nose, seen mainly in the big cats. She is extra large - bigger than some toms and gigantic for a female. She is spayed and weighs about 22 pounds.

Most of the time she eats or drinks by dipping her paw into her food or water and licking her paw. I have never seen any other cat do this and have captured this on video tape.

OLNEY   76374
Kyletta Miller, 200 Ave O Apt #1
Pussom [aka **Puss**]
F, 11, Calico
Domestic longhair
Loving, calm, sweet
I am Pussom's human. She adopted me. One of many strays that a neighbor was trying to feed, she just walked into my house one day and sat on my heart. She is very easygoing and laid-back. Sometimes she looks at me as if to say, "Chill out, wouldja?" She is very verbal, which delights me. She is spoiled rotten, and deservedly so. Sometimes she sits on my lap and does the "kneading thing." She almost goes into a trance; she gets so relaxed. She is spayed and strictly an indoor cat.
Dixie
F, 7 dec, Blue point
Siamese
Loving, independent, smart
Dixie deserves to be mentioned because she went through so much in her life. She had hypothyroidism and had to be medicated daily. Being Siamese, she was a "one-human" cat, and I was her human. She died two years ago, and left such an empty space in my heart. Credit goes to the wonderful veterinarian who diagnosed Dixie and helped her live as long as she did. It's such a shame that cats' life span is so short compared to ours, isn't it?

PEARSALL   78061
Ursula K Martinez, PO Box 1148
Boots
M, 4 or 5, Yellow/white
Domestic shorthair-tabby
Affectionate, sensitive, sweet
Because he is a survivor, Boots was found as a stray (with large whiskers) near a restaurant. Boots became the second cat our family owned. He had an injury to his back and a respiratory ailment, which caused the fevers with laryngitis that he suffered with for several days.
Our veterinarian offered two options: euthanize or more thorough testing. Boots tried different prescriptions - nothing seemed to help - only for a brief time, except for the small blue dephatabs. Boots' health improved, he started eating, playing and loves kneading his paws. Plus his meow is as load as a lion's roar.

Whitey
M, 2yr & 3mo, White/black spots
Manx / domestic shorthair
Mysterious, playful, jealous
Because Whitey was photogenic ever since he was born, it seemed there was a natural instinct for posing - with a tail, nubbed on the tip. He likes to stretch flat on his stomach like a ruler; especially on our blankets. Two of his favorite tricks are: (1) hide & seek; he hides in our kitchen or bathroom, quietly waiting for me - jumping out to scare me and (2) ghost cats; likes to chase my feet while I'm walking, using his left paw, trying to take a nip at my ankles - that's why!
In memory of my "Buttons", July 4, 1992.

ROANOKE   76262-9136
Kathleen Chaplin, 1875 J T Ottinger Rd
Hiker
M, dec, Brown tabby
DMH
Dynamic!!

Talented singer when his mouth is not full

Someone left him for "buzzard bait". Found him in late July on a dry Texas road.
He played hockey; volleying an ice cube down the kitchen & pop it into his water bowl! He played follow-the-leader, and preferred to lead. He would wait patiently for you to catch-up and off he'd go again. If being ignored, he would jump behind you and nip at your buns! No nibbling at feet, just bun-nipping. He would also jump up and hang from your arms if you stood with your hands on your hips.
He opened cabinets, opened doors, stole dish sponges, candy wrappers, paper towels, anything that you would chase him for.

His favorite trick was to jump up and down under my mother's (she is 75) nightgown! He could also sing. His little voice would, honest to God, move up and down in scale. From the day I found him, until the day he died, he always greeted me (and mom) by shoving his nose up mine!

ROSHARON   77583
Susan F Bailey, 18510 Pecan Bayou Dr
Mickey Mouse
M, 2.5, White with flame points
Mixed - shorthair
Flirtatious, gregarious, loving, communicative
While each cat is special, every once in a while one so extra special comes along that its very soul shines right through its eyes and leaps out to connect with you, becoming your alter ego. As the only surviving offspring of a stray, pregnant mama cat I took in, Mickey Mouse is such a cat.

Mickey loves to tease

My husband and I learned early on that his favorite daytime activity (other than eating) is retrieving a wadded-up paper ball. Whenever we are eating, Mickey Mouse will come and lightly poke my backside through the chair to indicate his specific need. And he is specific! If he wants food, he goes to his bowl to show me it's empty. If he wants to play, he "takes" me to his ball. But his funniest "game" gets played every night at our bedtime. He will tease and entice me to catch him for bed, then "laugh" at my inability to do so. But later on, he will come creeping stealthily into bed, lick my arm, and snuggle up under it to sleep with me. He has never failed to do this and I could never sleep if he did!

Leo
M, 18 dec, Taupe with dark points
Siamese
Old, cranky, demanding, cantankerous, lovable
When my vet clinic telephoned me one day 6 years ago to ask if I would adopt an old, stray Siamese cat they had taken in, I felt I could not, since I already shared a multi-cat household. When they indicated the cat would be euthanised if a home could not be found, I went to see him anyway.
The cat and I had an instant rapport, and I felt a very strong attraction to him. I told the clinic that if I could not find him a home, I would take him. I found him a home with friends of ours, and although I very much regretted not taking him, I knew he would be well cared for. He was, and he lived with our friends for about 3 years. They named him Smokie.
As fate would have it, a job transfer necessitated an out-of-state move for our friends at the same time that my husband and I were building a new home. Before our friends moved, Smokie disappeared. Several weeks later, a stray, skinny, starving, Siamese cat moved into the attic area of our home under construction. We named him Leo, and it wasn't until a month or so later that we learned our Leo was in fact our friends' Smokie! Three more years have since passed, and we still have Leo!

SAN ANTONIO
Whiskers
M, 5, Grey
Russian Blue
Unique
Whiskers has never been an ordinary cat. He has a passion for food and a really bad sweet tooth. If we leave donuts, brownies, or anything sweet on the table, he will tear the container open and eat one. On several occasions he has opened the pantry door, climbed on the shelf and helped himself to cat food.
But his real weakness is ice cream. Because of his obsession with ice cream we have to tie our refrigerator door shut. If not he will open the freezer and refrigerator and pull food out in order to get at the ice cream.

Chapter Seventeen

Who's Who in the Mountain States

COLORADO

BOULDER   80304

Lady Cat Powers, 3816 Wonderland Hill Ave

Izabaeaux of Ladyhawke

F, 5, Chocolate point

Siamese

Intelligent, affectionate, "needy" for love!

See story in chapter 7: Wild & Wacky.

Captain Navarre of Ladyhawke

M, 5, Black

Havana Brown

"Demands" love & attention!

See story in chapter 6: Feline Fetishes.

DENVER   80221

Julia G Brown, 8678 Mariposa St

Callie

F, 9, All black

3/4 Siamese

Mischievous, very intelligent, playful, loving, loyal friend.

Callie is the smartest cat I have ever known. Some of her every day activities include flushing the toilets and trying to catch the water as it goes down, opening every door in the house, stealing and stashing anything she can carry, scooping water out of her bowl with her paw to drink then washing her face the same way, balancing on the banister, imitating a bird's chirping when she sees one, answering the phone when it rings. She's double jointed and can pick up things with one paw and pinch you when she kneads your leg. She never gets bored with anything but keeps trying until she figures out how to do things.

Rocky

M, 19, Black, gray, orange Tabby

Very loveable, and very mellow

15 years ago we moved from a house we had lived in for 11 years. Rocky had lived there his whole life. When we moved 12 miles away from the old house he got out of the new house and went back to the old house. He crossed heavy traffic to get to the old house. He was gone 9 days. When he returned to the new house which he had only lived in for about a week, the only thing that was wrong with him was he had lost the tip off of one of his fangs. He has never strayed far from home since.

DENVER   80210

Kris Field, 3131 E Evans Ave

Alexander Bojangles

M, 7, Brown mackerel w/white Tabby DSH

Warm, loving, gentle and kind to other cats

Alexander Bojangles was dumped at a feed store after someone tried to drown him. He was a tiny ball of fur that purred when anyone so much as looked at him. At four months old, he went to a cat show and was "Best Cat in Show" because he was so sweet and purred continuously. He still goes to cat shows, but he never gets bathed because he is terrified, still, of water.

Several years ago he started an endearing habit: he bathes me every morning before I'm allowed out of bed. He sleeps with his head on the pillow next to mine, and when

I start to wake up, he takes his paw and holds my face still while he licks my cheeks, eyes, nose and mouth. ONLY then can I get dressed!

Clancy McTabby
M, 4, Red mackerel w/white
Tabby DSH
Loves other cats, very affectionate w/people
I found Clancy in the lost & found department of a local humane shelter in May 1990. It was love at first sight for both of us, so I put a "hold" on him and came back 2 weeks later.

He was a strict vegetarian and would eat no meat. He loves lettuce, and didn't take him long to figure out that lettuce scraps for my rabbit are kept on the bottom shelf of the refrigerator. Imagine my shock when a friend and I were chatting, when I opened the fridge, he jumped in and sorted through the lettuce for a piece he liked.

He's now expanded his diet to include fish and chicken, but he still loves lettuce and seldom misses a chance to "select his own" by leaping into the refrigerator when I least expect it!

FORT COLLINS 80524
Kim Walker, 820 East Laurel
Stri
F, 7, Tabby
Norwegian forest
Friendly, quiet, dainty
Stri has an intellect far greater than that of the average cat. She seems to "understand" what is being said to her. If told to "go get a mouse", she will go to the shed, catch a mouse, bring it back to you and drop it at your feet with pride!

Having a thick coat, Stri has had problems with hair mats which require intervention. After making an appointment for grooming, I was talking about it while she was asleep nearby. She immediately sat up and stared at me with terrified eyes. She had her coat looking so good the day of the scheduled grooming that I had to cancel the appointment!

Stri was trained at a young age to "wave". She actually lifts her front paw and moves it up and down in a waving motion. She spontaneously waves at friends she is most familiar with. During the summer she "pulls weeds" with us in the garden. Stri

does many inventive things and constantly delights us. She is a major aspect of our family life.

Tevin
M, 2, Seal-point
Siamese mix
Timid, loving, spoiled
Tevin was adopted from the Humane Society after the death of our cat Smitty. Tevin is harness trained and is very cooperative when putting on his harness to go outside. He will lift his legs in succession to allow the harness to be worn. If I don't get it on right the first time, however, he will "huff" in a very disgusted tone.

Tevin is very spoiled and babied and has been taught to give kisses. He will wait patiently in the bathroom while we get ready in the mornings just to be with us. Tevin is very fearful of people he does not know, especially the mailman. He will throw open the door and run inside at the sight of the mail truck! Tevin is a handsome cat with a sleek mink coat and big baby blue eyes. He has truly stolen our hearts.

LONGMONT 80501
Deb Baumgartner, 1731 Foster Drive
Muffin
M, 2.5, Black & gold tabby
Domestic shorthair
Introverted yet mischievous

The Crab Apple Cat

Muffin is our "Crab Apple Cat". His favorite game is to chase and retrieve -- you guessed it -- crab apple. We discovered Muffin's love for crab apple while playing outside one day. Trying to think of ways to amuse our cats, we tossed several crab apples their way. Muffin proceeded to chase and pounce on them, while the other cats ignored them. Crab apples have become Muffin's favorite indoor sport. We throw a crab apple across the floor and Muffin zips after it, carefully picks it up in his mouth and brings it back, dropping it in front of us. (He rarely shows any interest in the balls we toss his way.) We even went so far as to collect some crab apple this fall, storing them in the fridge so Muffin can enjoy his favorite game into the winter months.

WESTMINSTER   80030
Max & Betty Sullivan, 9937 Grove Way #C
Tipsy
M, 6.5, Seal bi-color
Ragdoll (not purebred)
Playful, lovable, loyal, best friend
We acquired Tipsy in 1985 from an ad for free kittens. I leash trained him and within 6 months, I did not have to use a leash. He responds to my commands to come, sit, stay. If he starts to wander, I say "no" and he immediately returns to my side. We play tag and hide and seek. When snack time comes, I line up 4 or 5 different snacks. He sniffs them all and then points to the one he wants first, second, etc. He tells me when he wants a drink by jumping on his stool in the kitchen and pointing to the faucet.

```
+------------------------+
|                        |
|        IDAHO           |
|                        |
+------------------------+
```

NEW PLYMOUTH   83655
Penny Goss, 410 Ada Road
Squeaker
F, 17 dec, Gray tabby
American shorthair
Very articulate, loving, opinionated, adorable
Squeaker was a birthday gift to me seventeen years ago.   She arrived in my husband's lunch box. She was part of a large litter raised by a good friend.

As the years past, Squeaker stole the hearts of every family member - but she was always first and foremost - my cat. She could read my moods better than any human could and her deep sense of my needs always overwhelmed me. She loved to participate in all discussions, placing herself in the middle of a situation and becoming very vocal.

If I was withdrawing to a quiet place to shed tears for any reason, she was always close behind and would jump up on my lap and do her best to dry those tears with her soft-sandpaper tongue. She always knew what I was thinking and often kept me in line. Her death last summer was rather sudden and I don't know if my heart will ever heal.

Max
M, 5, Orange tabby
American shorthair
Articulate, sweet, a little spoiled
Max was an only kitten. He has grown into a muscular orange tabby. He provides many hours of companionship and entertainment. His performances include a particular scenario in which upon spotting his tail, he begins a whirling frenzy during which he grasps his tail in his teeth and lets out a wail of displeasure - this may be repeated a number of times.

Most of the time, though, his favorite pastime is curling up on my lap after sharing his "kitty kisses." Max is all personality, wrapped up in a beautiful butterscotch coat with white accessories.

PLUMMER   83851
Patricia Amador, Rt 1 - Box 73C
Silver Gray
M, 3, Solid gray
Russian Blue Persian
Typical cat
Silver Gray is one of 3 gray cats in our family of 7 cats. I named the 3 gray cats Smokey Gray, Silver Gray, and Kitty Gray. As Silver Gray was growing up, we noticed that his two bottom incisor teeth came up from the bottom and stuck out rather than the way a normal cat's teeth come over the top. Because of the way his teeth look, Silver Gray looks like "Beast" on "Beauty and the Beast." His teeth don't seem to create any problems when he eats, except he is a bit more sloppy than other cats. Silver Gray loves mice and will come if I

call "mouse", as we catch mice in traps for our kitties. Silver Gray is a typical cat and loves to be petted. He follows me around the barn yard as I do my chores just as all the other cats do, and he loves goat milk.

Smokey Gray - Silver Gray - Kitty Gray
Three spooky-looking cats

Garfield Kitty
F, 3, Orange tabby
Tabby
Shy
Garfield Kitty has a Chinese look to her face and my son calls her "Connie Chung." She hates that name and will run and hide any time anyone calls her "Connie Chung." But if anyone calls her Garfield Kitty, she will stay. She is shy, loves goat milk, and is a smaller than average cat.

POCATELLO   83201
Russell O Simmons, 450 W Griffith #36
Sinbad
M, 8 months, Jet black w/ white toes & whiskers & half a mustache; blue eyes
Half Siamese / alley cat mix
Loveable, outgoing, playful, aggressive
Sinbad came to me one summer night. He somehow got in the house. He came running out of my bedroom. It really was quite a surprise. No one claimed him, so he just stayed. He fell in love with my dog Shasta. He plays with Shasta just like another dog. He's very friendly and loves people. He plays with my next door neighbor's dog. Shasta and Sinbad are the best of pals. When they're outside, Sinbad will wait by the shed ready to jump out at her when she comes around the corner of the shed. I just recently got a new puppy, and Sinbad

accepts him as well. I get complimented on Sinbad by my friends and relatives, and how pretty he is, especially his blue eyes.

MONTANA

GREAT FALLS   59401-1920
Gayle Richardson, 2308 7th Ave N B#1
Clown
M, 3.5, Dark brown, brown & white
Half Siamese, shorthair
Shy & aggressive
He was 9 months old when he came to live with me. He wants to smell each and every food you eat. He doesn't want any - just wants to know what you are eating. I talk to Clown nearly all the time, so when I don't talk, he taps me on the leg as if he wants to know why I'm not talking to him.

He races through the house growling loudly. He reaches up through the mail slot when the mail is delivered and sometimes gets it all on his head. He sleeps on the TV but he's too big to sleep there, so he hangs off on both sides. He also sits on the TV to look out the window.

He sits on the couch arm and watches me; sometimes stays there all night as if he had to watch over me. He goes everywhere I go in the apartment. He loves to be brushed and combed and he taps me on the leg to remind me when he's ready to be brushed and he sleeps with me sometimes.

Skizzy
M, 12 dec, Blue grey & white
Half Siamese
Very affectionate, loved everyone
He was special because I had him from the very moment he was born. He never met a single person he didn't like. He expected everyone to hold and pet him when they came to visit. He didn't care if they did not like cats. In fact he seemed to pick out the cat haters to be his first conquest. And because of him, a few cat haters live with cats now.

He always slept on a pillow by my head at night. He would run up and scratch the back of my legs if his food dish was empty.

If that didn't work, then he'd sit in the middle of the floor and stare at me and rock.

I miss this cat very much because he was so loving and affectionate and I had him all of his 12 years.

NEVADA

LAS VEGAS   89115
Kathleen Chandler, 2855 N Walnut Rd 272
Junior
M, 5, Grey-striped
Tabby

Overflowing with love

Junior is my handicapped kitty. He is unable to jump, and waddles when he walks. Instead of being able to run, he puts his hind feet together and hops exactly like a bunny rabbit. Let me not forget . . . he LOVES to eat! This special kitty has given me years of love and devotion.

His being handicapped is due to distemper at 6-1/2 weeks. The other kittens in his litter died. The distemper has left him with what humans call cerebral palsy. On top of that he has had two bad bouts of FUS. He is my miracle survivor, and charmer to all he meets.

LAS VEGAS   89119
Elizabeth Hardouin-Arnold, 1773 E Harmon #2
Elwood
F, 5, Tortoiseshell (black & red ticking)

Very affectionate, very curious & very jealous

Elwood does two things that are interesting. One is that she "cleans" (licks) everything she can. She is constantly cleaning the other cats. She will also clean my skin, hair and sometimes even my clothes.

The main "thing" Elwood does is very unique to her alone. Her FAVORITE thing to do is lay on the floor on her side (it must be a carpeted floor). She wants you to "spank" her on her rump and THEN she pulls herself along the carpet with her front

paws. She will scream at you to continue until she is across the entire floor!

LAS VEGAS   89104
Linda Hoskins, 1404 Atlantic St
Grumpy
F, 3, Black
Shorthair

Very intelligent, affectionate, inquisitive

Grumpy's story is of survival. I rescued her from a parking lot. She was a tiny, starving kitten with one badly mangled eye. The vet had to remove the eye and found a pellet in it. Two weeks later, Grumpy developed a respiratory infection. As my vet examined her, he found another pellet in her upper lip. He was amazed, and so was I, since this hadn't interfered with her eating. Grumpy survived it all and is now a happy indoor cat. She has very strong hunting instincts and keeps our home pest free. She gets along fine with my five other cats and gets into everything.

Bernard
M, 7, Black
Unknown

Independent, Bossy

Bernard is a tattletale. Whenever one of my other five cats is into something they shouldn't be, or is misbehaving, Bernard will find me, tell me about the problem, and lead me to the offender. He's the only male and keeps the girls in line by hitting them on the head. He'll walk up to one of them, hit her on the head, and walk away. The girls usually accept this, but once in awhile one will hit back. It's really funny to watch.

LAS VEGAS   89115-0108
Tracy J Johnson, 4139 Fernleaf Dr
Tigger
M, 2-1/2 dec, Tiger striped tabby
Tabby

A loving, quiet prankster

When I rescued Tigger as a kitten, he was afraid of my other cats and the unknown world - but not me . . . so he followed me everywhere. Soon we were taking showers together, eating together, sleeping curled-up together - he even used the bathroom when I did. We soothed each other when one had a bad day. As active as he was, he never minded traveling by way of my shoulder, since he had to give me hugs that way. He was truly uncommon. I have yet to meet another cat like him.

UTAH

WEST JORDAN   84088
Cariann & Floyd Hiatt, 795 South Linton Drive
Adam Hiatt
M, 8 months, Orange
Tabby

Pushy, stubborn, spoiled and very affectionate

Adam has been experiencing his "terrible 2's". He terrorizes his sister, and cannot keep his nose out of any food, especially if you haven't eaten it yet (including Peanut Butter Crunch, Mexican food, bananas and oranges, Cheetos, spaghetti, and even flake fish food). Adam also helps feed HIS fish every night and watches them from the couch before he takes a nap.

Also he cries. If you tell him "no" - he goes to another room and cries; if he's awake and you're not - he cries; if he's not getting all your attention - he cries. However, I've never seen a more adorable and affectionate cat. He enjoys sleeping on my lap or has to keep his hand on someone he loves, to be sure they are there: me, my husband or his sister, Rooby.

Roobylyn Hiatt
F, 5, White & gray (with big blue eyes)
Persian/Siamese

Snobby, gentle, and sweet as can be

Rooby likes to know she's in charge - which, of course, she is. As long as it suits her, she's always on your side, protects you when she hears noises and she waits patiently to eat breakfast until I do, although she wakes me up every night at 3:00 am to get her a drink from the bathtub. I'm sure she knows she is doing what we want her to do, but I'm sure it's always on her terms. I know that she loves us very much, but we love her even more!

WYOMING

DOUGLAS   82633-2825
Debbie Alberts, 922 Jefferson St
Tommy
M, dec, Orange
Domestic Short Hair

Demanding, small in size but lion-hearted. He loved being loved and treated kindly.

I saw him briefly through the window for about six months. He vanished when the door opened. A year after I first saw him, he let me touch him. Many months later I could stroke him quietly. Arriving home from work one afternoon, Tommy waited on the porch. He could hardly stand. He rose to his feet weakly and greeted me with his meow. I had never attempted to pick him up before. I gingerly carried him inside to assess the problem.

Tommy models his "contraption"

Due to the bruising on his hind legs, I assumed he had been knocked down by a car. His tail was paralyzed and his bladder control compromised. The nursing care I provided to him while he recovered created a bond which will never be equaled. When able, he made the trip to the veterinarian for tail amputation and neutering. Tommy was not happy if he could not be inside periodically. To address the bladder control problem I had to be very creative. I tried numerous products advertised for animals "in season". Trouble was, Tommy had no tail to hold the contraptions on. An infant T-shirt pinned to disposable diapers worked. At first he walked like Chester from the TV series "Gunsmoke", stiff-legged on one side! He never seemed to mind and marched through the house daring my other cats to test him.

Tommy developed fatty liver disease in 1988, but his condition was not diagnosed until after his death. I have read some theories which may link the disease to injury. I am the first person who ever loved Tommy - the only one he trusted in return. He enriched my life with much joy. Tommy has a star listed with the *International Star Registry* in his honor. Oddly enough, his star is in the constellation "Lynx."

Oscar

M, dec, Gray and white

Domestic Short Hair

Outgoing, loved people, vigilant watchcat, long-distance traveller who knew where HIS home was.

The handsome gray cat came and went. He was big and friendly; appearing to be well cared for. He appeared one evening with a gaping throat wound. I presented him to my veterinarian the following day for treatment. We made great efforts to locate an owner. He was considered a stray; asked if I wanted him back, I said yes. I offered to have the cat neutered and vaccinated in exchange for a good home.

He was placed on a ranch some 12 or so miles north of town (after he enjoyed a week of recuperation in my home). His first day at his new home was his last. He was not seen again. Two months and three days later, he was on my porch. I went out, picked him up, hugged him close, and took him inside.

He was my new house cat and his name was Oscar. Oscar was diagnosed with FIV in 1991. I gave him the best care I could each day; on January 16, 1992, the best I could do for Oscar was to say goodbye - it was time. He rests close to Tommy. His long journey was finally over. My home and heart will know Oscar's presence always.

Chapter Eighteen

Who's Who in the Pacific

CALIFORNIA

CALIFORNIA
Elida
Nephthys
M, 18 dec, White w/grey markings
Siamese mix
Distinguished, caring, demanding, sweet

A devoted friend

I'm writing about my dear friend Elida's special cat, Nephthys Nephertum Macy. He was the most intelligent and sophisticated cat I'd ever met. He spent his whole life being Elida's devoted friend. He protected her from danger, and comforted her through hard times. When she least expected it, and needed it the most, he'd pull something cute and spunky - just to make her laugh - while always being dignified about it.

Although he is no longer with Elida physi-cally, his wonderful spirit lives on in her heart, and the hearts of everyone who had the pleasure of making his acquaintance.

ARCATA 95521
Grace Marton, PO Box 848
Casey Jones (Nickname: **Jones**)
M, 14, Brown tabby
Domestic shorthair
The best boy cat in the world!

Jones and I met at an animal shelter in Sanford, Florida in 1979. Only he wasn't Jones then. Shelter workers had named him Little Hitler. It was a terrible name for such an affectionate cat. His purring seemed loud as a train whistle so I promptly renamed him Casey Jones after the legendary railroad engineer.

Jones and I relocated to northern California in 1990. While I'm working harder than ever during this recession, Jones has eased into semi-retirement. He no longer engages in cat work, like climbing drapes or scratching furniture and now spends most of each day sleeping on the bed.

BEAR VALLEY 95223
Ellie Hawkins, Box 5257
Calico Doe
F, 13, Black with white & orange
Calico
Shy and intense

Calico Doe: Rock Climber Extraordinaire
On March 25, 1980 we watched as Spunky gave birth to three wonderful kittens. Little did we know that kitty Doe would become one of the best feline rock climbers in the country. When the kittens were six months old, they began walking cross country with

us over a mile to a rock climbing area, a 25 foot vertical Basalt cliff. Her passion and talent for climbing amazed us. We learned and copied many of her intricate rock climbing moves.

Ricky the rock climber

Ricky
M, 13, White with a little orange
Happy-go-lucky
Ricky: Entertaining Learning Disabled Kids
Ricky, along with his talented sister Doe, enjoys rock climbing. Ricky - more than anything else - loves to give and receive attention. He was kind enough to let us take some slides of him climbing granite boulders. These are featured in a slide presentation for learning disabled adults and school children which has been seen in many different parts of the country.

BELMONT SHORE 90803
Melysa Newberry, 46 Ximeno #4
Romyo
M, 3, Black
DSH
Loving, playful, and yet very strange
My cat Romyo is special because he not only plays with balls, he also fetches them . . . just like a dog. Any kind: cat toy balls, wads of paper, wads of tin foil, anything he can fit in his mouth. I am a vet. tech., and when I get ready for work at 5:00 AM, he always insists on bringing EVERY ball to the bathroom, dropping them at my feet, and meowing over and over again until I throw them for him to fetch.

Romyo is very strange because he is afraid of everyone but me and also every strange noise. When he hears either of these, he runs and hides under the covers on my bed - sometimes for hours and hours!

BEVERLY HILLS 90213
Beverly & Thomas Miligan, PO Box 2484
Zuñi
M, 8 months, Ruddy
Somali
Loyal, fun-loving and curious
Zuñi loves his playmate, a box turtle named Eve. He will sit atop her cage and try to steal her food, a slice of avocado. He'll even squeeze into the cage through a narrow opening to get it. He also follows her around the floor.

Zuñi also loves to play hide and seek. He'll run off and hide somewhere, then call out with a mischievous meow as if saying, "come and find me". When I walk past his hiding place, he jumps out to scare me, then scampers off to hide again. He sits up and is very bright.

CERES 95307
Lynnette Crain, 3105 Rose Ave
Little Girl
F, about 2, Grey & black mix
Tabby - longhair
Very friendly & affectionate
She was a stray that came to our house. I could not locate the owner through a news-paper ad or the SPCA, so I kept her. What's strange is, I had recently lost my 8 year old neutered male tabby (Blue). I was in tears for days; my other tabby (Black) mourned him; he went up and down the fences with a howl that was unbearable.

In September of 1982, Black & Blue, at approx. 4-6 weeks of age, were left in front of our house. Blue disappeared in March of 1991. Little girl showed up in September of 1991, almost to the exact day the twins were dropped off 8 years earlier. She is almost identical to my cat Blue, who disap-peared. Since day one, she has slept at the foot of my bed (exactly where Blue slept), drinks from a running faucet in the bath-room (not just dripping - a flow) like Blue - very smart.

She's a house cat - we take her out. She doesn't leave the yard and if she goes out of the fence, she lays down and she knows she has to go in the house. Black has never accepted her. She constantly messes with him in the house trying to fight him etc. He will not do anything to her at all - he never fights back. Now outside she won't touch him. We have two other males besides these guys - Black will not hesitate to fire them up.

It is hard to believe - even our friends know that she is special. A beautiful stray kitten - smart & friendly, shows up the same month and almost exact day as the one I lost. Almost identical markings, the same breed, only she's a female. She sleeps exactly where Blue did. It's like one of their nine lives. That's why she really is something special.

Midnight

M, 3, Black

Some Siamese (DMS)

Arrogant

Midnight is the first kitten I got after Blue disappeared. I thought I got him for Black, but I guess deep down I knew I did it for me.

Blue, my missing cat, would fetch a ball. The second day after I got Mid, I threw the ball for him. He chased it and I could not believe what I was seeing. He had the little red ball in his mouth and brought it back to me. I cried, because my Blue always fetched that ball and brought it back to me. The memories you never forget. I knew then that this was a special kitten. I also knew somehow Blue made this happen.

Midnight tries to open the door coming in from the garage to the house, so when he's out there, I just close it - just enough so it doesn't latch. When he is ready to come in, he stands on his back legs and hits the door with his front ones and in he comes. He has a special way about him. He is a one owner cat; he does prefer me and he is a bit jealous of the others at times. But all in all I feel that he was meant for our family just as I feel that Little Girl was. This is why he too is so special!

CHICO   95927

Koshka Delgado, PO Box 4119

Harri

M, 2, Seal-point

Siamese

He thinks he's a two-year old child with no thumbs.

Harri and his Medieval Pavilion

Harri is a member of the Society for Creative Anachronism, a non-profit medieval re-creation group. Harri has participated in the SCA (including camping frequently) since the age of nine weeks. Harri is squired to a knight and he served as princess' escort, an honor bestowed upon worthy fighters. Harri has a medieval encampment to rival anyone's - complete with period pavilion, rope-bed and miniature brazier. People treat Harri more like a child than a cat, and he's often invited to parties -- even his human mom and dad's wedding (he wore a tie!) "Harri" is short for "Harakka", meaning "magpie" in Finnish.

CUPERTINO   95014

Grace & Marcus Johnson, 175 Calvert Dr

Flash

M, 1, Orange tabby-tux

Domestic shorthair

Flash is a working "Hug-a-Pet"

Fearless, friendly, and full of life!

I found my little orange and white fur ball from the foster home of a local rescue group. My husband chose the name Flash in honor of his best friend who had recently died and who had liked the comic book character.

Flash is an unusual cat who is quite intelligent. He has learned to do a variety of tricks including sitting, begging and waving. Flash is also a working cat who travels to convalescent homes as a Hug-a-Pet with the local humane society. He has two other feline brothers, a brother rabbit and guinea pig and is friendly with them all!

CUTTEN   95534
Jacalyn King (Ford), PO Box 351
Mo
F, 1.6, Black
"Humboldt County pure bred"

Quite curious & most mischievous

"Mo" is a couch potato. She loves to watch rodeos and music videos. She is also a retriever of small toys. She learned this trick by copying a small dog ("Pocket") I used to have. We call this game "Boomer".

"Mo" is also noted for her "mask" wearing. Any lightweight material she can see and breathe through - I'll make a small slip cover out of it and paint a face on it, slip it over her head and off she goes around the house spooking the other seven cats she lives with.

That's my wild and wacky kitty "Mo".

DULZURA   91917
Kathie Cain, PO Box 384
Bill
M, 4, Orange tabby
Mix shorthair
Unique - assertive - he owns us

I found Bill by a country road late one night. He had been dumped at approximately 6 months. He was so scared but very vocal, wrapping himself around my legs, begging for help. I took him home and introduced him to my husband and my other cat, an elderly female. She wasn't pleased, to put it mildly.

When Bill wants to get up in the morning, he'll knead on your arm. If that doesn't work, he'll put his paw on your mouth. If

that doesn't work, he'll try any number of things such as rattling the glass door on my jewelry box, tipping over trash can, chewing on my paperback books . . . you get the picture!

We give "Pounce" as a treat and he knows what cupboard it's in. When he wants one, he'll get on the kitchen table and scratch at the cupboard, all the while meowing in piteous tones. He's a beautiful 14 pound cat, too smart for his own good, I sometimes think. He loves attention but only when he wants it. (Multi-cat house: nine)

EL CAJON   92021
Tina Ayala, 1480 D Naranca Ave
Homey
M, 3, Orange striped
Maine Coon & ?
Talker & always purrs when you touch him

Homey knocks to enter

Homey knocks on the door and sounds just like a person knocking. When he first started it, I expected a person on the other side. There's been an occasion or two when I'd be talking to someone I thought was Homey, but there was actually a person there. When I have guests, they always expect to see someone too, and they think it's unique.

When he was a kitten, I would comb him when he was snacking on his crunchies. It was the only time he would tolerate being combed. He would even come and get me when he was going for a snack. Whenever I walk into a room where he is, Homey always gives a "Purr", and always greets me when he hears my car. He's real loving and is a lap cat. He is only that way towards me and a few choice people.

ENCINO   91316
Frankie Wolf, 17925 Collins St
Precious Cat (P.C.)
M, 6, Black & white
American shorthair tabby
Shy with strangers, loving with family
P.C. was found inside the Panorama City post office playing amongst the letters. I took him home with me, placed an ad but kept him. I couldn't resist the way he'd greet me at the door. The minute I'd walk in, he'd climb my leg up to my neck with a paw on each side and I could feel him squeeze to give me a hug. He loves newborn kittens and thinks he's their mother by trying to nurse and bathe them. He's a great teacher and the best baby sitter I've had for my kids.
Bear
F, 14, Black
1/2 Siamese & Persian
Loving, demanding, wise old woman
Bear is strong-willed with a mind of her own. She's tiny and agile which is an asset for a thief. By the age of one, she was stealing bread - then she wanted it buttered. Not long after she graduated to french fries and Dorito chips.
A kitten who wasn't supposed to make it from day one, stole my heart, by pretending to be a parrot. Whenever she can steal your attention, she will perch on your shoulders for hours. At bedtime, no matter what position I'm in, she manages to get comfortable sleeping on top of me.

ESCONDIDO   92025
Marie Bloom, 500 N Grape St #301
Taz-manian Devil (AKA Tippy-Toe)
M, 1.5, Gray w/ white markings
Mixed
Short spoiled child
My cat Taz-manian Devil (AKA Tippy-Toe) thinks he's a human. Ever since he was big enough to jump over two feet, he's waited each morning for my husband outside the bathroom door. After Bob gets up, if he's not in the shower within ten minutes, Taz really pouts. That's because Taz jumps up on the top rail of our sliding glass door and plays while Bob (or anyone)

showers. Taz either sits with his front legs hanging or tries to catch the droplets as they run down the door.

ESCONDIDO   92025
Deborah L McCaleb, 500 N Grape St #503
Tiger
M, 3, Shades of grey, tiger striped
Ragdoll mix
Tolerant, especially with our Sheltie puppy.

TAKE THAT ! !

He thinks he's a dog. He loves to play ball - he will bring it back to me. He will only play with one kind of toy - a ball with a bell in it.
He loves a bath. He also plays with our dog - they run all over the place. He loves to get brushed, but after the brushing he starts to get into stuff and push it onto the floor. Once in a while he's not very loveable.
He eats only one kind of cat food. He only will use one kind of litter. He won't drink out of a bowl. He will also knock on the door to go out or in. Tiger is a very big kitty - 35 pounds! I have had 16 cats. They are all my kids.
CoCo
F, 5 dec, Black
One of a kind
She loved to ride on my shoulder or on the backrest of my wheelchair. She also stole anything left around - like rings, make-up - anything she can carry. She is deceased now and I miss her a lot.
She didn't like to be rubbed or petted - she liked to be patted to the point of being beaten. Some kitty. She also wet on our

bed every time we got a new cat. She would only eat one kind of cat food and would drink water out of a glass not a bowl. She also had to take a bath with me. We loved her a lot.

FONTANA   92335

Michelle & Rusty Peery, 8469 Cottonwood Ave

Dwezil

M, 3, Brown, black, tan, white

Shorthair Tabby

Ambitious, outgoing & extremely talkative

When we went dog shopping for a companion for our cat Nikki (he thinks the world revolves around him), we stumbled across Dwezil. We knew he was an uncommon cat. At first sight he meowed at us. Three years later he hasn't stopped yet. We're not sure if he likes to talk to us or if he just likes the sound of his voice. Whenever we ask him questions he responds with a meow. Each question has a different meow accompanied by different expressions. He's also been known to have conversations with us. We love Dwezil our "Uncommon Cat".

GLENDALE

Marilyn Baker

Jackie

F, 1, Black & white

American shorthair

Shy, but very curious and alert

Jackie likes the action shows best

My cat Jackie has an extra keen sense of curiosity. Her big round eyes are always alert, looking for some new, interesting discovery. She will be sitting quietly on the floor, and suddenly dash over to the TV and reach up with her paws against the screen to get a closer look at some moving object. Other times she'll run to the bookcase that holds the aquarium and stretch her front paws up as high as possible to inspect those strange, wiggling creatures in the water.

HUNTINGTON BEACH   92649

Giselle White, 3674 Montego Dr

Lucky Bandit

M, 3, Black & white

Domestic - mixed longhair

Sweet, loving, determined, very smart

See story in chapter 5: Working Cats.

LAGUNA HILLS   92653

Ernie & Alice Jacobi, 658-B Avrnida Sevilla

Dusty

M, 7 dec, Blue grey

Persian

Pleased us. Loved us.

After driving to Indiana, Dusty sat on my lap getting to Illinois. Being tired we took the kitten to bed. His mother taught him well - he used my husband's shoe for a toilet!

When we went on trips he was always with us. Except on one cruise. Well, he was nearly dead when we picked him up. He was seven when we decided things would have to be different. I made a plastic cover for the toilet (cut a hole in the center), put kitty litter in it. It took an afternoon to train him. After that he went everywhere with us.

Onboard ship the cook sent up food for him each night and the deck steward conducted tours each day to see him perform on the toilet! He ate baby food until we reached home, then sat quietly until his food came from the freezer. FUS did him in at the end.

LODI

Karen & Adam Farrow

Sox

M, 8-1/2, Black & grey striped w/ orange

Tabby

Demanding, fun-loving, enthusiastic, a good friend

Sox the Boat Shop Cat

Sox is a cat with an incredible personality. He came to our boat shop eight years ago. He walked in, sat down like he owned the place, and we loved him immediately. Most of his day is spent sitting in the office chair greeting customers, and keeping my husband, Adam, company. He's content sitting in his chair while Adam noisily works on motors.

Every morning when Adam eats his oatmeal, Sox joins him with his own bowl. If breakfast is late, he lets me know by pacing and "yelling" at me. Sox is a wonderful and loyal companion.

Tahvi
F, 7, White, grey & brown w/blue eyes
Persian mix
Sweet, spoiled, loving, demanding

When Tahvi was born we knew she was special. She wakes my husband, Adam, up every morning by sitting close to his face and just staring at him! And it always works! Then she snuggles with him till he gets up.

Every evening she brings him her favorite toy of the day, so he'll play with her. Adam puts his change on our dresser at night, and by morning our little thief will have made off with a dollar - or more. She hides bills all over the house, so if we need money - we just go to Tahvi's secret places!

LOS ANGELES   90025
Carrie Lensner, Hearst Entertainment, 1640 S Sepulveda Blvd, 4th Fl
Pumpkin
F, 7 months, Cream color w/ brown tail, ears and paws
Siamese mix
Friendly, funny, loving & does the craziest things.

Last summer I decided to become a foster parent and adopt my very first cat. From a litter of about eight kittens, all furry fluff balls, I chose a beautiful blue-eyed, beige and brown Siamese mix, approximately seven weeks old. I named her Pumpkin. It is now going on six months and every day with Pumpkin is a joy. I never realized just how funny, amusing and endearing cats can be.

Pumpkin – my best friend

When I have a bad day at the office and I walk through my front door she is there to greet me. When I am feeling sad and depressed she is there to cheer me up and when I want someone to talk to, she is there to just listen. Pumpkin may not have an unusual talent, trait or story nor is she able to leap tall buildings in a single bound but she is special to me. Pumpkin is much more than a feline that shares my home - she is a best friend.

When I look back I used to say I could never imagine my life with a cat - now I say I can never imagine my life without one. I like the way that sounds.

LOS ANGELES   90069-5215
Kari Winters, 700 N West Knoll Dr   #101
Nicky Arnstein
M, 1, Buff
Tabby
A character!
Nicky was adopted when he was 7-½

weeks old. Ever since he came home, he has been a "puppy" cat. He now sits on command, fetches, shakes paws, sits up and says "please", and loves to ride in the car. Recently Nicky and I adopted a new cat, named Nora, and Nicky is teaching her to sit and to fetch. Yes, he's doing this without any help from me!

When he meets new cats, he usually takes about 10 minutes or so to get to know them, and then they become friends. His friends now include Elsie, Ernie, Sinclair, Charlene and of course, Nora.

MARTINEZ   94553
Paul & Kim Gangwisch, 149 Woodview Ct
Strawberry

F, 11, Tiger striped - brown, tan, black
Quite the beggar

Our cat Strawberry is our beggar, but she does it with her own style. She casually perches atop an adjoining chair at the table during meals. At first she sits, apparently disinterested, eyes half closed. She doesn't want to be obvious, giving her human friends the chance to "volunteer" some tasty morsel if they see fit. If the morsel is not forthcoming, she eventually begins to wave her paw in the air, saying "Hey! I'm here!" If she is still ignored, she will tap the nearest person on the arm with her paw insistently until she gets what she wants.

Jenny

F, 8, Black & white
The outspoken enthusiast

Jenny is a black and white terror at one moment and a lovable pal the next. She will cuddle in bed every night, and also tease Strawberry and play a lively game of tag. Other favorite pastimes of hers include chasing moving objects and rolling in some nice fresh catnip. Sometimes it seems that her favorite state, though, is just relaxing and being lazy.

MENIFEE   92584
Linda K Dyer, 29918 Greens Ct
Irma

F, 2, White - black tail
Turkish Angora (except black tail?)
Regal, independent, intelligent, loving!

Irma, a contradiction to most beliefs about cats! Irma was five weeks old when I

brought her home, hungry and dirty. Tenderly and with patience, gave her a bath, which she has become accustomed and likes to play with the bubbles.

I'm ready for my bubble bath

Irma enjoys traveling and is trained on a leash. When necessary to board her, Irma creates such a ruckus on the feline side, so is placed on the canine side, where she is content and enjoys watching the dogs being groomed.

Irma fetches her favorite toy, drops it at my feet, meows "playtime". Irma warms my life!

MENLO PARK
Barbara
Chelsea

F, 0, Solid bluish-gray with bronze-colored eyes
British shorthair
See story in chapter 5: Working Cats

MONTROSE   91020
Angela Visser, 4321 Ocean View Blvd #5
Oz

M, 3 ?, Grey
Maine Coon
Very loveable

When I first went to save this full grown cat on death row, I had no idea of his love. I picked him out of several at the pound because of his size. He was huge. He bit the pound worker and they suggested I choose another cat. I said no!

I took him home and after a very short period of adjustment he began to learn to live. Because when he came home he was thin, very thin for his size. He learned here in my home he could eat, be loved and play. Now he is 17 pounds and very healthy. He is a lap cat - a very large, uncomfortable lap cat. He dominates the house (all 8 cats) and breaks my ribs in the morning, just to be loveable and say, "thanks for saving me."

Magic

M, dec, Black & white

Domestic longhair

Special

I was looking for a lost kitten in the local pound when Magic said, "Take me!" I was so devastated about the kitten I reared, I needed someone to love.

Magic started with me at a new school. He slept on my desk in classes. He comforted me when down. He went everywhere with me and wanted to be with me 24 hours. My new boyfriend fell in love with him. He walked on a leash everywhere. I loved him more than anyone.

He then started coughing. I took him to the vet - he had FIP - and was suffering. That day I had to hold my best friend while the vet put him to sleep. Some day I hope to see him in heaven.

OAKLAND 94601

Debbie Devney, 706 36th Ave

Stumper

F, 5-7, White, peach

Alley

Model cat, affectionate lady

When we first moved here, I saw a 3-legged cat running around the neighborhood. As I am an animal rescuer, I sat a bowl of dry food on the front porch morning and night. Several months later Stumper was pregnant again and slowing down. My children ambushed her at evening bowls and put her in a cage. She got out 2 weeks later. A few days later I caught her with virtually no effort. Since she hadn't been tested yet, she went back to the cage, but seemed glad to be there. She delivered 4 kittens 2 days later, by which time she had decided to be tame - I even handled her newborn kittens! Since then, the Stumper has lived here. She loves scratches, especially on the stumper side, dry food, and the kitchen chairs.

Stinky/Lady Di

F, 5, White, black, orange

Domestic longhair

Very loving

Stinky was found about 5-1/2 yrs. ago on a neighbor's car mewing like someone was killing her. She was sick and dehydrated, had the two-step. We'd been out of work for over a year, so we couldn't take her to the doctor, but fed her and gave her all the water she wanted. I spoon-feed her yogurt. That sick kitten no more than 8 weeks old is now 5, fat, spoiled, and gorgeous. She will comfort you when you're upset - even put her front paws around your neck to hug you.

OJAI 93024-1201

Rena Jones, PO Box 1201

CJ (Claws & Jaws)

M, 11, Striped Tabby

Domestic longhair

Like Garfield . . . fat, lazy & proud of it!

CJ is one tough kitty

CJ is very special. He's been through a lot over 11 years. In 1983, he was hit by a car and had extensive damage, but we managed to fix him back up. He's a tough little kitty and my best friend. CJ is most famous for his job as the editor of *PET PALS!*, a pet related pen pal newsletter. The whole thing is featured in CJ's voice, even though all types of pets are included. CJ takes his job very purrsonally and, guess you could almost call him a purrfectionist! He idolizes Garfield. He's the greatest kitty!

ABBY-gal

F, 2, Striped Tabby

Domestic shorthair
Snooty & Tooty!

Abby is special because she is my other cat's friend. CJ has been with me over 11 years and up until the births of my two children, CJ had been "the baby" in the house. Abby moved in and CJ really welcomed having another kitty around. Abby also works for *PET PALS!* She is featured in a comic strip called "Abby The Gabby Tabby". I rely on her crazy behavior to keep that going strong. She's sure got purrsonality.

ORANGE   92667
Jane Krukowski, 3438 E Collins #10
Scooter

M, 1, Gray w/white on throat
DMH

Molly was vaccinated the day I adopted her from a shelter. No one knew she was pregnant. The panleukopenia vaccine caused one of her kittens to be born with "cerebellar hypoplasia", which is lack of control of the motor skills.

When the kittens began to walk, one of them could not stand up. After seeing two vets, the decision was made to see how this kitten would develop, since he was not in any pain, and was growing normally.

We fell in love with this kitten whom we called Scooter. What he lacks in motor functions, he makes up for in his determination. He pulls himself around, uses his litter-box, plays ball, eats and drinks by himself. He gets in and out of his cat beds, likes to "wave" his paws at you when greeting you, and plays hockey with his ping-pong balls. He loves to cuddle and his purr is louder than my other 7 cats combined. He has the unusual ability to propel himself through the air. In the blink of an eye, he will "fly" across the room . . . faster than a speeding bullet, able to leap up off the ground . . . This has earned him the nickname . . . SCOOTERMAN!!!

Opie

M, 5, Orange tabby
DSH

Opie was given to me when he was almost 1 year old. His unusual activities include: laying completely flat, front legs tucked under, elbows sticking out, rear legs extended straight back - his face flat on the surface. This makes the base of his tail hump out. He runs up the stairs and leaps onto the balcony railing and struts to the end and then turns around perilously, all without front claws to grasp the railing!

Opie pretends he's a rug

He runs to the door when you come home and stands against your leg like a dog, while you roughly pet his head. He makes grunting sounds while you pet him. Although he never got along with my other female cat, since another adoptee had 5 kittens, he has consistently groomed and cuddled them, and generally thinks he's their father.

REDDING   96001
Kelley Slutts, 15330 La Paloma Way
Amel Nitro

F, 9 months, Black & gold
Calico mix

Affectionate, spirited, energetic

When we found Amel she was only 4 weeks old and she was very sick and very hungry. I rushed her to the vet and after a month of nurturing her back to health she became mine forever.

She is not like most cats in that she was raised by a human; there was no cat influence at all. Now Amel loves to retrieve things (i.e. caps, balls, pencils). She likes to play with the bubbles and the water when I take a bath - she even fell in once. Amel loves to ride in the car with me. If it's a nice day, I roll the window down and she sticks her head out like a dog. Most of all she makes me happy when she greets me at the door by clawing up my leg, and when we go for walks on her leash.

REDLANDS
Andrea & Kobbe Titera
Tiny
M, 4, Gray & black
Tiger striped tabby
Rules over other pets & humans alike

Our tiger striped tabby, Tiny, was thrown from a speeding car when only 4 weeks old. He suffered two broken hips and a broken tail. This pathetic little feline had an amazing will to survive. From the moment we brought him home from the vet, he wanted to be with us every second. He was unable to walk, but could drag himself with his front paws over to where we were, purring all the way. The doctor had said to keep him confined and still to allow his bones to heal - but this was an impossible task. We tried to keep him in a box, but he kept escaping . . . so we put a big heavy book over the top of the box, which turned out to be no problem for Tiny. He somehow managed to push the book off and climb out of his box. I don't know where he got his strength.

At four, Tiny is now a strong, healthy 10-pound cat who rides around on my husband's shoulders, sleeps in our bed, and bosses our other cats (plus two large dogs) around. Tiny is definitely Top Cat in our family!

Velvet
M, 3, All black
?
Happy-Go-Lucky

Our Crazy kitty, Velvet, has a built-in alarm clock. At 5:30 on the nose every morning, Velvet wakes my husband and I up. It's not because he's hungry - because we leave food out all night. I guess he feels that the sun is up . . . and we should be too! This wacky kitty has a strange craving for vegetables - especially green ones. We have to be very careful when eating broccoli, zucchini, or spinach because Velvet will come up and steal a bite right from our forks! Velvet makes sure he gets his five servings of vegetables daily.

RIALTO
Mantha
M, 2, Black

American shorthair
Let's "do lunch" occasionally, shall we?
Alias: Monster Mantha.
Background: 2 year old typical black cat. Homeless stray.
Favorite scratching post: The dog's nose.
Favorite activity: Playing in the toilet.
My best trick yet: A somersault.
I like to spend time: Sunbathing at the pool with my parents.
I'm obviously intelligent because: I climb the tree outside to the second story window to look in at my dad's finches.
Naps are great on: Stacks of old newspapers.
On a good day: I'll let someone hold me.
I'm especially loved because: I report when called, and I like to take walks with the dog.

Jewelie
F, 6 months, Gray, black, orange, white, etc.
You name it.
Learning student

Jewelie is my "some assembly required" kitten. God took a number of breeds, mixed them up, then attached orange & white hind legs. We trapped her only two weeks ago when her guardian, our beloved Gretel, also feral, was run over by a car.

Ours is a relationship of teacher/student as we teach her to play, eat and cuddle in the human world. May she outgrow the size of her I.D. tag and this incredible shedding phase! Her name is for "Little Jewel" and her favorite song, "Julie, Julie, Julie" by Bobby Sherman.

SAN DIEGO   92120
Stan & Sharon Chrapkowski, 8030 Deerfield St
Callie
F, 6, Multi-color tortoise shell
Mixed
Playful, loving, sweet, mischievous

We got our petite Callie 5 years ago from Friends of Cats. She was rescued from a coyote's mouth at 2 months old. The coyote had already killed her mother and sister. A passer-by scared the coyote away and saved her. She was sick for a long time. I knew she was meant for us to adopt, when she ran over to me and jumped in my lap and put her paws around my neck and gave me a big hug. She still "hides" her toys in the water dish to keep them "safe", just like she did at Friends of Cats 5 years ago.

Sami & Callie share a moment

Sami
F, 2, Black
Unknown
Shy & loving
Sami's thing in life is to carry around stuffed teddy bears in her mouth, stack them up in a pile with her blanket and give them a bath. Her favorite treats are Ritz crackers.

Sami is 15 lbs., totally black except a small white triangle on her belly and one white whisker.

SAN DIEGO   92101
Anthonette Kosmas, 1831 Fourth Av Suite B
Wyatt
M, 4, Black & white
No known breed
Really affectionate, mischievous
Wyatt has fallen from the second story window twice, been shot in the shoulder by a BB gun, and hit by a car, and suffered nothing more than a fractured hip and a few broken teeth.

The most unusual experience I had with my cat was the first time he fully demonstrated how protective he is of me. My boyfriend and I had gotten into a tickling/wrestling match one day when he suddenly started shouting "Ow! Ouch!" Wyatt must have thought he was hurting me because he was biting Scott's bare feet, attempting to get him to stop!

SAN FRANCISCO   94122

Susan Marshall, 6 Locksley Ave #6H
Giggles Marie
F, 2, Black/white/red/brown
Calico (not pure breed)
Intelligent, reflective, resourceful
Giggles was born on Feb. 20, 1991 in San Francisco. She is one of four. Giggles is my alarm clock. All she needs to hear is the radio and she begins her wake-up routine. She begins by meowing at me. If that doesn't work, she claws on the laundry basket. She will then go to the closet doors, which must be kept closed with a bungee cord, and snaps the ends of this bungee cord against the closet doors. If I still ignore her, she stands on my chest. She will do this no matter what time of day. I have not been late for work in the past 16 months.

Amber Jean
F, 2, Red over white
Attentive, alert, loving
Amber is the sister of Giggles. She is deaf. Amber knows sign language. Her name to her is a high-pitched whistle. If I have a bad day or are not feeling well, she jumps on me and wants to snuggle. She lays her head on my shoulder and begins to purr. She is my lover. She only weighs 6 pounds. I can carry her with me anywhere. She sits on my shoulder. She is my marmalade kitty.

SAN JOSE   95119
Martha Benco, 297 Esteban Way
Verser
F, 4, Pure gray
Domestic shorthair
Independent, affectionate, and alert
Verser is an outdoor cat. She has cat friends everywhere and roams the neighborhood via trees and fences at all hours. Her most memorable moment was when she leapt out of a second story window and landed on her feet. Days later, we took her to the vet when we saw her favoring a hind paw. The vet told us her very life was in danger. Verser had major surgery on her retractable claws, but she is now as playful and happy as ever.

SAN JOSE   95117
Patricia Schulke & Tom Heath, 3615 Gre-

enlee DR. #12
Sheba
F, 9, Black-brown
Tabby
Friendly, outgoing to people only, not cats - male or female.
Sheba GAGS! By opening mouth, sticking tongue all the way out, eyes bulging over food and smells - people or cat. Even Sheba cat food! Sheba fetches and catches Superballs, brings it to you, says "ya" when she wants to play. She puts the ball in her mouth with front paws, sometimes sits up too, then drops it in your hand. Sheba takes baths and sits in Pat's lap for nail cutting. Sheba understands "GO OUT-SIDE" means: carry out garbage or laundry, shake car keys or yell "GO OUT-SIDE". And she is buddies with Oscar our 6 year old Australian carpet python.

SAN JOSE   95129
Rich Williams, 4681 Albany Circle #123
Coony
F, 3.5, Cream, dark brown, black, and white w/ blue eyes
Siamesoid
Bright, talkative, athletic
Coony's absolutely favorite thing, even more than food, is light. No matter what she is doing, if she sees a flash of reflected light, she races over to it and tries to hit it with her paws. On sunny mornings, she sits over against one wall, waiting for some light to come through the partially open blinds and reflect off something. I can drive her up and down the walls and in circles on the floor just by moving something shiny, like my watch, so the reflected light moves in patterns. I always tire of the game before she does.
Notty
F, 3.5, Black with a white belly & gold eyes
Siamesoid
Slow, sweet
Notty loves the sound of my VCR's loading and unloading functions. Whenever I load or unload a cassette, if she can hear it, she turns to the VCR, raises her head and perks up her ears. Then as the cassette thunks completely in or out, she kind of hunkers down and drops her head, with her ears still up. I invite her over to the VCR and

cycle the cassette in and out. When it's out, I tap it, and then she pushes the cassette in all the way. Other than food, the VCR is her favorite thing.

SANTA CRUZ   95062
Patricia M Crawford, 425 34th Ave
Shy
M, 4, White with green eyes
American shorthair
Shy, sly, frisky, and neurotic
When I first got Shy it was September 1989, one month before the 7.1 earthquake. I wanted him because he is white and I have had several white female cats in the past. I was starting a new job and needed someone to love and to love me. Well, instead of getting loved, I got bit, hissed at, and scratched. (He probably sensed the coming quake.)
After much prayer and calling the lady who gave him to me to complain and try to give him back, I remembered the saying "If you love something, set it free. If it does not return, it wasn't yours, but if it returns, love it forever." I looked at Shy and asked God for a sign and he went back to the screen door and looked out and back to me. He was out on his own for 2 weeks and then came to the door wanting in. He has been my cat companion ever since.
He sleeps next to me, hugs my hand to him, waits for me to come home, and comes running when I whistle for him or he hears my voice if I have been gone for a while. He will not take food from other people or let them pet him. If anyone comes to visit, he runs and hides, only coming out if they stay for more than one hour. If we hear any sounds during the night, he will growl and get in front of me when I investigate. I pray for him every morning after we get up, and he knows at the word "Amen" he can get down.

SIERRA MADRE   91024
Lili Anonuevo, 128 Esperanza #A
Ginger
F, 3, Ruddy
Abyssinian
Very affectionate, loving, beautiful
I live with my cats Ginger and Candy. I call them my "attack cats" or "sentries". Whenever they hear footsteps outside my

apartment, they immediately spring from their resting positions and approach the front door. Their stance is like a statue: poised on stiff legs, eyes alert, ears zoning into the sound, low growls coming from their chests.

Ginger – one of the attack cats

Usually those "footsteps" turn out to be a visiting friend, so I disperse my two "guards" with a smile of amusement. However when they start growling in the middle of the night or while I'm taking a quiet bath, it's not so amusing!

Candy

F, 3, Red

Somali

Inquisitive, mellow, relaxed

Candy displays the same behavior as described for Ginger. But Candy does something else: she has a really loud purr - so loud that I decided to record her thunderous purr and use it as my greeting on my answering machine!!

I have since removed that recording and replaced it with a human voice. That phone line doubles as a business line and clients might be a little confused to hear loud purring when dialing a business office!

SIMI VALLEY   93065

Grace Getzen, 1377 Village Ct

Thaddeus

M, 2.5, Brown, black, white

Looks like Norwegian forest cat

Gregarious, mischievous, bratty

Thaddeus has an interest in my bathroom. He likes to sit in the sink while you fill it

with water. He likes to chew on toothbrushes so I gave him one. If you hold the toothbrush next to him, he will lie down, wrap his paws around it, chew on it to get it wet and then brush his face with it.

He's the only cat I've heard of that will use a tool for grooming. He uses the toothbrush as an extension of his paw to groom his face and will even open his mouth so you can brush his teeth.

SO EL MONTE   91733

Stephanie Bezaire, 1810 Parkway Dr

Kitty Kate

F, 2, Silver brown

Tabby

Always ready to hunt

Kitty Kate was born and raised outdoors. She was "adopted" one day when she wandered into an open door, and then my heart. After seeing her eat, I knew she was abandoned. Later, I picked her up to notice she was pregnant. We also discovered her first litter living in our shed. We turned the kittens over to the Humane Society, and I refused to allow my parents to turn my "baby" in. After her second litter was born, I took her for shots and spayed her. We kept "Tigger", an adorable, and very lively, black and white kitten.

Tigger

F, 1, Black and white

Tabby mix

PLAYFUL !

Tigger is the daughter of my Kitty Kate. She is a mouse-loving, yarn-chasing, crazy little kitten. She is very well noted for her extremely fluffy tail, which she is most proud of. You can tell when Tigger's on her way by the deep-throated purr from which she gets her nickname "Mack Truck". We enjoy tossing around her fuzzy play mouse which she goes wild for! She is still very much a momma's baby, and hangs by her side whenever she can. She is the most adorable and loveable kitten you could ever want to meet.

SUNNYVALE

Grace

Chelsea

F, 3.5, Calico

Mixed

Energetic, brilliant, devoted

Chelsea is special for many reasons. She is a pretty cat with an interesting personality. She has regular play dates at monthly intervals with her canine pal Mac and they stay together indoors all day while their owners are at work. They romp in the garden together and Chelsea always picks up her ears when I ask her where Mac is. She is happy to share our bed whenever Mac has a sleep over. She comes running for a treat when I ring a dinner bell. Most unusual, however, is that she lets me brush her teeth with her kitty toothpaste and my electric toothbrush! I do this every few weeks.

TOLUCA LAKE   91602
Stephanie L. Sterba, 4310 Vineland Ave #202
Princess
F, 18, Black, brown, red, green, white
Maine Coon
Laid back, with abash of high-strung nerves.
Princess will lie on the floor at my feet whenever I'm sick or upset. She has done two things that seem to me to be silly. The first is that she will race down the loft of stairs and into the bedroom at breakneck speed as if she is being chased by an imaginary playmate.

The second is - I have a bird feeder on a stake in a potted plant on the terrace. When Princess goes out in the darkness she thinks the clay bird on top of the feeder is a live bird and will stand on the base of the plant very still as if she is going to pounce on it. I've lifted her up to show that it isn't a live bird, she just hasn't quite grasped the concept yet.

I am not Princess' first human companion; someone else named her, but by her behavior, she has shown me that a royal name is very appropriate.

VACAVILLE   95687-5862
Tim & Kim Allen, 591 Peabody Rd #201
Alexander
M, 3, Orange
Not known
Extremely loving and sweet
Alexander craves attention. If I am reading and he wants attention, he will sit next to me and put his paw on my arm to first get my attention. Then he will guide my arm over to him and he will duck his head down under my hand for a pet or scratch. Also, if one of us is holding him, he has to put his paw on the other person. He is definitely a person cat. He also seems to sense when one of us needs some extra attention. He will always cuddle up with us to make us feel better.

VENICE   90291
Joelle Steele, 30 Dudley Av #15
Twinkle
F, 16 dec, Grey/white tabby
Domestic shorthair - mutt
Affectionate but temperamental
Twinkle was orphaned at two weeks of age. While I was seriously ill some years ago, I became suicidal, but Twinkle was also ill at the same time and I was worried that leaving her might result in her death too. But, I was desperate.

One night I tried to take an overdose of my medication and Twinkle was trying very hard to get my attention. She cried when I wouldn't pet her and stood up on my chest and tried to nuzzle my neck while her motor was roaring loudly. I realized that I couldn't do it. I couldn't leave this beautiful, loving friend. I owe Twinkle my life. She was all that kept me from ending my existence.

Muffin
F, 8, Grey/white tabby
Domestic shorthair - mutt
Shy, nervous, affectionate
Muffin is very sensitive to changes in her immediate environment - not limited to growling at strangers who pass by our front door and pacing and crying just prior to earthquakes.

She is an excellent judge of character. She can tell if someone is a good person right from the moment she meets them. She hides from people that I don't like too.

She has accurately predicted every major earthquake in California, including the Sierra Madre and San Francisco bay area quakes, since I got her in 1985.

WELDON   93283
Don & Pennay Johnson, 15455 Cottontail Ln
SirVester

M, 6, Black/white markings

Purebred alley cat

Timid with people - aggressive with our 4 other cats

While holding Vester I ask him to sing. He starts with a very high meow that goes down the scale. After he sings a few measures I ask him to yodel. He then yodels down the scale. He usually sings and yodels looking upside-down. I then ask him for a great big hiss. He throws his head back and gives me a hugh hiss. I then let him down and he promptly goes to his "sister" and slaps her or if she's not in, he goes to the door, stands on his hind legs and "opens" the door.

Miss Mugs McMuffin (Puff Puff)

F, 9, Chocolate brown & fawn

Ragdoll

Friendly, affectionate, jealous when her person loves another cat

Puff is quite a talker. Not like a Siamese, but she answers me every time I talk to her. When the phone rings, Puff runs to it and "chirps" (meows) while purring loudly and rubbing around the table legs. She continues this until the phone is answered. Her brother SirVester taught her to stand on her hind legs and "open" the door. The two of them wait, hide and then ambush each other. They chase each other up and down trees and around the yard or house.

Miss Mugs McMuffin is quite a talker

WEST COVINA   91790

Donna Kentnor, 800 South Sunset, #177

Daisy

F, 11.5, Tortoiseshell

Imp! Frisky! Noses into everything.

Daisy from an animal shelter is as much of a kitten at 11-1/2 years as she was at 1 year! I have never taught her the tricks she knows - fetching balls, "scooping" her food (like a raccoon). She opens kitchen cabinets to retrieve her food - rolls can onto floor, pries off plastic lid. All this because I was late coming home!

She knows when I'm sad. Climbs on me, looks me in the eyes, and puts her paw on my face. She is 'uncommon', but more importantly, she brings me life!

Twinkle

M, 12, Black/white

Serious thinker

A proud and serious cat who never loses his dignity. He resembles the Egyptian cats of old.

Smart to the point where I cannot put anything past him. All I have to do is say the word "vet", and I'm left standing alone! He seems to read my thoughts.

Great courage to face life's bumps in the road, never losing his patience. He is my inspiration

WESTMINSTER   92683

Shelley McLaughlin, 13811 Locust St

Kinison

M, 9 months, Black/white

Alley (for sure)

Most loving, great quest for life!

Kinison was named after the late Sam Kinison because when my boyfriend and I rescued him and his brother (they were 4 days old) all he did was SCREAM. Kinison was barely alive and most definitely used one of his 9 lives.

He is unique in features because his face and legs are all white but his nose is in the shape of a heart and is all black. And his pads are all black which is highly uncommon. He is black on his back but has a black skunk-type stripe down the middle of his back.

Kinision has used up the 2nd of his 9 lives, for he was diagnosed with feline leukemia. Some days he doesn't feel too hot but still manages to walk up to caring souls, look up with the sweety-pie face and plops right over so they will scratch his belly. Someday Kininson will be with his namesake, but for now I'm happy to share his quest for life!

Rocket

M, 9 months, Black & white

Alley

Totally uncommon

Rocket, like Kinison, was rescued by myself and my boyfriend. Rocket knew nothing but humans. Human sound and touch or at least touch.

We have neighbors who leave bread out for the pigeons and they tend to come near our back screen door. Rocket enjoys sitting at the screen watching these pigeons. This was fun to watch but then one day Rocket made a strange noise. You got it - pigeon noises. Rocket mimics the pigeons all the time. You call his name and he calls back in pigeon talk.

He got his name because when he was a baby, we had to bottle feed him and Kinison. Whenever Rocket would see the bottle he would shoot up and scurry fast around his box like a rocket. Maybe I should have named him Pigee or Birdy.

WOODLAND HILLS   91364

Douglas W Topham, 5151 Penfield Av

Panther

F, 7, All black

American shorthair

Playful, highly intelligent

See story in chapter 9: Catmunications.

Tiger

M, Dec, Black & grey

American shorthair / Manx

Playful, devoted

[Included in story in chapter 9: Catmunications.]

HAWAII

HONOKAA   96727

Purrcynth, PO Box 1464

Giggles

F, 6, Silver black tabby w/ blue eyes and white tummy

½ Pedigree Himalayan & ½ tabby

She's my fuzzy human baby.

Giggles is six years old from a pure Himalayan pedigree Mom who was in the mood

The amazing Giggles ready for the surf

for a street-wise tabby. This mix of breeding has created a unique, highly aware cat whose range of perception borders the edge of the human realm. She does a lot of things so I couldn't name just one . . . Here's a partial list:

1) She is the only CAT on the block with her own gray Arabian horse named Asian, whom she rides occasionally . . . walking is a breeze and she has mastered the art of Cat Posting at the trot.

2) She talks on the phone.

3) She cries like a human baby.

4) She says, "I love you" and "I want down."

5) She has a full wardrobe including bunny slippers & rain boots.

6) Her favorite pastime is sitting in her stroller and will watch TV till she falls asleep.

7) She turns the pages of my book while I'm reading with her tail.

8) Being a Hawaiian cat, she does like the beach and has her own Boogy Board - swims well.

9) She poses for pictures being the star that she is and wants her own fan club.

10) She has a big blue bathtub and enjoys having her hair blow-dried too.

11) She says Garfield is her hero.

12) She was Santa's helper this past X-mas, delivering gifts to stores nearby.

13) We are working on her new video titled "A Day In The Life Of Giggles!"

14) She barks like a dog and growls like a tiger.

15) P.S. She does giggle too!!!!

OREGON

BEAVERTON   97005
Winter Drews, 4955 SW Normandy Pl
Zonker Harris
M, 3, Black, white, and tan
Unknown
Loving, wild, funny, and nice

Zonker is my cat, and he lets no one forget it. He grabbed hold of me at the pound three years ago, and hasn't let go since. This cat is big, and I mean B-I-G! He's an excellent hunter and has steadily reduced the mouse and shrew population of a nearby meadow. He often "helps" me with my homework by flopping down on my book.

If I shut him out of a room for more than five minutes, he tries to get in, even to the extent of trying to pull himself under the door! Eventually, if I don't let him in, he starts frantically throwing himself against the door. Doors are always left open in our house!

BEAVERTON   97005
Valerie Fouladian, 12390 SW Center #57
Gonzo
M, 9 dec, Black & white
Longhair domestic
Sweet, clever, funny and easy going

This is *r e a l l y* tempting!

Gonzo was black and white with the shape of South America on his face. He had a funny way of tilting his head to the right whenever he wanted something. Any time

I would say - "Are you hungry?" or "Do you want to eat?", he would spring to his feet, meow and zoom to the kitchen.

He learned to shake hands like a dog. I'd hold out my hand and say, "Gonzo, can you shake?" Almost immediately, he'd put his paw across my hand. Once we took him fishing with us, and he had a wonderful time inspecting the fish.

BEND   97701
Lillian H Mason, 64945 Glacier View Dr
Quigley
M, 19, Beige w/ tabby points
Siamese cross / domestic tabby
Me Tarzan, you Jane!

Quigley is almost nineteen years old, weighed 16 pounds in his prime, and is a Siamese cross with tabby points and blue eyes. He has big jowls like a tiger, and his attitude is "Me, Tarzan - You, Jane!" He has always been loved by everyone, even those who swear they don't like cats.

At an early age he showed a desire to chase and retrieve paper wads, laying them carefully in front of the thrower. The game quickly evolved into something more complex, due to Quig's insistence that each throw be different from the one before; then it had to be harder for me to place the throw and him to retrieve it. If I failed in any part of this Quigley just refused to retrieve. Somewhere along the line I realized this was definitely Quig's game, and I his willing pawn. Sadly the game was ruined when we left for three weeks, leaving our animals in the care of family members; she would just throw out more paper wads if Quig was slow in retrieving. Later we found over a hundred paper wads under our refrigerator!

However, Quigley wasn't through. He took up new habits, decorating and petty larceny! One Christmas he pulled 20-foot vines through the kitty door and stretched them from room to room. Soon he amazed us by retrieving Kleenexes, one at a time, then a whole box, then a little white bag with dentures inside! We learned eventually they had all come out of the back seat of a car parked nearby with a window partly down.

Quigley's most recent phase started when we moved onto 2-½ acres here in Oregon. He wiped out all the "varmints" on our property, which was a massive task which took about three years to accomplish. For the last 3 or 4 years he has rested on his laurels as the "mighty great hunter of the North."

Jezebel

F, 18-½, Smoke/off-white

Siamese cross

Billie Burke reincarnated (Funny Blonde)

See story in chapter 9: Catmunications.

LA GRANDE 97850

Glennys Grapengeter, 803 14th St

Bugger

M, 9, White

½ Manx - ½ Persian

Easy going, laid-back attitude

Bugger has been a constant calming ingredient in an otherwise hectic, stormy environment. He made the thousand mile move from Missouri to Oregon with me - draped across the top of the back seat in our station wagon. He plays the part of "Big Brother" to the other felines in our household.

Bugger is the Big Brother

Beefer

M, 6, Black & white

Manx

Standoffish, loner

Beefer was a very solitary, standoffish six-week old kitten when he joined our family six years ago. He has become a more sociable feline who is very vocal and now initiates the interaction with the human members of the family. He now stands at the back door and yowls to let you know he wants outside.

SALEM 97301-5769

Arlene & Norman Walters, 4921 Trails End Ct SE

Ricochet

M, 3, Blue-point

Siamese

Extremely friendly and loving

Ricochet loves hide & seek

Is he uncommon? He plays hide and seek with my son, running from one end of the house to the other. He jumps up and bumps me for attention. He sits on my jewelry box and waits patiently for me in the morning. He loves my lap but if he wants the chair he digs behind me until I get up.

He greets all visitors and is the center of all activity in the family. "Richochet, George is here," and he RUNS to the glass doors. Yes, he knows the neighbor cat by name. He is truly special.

SCAPPOOSE 97056

Tom & Allene Severtsen, 32905 James St

Keetah

F, 12, Seal point & white

Because of her mittened feet / Birman

Demanding - talkative - a people person

1981 - Adopted at two years of age from pet store.

1979-81 - Former homes, elderly couple, girl with five Siamese.

1981 - Twenty-five days after adoption, litter of five.

1984 - Lost collar in Montana, returned from Minneapolis - answered letter - received invitation for all to visit.

1987 - Moved to full time RVing - tore out screens - now out of wire - almost hung myself tumbling out of window.

1988 - Met grizzly in Yellowstone (15" paw print) during big fire.

1989-91 - Enjoyed riding on golf cart at Death Valley.

1991 - Escaped from coyote in Death Valley by breaking leash.

1992 - Oh, yes, I drink my water out of a cup.

1993 - Looking forward to more adventures.

There must be something I can get into!
Keetah - 1984

SPRINGFIELD   97477
Sharon Boggs, 2536 Debra Dr
Teddy Blue II
M, ?, Brown McTabby
Devon Rex
Very, very lovable

Goodwill Ambassador

Ted is the goodwill ambassador in our home. We have two separate households of cats. Ted is the only cat who moves at will between the two. It's his choice to stay with the big cats - strays we took in, who have a spraying problem. Or he stays with his harem of five spayed females. He gets along well with all eight cats. Ted also accompanies us on any overnight trips we take to the Oregon coast or to Washington state to visit family.

I love all my cats but Ted's the most precious.

WASHINGTON

ARLINGTON   98223
Janie Acton, 13628 152nd St NE
Mr. Stretch
M, 6-1/2, Black/brown tabby
American shorthair
Demanding, social, and stretches legs frequently

Mr. Stretch is perfectly marked (looks like an ocelot) and weighs 16 pounds. He enjoys being brushed and occasionally bathes with me and seems to enjoy the warm water running over his back. He jumps into the wash basin and calls for me to turn in the water for his drinks. He seems to enjoy rides in the car and feels at home both at my parents' house and here on the farm. He refuses to get out of the car if I make any stops in between. He stands on my lap with hind feet and front paws on the window to watch the scenery.

Every morning in bed he paws at my shoulder for me to lift the covers. He often sleeps on his back, head on pillow, and snores. When I say "Hungry?" and "Canned cat food?", he rushes to his bowl. He climbs a ladder onto the roof but is fearful of coming down the same way. So when I stretch out my arms, he jumps into my arms. He always demands my undivided attention. When I'm grooming my horse or talking on the phone, he definitely exhibits some jealous behavior. One morning I was even awakened by his standing over me licking my lips which I really didn't appreciate. We really do have a very close pet/human relationship.

EVERSON   98247-9461
Lynne Marschke, 3869 Cabrant Rd
Mitzie
F, 1, Grey blend
Mixed but looks like small Maine Coon
Loving, very vocal, a tease, sometimes bitchy and independent.
Mitzie was doomed to ill fate on DuPont Street, if she continued to cross it. I carry mail, and as a kitten, she jumped out (talking of her woes) from under a bush. I'd pick her up, satchel on right shoulder, kitten on left, up the walkway and steps - drop the mail - back down to the sidewalk. When I put her down, she was seemingly sad to watch me go.

Her hunger and lack of affection was evident, so a week or two later, I was determined to save her and discovered very quickly what a delight and joy she was. At home, she showed her pleasure in a loving environment. Mitzie is a treasure and keeping her has been a most rewarding experience.

GIG HARBOR   98332
Deborah Reimann, 9615 Moller Dr NW
Sir Lancelot
M, 11, Black w/gold eyes
Bombay
Very shy, but affectionate with me.
Now, about my Lancelot: He is a very spoiled Bombay cat who runs my house. He was accepted into *Who's Who In American Pets For 1992,* appeared in articles written in the *Philadelphia Inquirer, The Kitty Letter, Pet Pals Newsletter, Tabby Talk, The Everett Herald, The Wall Street Journal,* and a few other kitty newsletters. There is a possibility that Lancelot may get on a national TV talk show because of being in *Who's Who In American Pets,* but we aren't sure about that just yet.

When I joined ACFA, I wrote and told them about Lancelot, inquiring about his picture appearing in their *Parade of Royalty.* It took a few weeks, but I did hear back from ACFA's executive director. She advised that I was the instigator, the person responsible for creating a new section in *Parade of Royalty* for cats who are special.

Needless to say, I am very proud of Lancelot and my life would be so empty without him. Lancelot is very much a part of my

life. His big gold eyes reassuring me that he will always be there. It seems that people come and go in our lives, but the kitty is always there, with no condition on his love, his purring so comforting and those unforgettable big gold eyes that are so much a part of my life. This perfect angel kitty that has always brought nothing into my life but love and joy.

Missey Kitten
M, 15 dec, Blue/white/silver
All American tabby
Loveable - a real baby.

Missey Kitten was really one of the guys

My husband had promised me a kitten for my birthday, Christmas, Valentine's Day and Easter and on Mother's Day I went and got my own female kitten from the vet or so I thought! Three months later I found that I had a male kitten named Missey!! The reason I called him Missey was because I wanted a baby girl (but my husband didn't) and her name would have been Melissa because my name is Deborah which means bee in Hebrew and Melissa means bee in Greek. I wanted that unique connection with my daughter, but I never had her, but Missey Kitten gave me 15 years of happiness.

KELSO   98626
Michele Koethke, 705 S 6th
Bubba
M, 1-1/2, Brown/black/white
Tabby DSH
Playful, loving
To me, Bubba is special just because he is my cat. He is very playful and loving. I have taught him how to fetch and retrieve.

He is very clean.

He doesn't get to go outside very often, but when he does, he stays on a halter and leash, so he doesn't interact much with other animals. He loves to sit on top of the TV and look down at the people on the screen. He puts his paws on them and tries to "catch" them.

KENT   98031
Chris & Tracie Costenbader, 10607 SE 250th Pl #I301

Shaman
M, 9 months, Black & white
Very friendly - almost human qualities.
See story in chapter 2: The Good Samaritans.

MOUNTLAKE TERRACE   98043
Charlotte, Jack & Christine Hatfield, 4404 224th Place SW

Jaspár
F, 10 months, Grey and black
Bengal tabby
Independent, slinky, and loveable

Jaspár was adopted by our family in July 1992 from an animal shelter, along with Henrí. She helped us get over the loss of our 18 year old cat. Jaspár had experienced some kind of trauma before coming to us. She was very scared, ran from us, and hid. Now she trusts us and, though still very independent, likes to be petted and held on her terms.

Jaspár plays hockey with plastic bottle caps from seltzer bottles. They are deep enough that she can carry them in her teeth. She stashes them around the house. To play hockey, she bats them off a wall and under a towel stand that sits one inch off of the floor. She has spent as long as three hours at a time at this activity. If you slide a bottle cap towards her, she catches it in both paws like a "goalie".

Henrí
F, 8 months, Orange with stripes
Unknown
Laid back, cuddly, curious

Henrí was adopted by our family in July 1992 from an animal shelter, along with Jaspár.

Henrí likes to answer the phone. When it rings, she nearly knocks over the receiver. She is very curious - has to get her nose

into everything.

Henrí cries like a baby wanting to be picked up. She sleeps with her mouth open and tongue hanging out. Her favorite toy is a ball of scrap paper. She gets excited at the sound of rustling paper. When it's time to eat, Henrí stands by her bowl and points her right front leg out straight. Henrí will always be "the baby".

SEATTLE   98178
Diane R Goldsmith, 11711 Luther Ave S

Napoleon (Poly)
M, 16 dec, Orange & buff
Short-haired
23 Pounds, but gentle and loving

The most remarkable thing Poly did, which was witnessed by many, was to open our sliding glass door 9 inches by himself, and go in or out if someone wasn't there to open it. An average sliding glass door weighs 50 pounds or more. The amount of strength that he had to have in order to move the door is amazing. He terrified all large cats and dogs including a pit bull. But with little animals he was very gentle and even let wild squirrels eat on the porch while he just sat there.

There will never be another like him; he is missed tremendously.

SPOKANE
Brenda Danner

Cassandra (Cassie)
F, 1.5, Tortoise shell
Extremely friendly & outgoing

Rescued from the pound two days before her death date, she's been the most special of the cats we've adopted.

She fetches gold chains and necklaces that people throw for her and brings them back to their feet. She likes to turn overhead somersaults and carries "super balls" around the house to play with on uncarpeted floors. When sleeping, she likes to always have part of her body touching someone's legs or feet. When we sit in our recliner, she likes to sit on our shoulders. She doesn't like any human food at all except for grated cheddar cheese.

SUMNER   98390
Sonja Hendricks, PO Box 145

Tippy Toes

F, 14, Tortoise Shell Calico
Polydactyl

Cautious, aloof until she gets to know you.

Tippy Toes was an abandoned cat in the care of a rescue home in Puyallup, WA. She was 2 years old and very frightened of people. She has extra toes on her front paws - hence her name.

Tippy Toes – a woman's cat

Toes hid for a long time before venturing out into the house. It took her about four months before she would let me pet her. It was clear that she was a woman's cat. Tippy Toes now begs at the table, tapping her victim on the arm for bites. If she really takes to a person she won't leave them alone! She talks to anyone who will listen and always lets me know when the food dish is empty!

Tippy Toes has come a long way from the scared cage cat we adopted 12 years ago. Goes to show what a lot of love can do!

Pepper

F, 1, Orange, white, gray & black
Heinz 57

Friendly, tenacious & loving

Pepper came into our lives one evening last summer. She was wandering down the block and I called, "Kitty, Kitty." She came running 90 MPH. We noticed her long tail as she came toward us. But her unusual coloring really did it! We fed her and decided to keep her after she spent the night in our tree.

Pepper keeps our other 3 cats busy and helps exercise them by chasing them about! Pepper is our curious bathroom kitty. She sits on the tub while we shower, watches us brush our teeth and really loves watching the toilet flush. She also likes to play in the water as my washer fills! Pepper is a source of entertainment that keeps us laughing.

Chapter Nineteen

Who's Who in the World

ONTARIO, CANADA

ALTON   L0N 1A0
Krystal Jemmett, RR #1
Bunny
M, 2, Orange
Unknown
Aloof and unconcerned

The best place to sleep!

Bunny is the "King of the Hill" in my house - the dogs and the horses stay out of his way. He has been dubbed as "the cat from hell" by my friends as he is very aloof and unpredictable and dislikes strangers invading his territory. His one very peculiar trait is that he sleeps on top of my horse's back. He jumps up on his own and stays there all night, making himself quite comfortable. That's one way to stay warm on the cold, Canadian nights. I still laugh every time I see him curled up on his valiant steed, looking like he owns the world.

COBOURG   K9A 2V7
Bethany Butzer, 717 Murray Crescent
Frisky
F, 5, Grey striped
Mixed
Exactly what her name says!
My cat is special because she hates it when I scream! I must be quiet or talk in a normal tone around her. Once I got my head stuck in between two railings on our back deck. I didn't really think my head was stuck, but when I realized it was, I started to scream, calling my mom. Suddenly Frisky jumped out of nowhere, and began to bite my lips! That was when she was younger. But even now, if I scream, she will bite my lips (if she's up high enough) or push her head really hard against my back, head, knees, or anything she can reach!

May I have a little quiet . . . please?

KITCHENER　　　　　　　　　N2K 1K4
Norma McGrath, 30 Bridge St W - #205
Brodie
M, 5, Brown/black
Brown tabby
Loving, shy, bright
Brodie always wakes me up at 7:05 am on Monday through Friday. He does not like it when I try to sleep in on Saturday mornings. He rests his head on the pillow and gently pats my face with his paw until I get up. Then, after I make a cup of coffee and climb into bed to try again to sleep, Brodie will again lie down beside me, lovingly purr in my face, and continue to pat me with his paw. By this time it is nearly 9:00 so I will sit up for 15-20 minutes and read my book. This seems to satisfy Brodie and he proceeds to his spot on the corner of my bed, has a bath and goes to sleep. Then I quickly crawl back under the covers and snooze. By the way, I did feed Brodie at 7:06 am!

WINDSOR
Louanne Meloche
"Champ"ion
M, 1, Brown/black
Medium hair tabby
Loving, fun & devoted

. . . and now for the paperwork.
Champion

When I adopted my adorable kitten he was 6 weeks old. The lady gave me his adoption papers which read "Found in a dumpster inside a taped shoe box left for dead." He was approximately 2 weeks old and dehydrated. My heart went out to this little guy. Champion will always live like a "champ" and it is now he who runs my home. When I come home from work he's always patiently waiting for me at the window - then runs to greet me at the door. We play hide and seek daily, each taking our turn to hide. He always has to be the center of attention - especially when I'm on the phone. He'll cry for me or get into things he shouldn't be in and wait for me to come and get him.

He's my "never fail" alarm clock every morning! He turns the lights on at night for me if I've forgotten (I can always count on him for that). Many of my family and friends call him "part human". I will always love and do whatever it takes to make my little friend happy . . . I don't ever want him to suffer again.

MANITOBA, CANADA

WINNIPEG　　　　　　　　　R3J 1V9
Shirley B Roy, 319 Ferry Rd
Sidney
M, 4, Natural mink
Tonkinese
Talks a lot

Sidney is an avid fish & bird watcher.

My sister Darlene adopted a cat from the Winnipeg Humane Society. She moved from a house into an apartment and couldn't keep the cat. I, on the other hand, moved from an apartment to a house. Sidney has completely moved in. He also has a dog (cat?) house. His favorite hobbies are watching my fish and watching birds. He was entered in the Manitoba Cat Club as a household pet (as he has no papers) and won 5 first blue ribbons, a red ribbon for fifth place and a trophy for fifth place in the long hair cat division. Sidney also likes to listen to the ham radio, although he doesn't like "Morris" code very much.

WINNIPEG   R3L 1M4
Janet Drummond, 668 Rosedale
Griswall
M, 2, Grey
Long hair Norwegian?
Outgoing
He likes people. He pretends to be a great jumper. He adopted the Drummond family. The cats got along very well with the dog Clover. Since Clover passed away, Beth has adopted a dog from the Winnipeg Humane Society. The dog had six puppies. The cats and the dogs get along fine.

Shadow [owner: Beth Drummond]
M, 4, Black
Shorthair?
High-strung, very outgoing & territorial.
Beth found him as a kitten 6 weeks old. Very adventurous. Had him fixed when he was older. Very independent - likes to have cat fights with friend Griswall.

ISRAEL

REHOVOT   96100
Hanna Dershowitz, 7/A/3 Meltzar St
Ginger
F, 2.5, Orange & white
Tabby
Friendly & loves people
I had always wanted an orange Tabby. I told a teenager in my 4-H that I wanted one and to my surprise, she brought me one! My mon did not want to pay 30 dollars.

My dad said, "well, we can't return her." (My mom does not like to buy cats from pet stores.)

Ginger loves people. When we are in one room, there's Ginger! When we move to a different room, Ginger follows us. Ginger has extra toes. When she walks they go "Click! Click! Click!" (we have wooden floors). That way we always know where she is in the house. She also can open doors. When she opens doors, we think it's a person and in walks Ginger!

Rascal
F, 1.5, Grey, cream, orange and white
Calico
Very friendly
Rascal is the daughter of Ginger. My mom says she is very rare. She is a grey calico with tabby markings on some of her paws. We did not think Ginger would have babies. Rascal was the runt. It was fun watching her grow. It's fun watching Rascal and Ginger - they never fight. Rascal sleeps with me in my bed at night under the covers!

SWITZERLAND

BASEL
Carlee Marrer-Tising, Flughafenstrasse 40
4056

The sock baby

Aida
F, 14, Brown
Burmese

Affectionate, playful, very trusting

We call her our little "sock baby." Aida, my little shadow, began her career as a sock collector when, still a kitten, she sneaked a sock out of a packed suitcase.

She later made off with socks from closets, drawers, and laundry baskets and invented various games with them: fetching them and inviting us to toss them for her - even including our dog in these games. Her most impressive trick is to present visitors with socks that exactly match the colors of their clothes; this happens so often it must be more than mere coincidence! Only Aida knows for sure.

Sarah

F, 2, Seal point

Siamese

Terrific! Self-confident, saucy, very fun cat

Sarah, rather stingy with her purrs - except with our dog - is full of fun and brilliant ideas. (After having long since been weaned, she convinced our dog to produce milk just so she could nurse again.)

Sarah is a heroine

She is also a heroine: thanks to her ability to patiently observe anything unusual, she alerted me to a problem with the heating system, saving us from certain disaster due to an overheated furnace.

Whenever anything happens, she is right there; and if there is a CRASH anywhere in the house, it pays to investigate, because chances are she caused it!

Chapter Twenty

A Cat's Best Friend

What a wonderful friend is this animal – the cat. Each contributor to *Uncommon Cats* graphically expressed how their lives have been enriched by their furry feline friend. Cats are marvelous creatures indeed; ordinary, yet in the same breath, uncommon. They give so much while asking so little in return.

Let us not forget that every one of the 673 cats presented in this book was loved and cared for by someone. Some bore lives of desperation and loneliness for a time. But that ended when they found a human willing and able to reciprocate the affection they longed to provide.

And what of the rest? The thousands upon thousands of less fortunate cats. Those afflicted with feline diseases. The homeless, the hungry, the unwanted. Who will look after them? Will anyone love <u>them</u>?

The answer is YES! There are many individuals and organizations dedicated to the welfare of our feline friends. *Uncommon Cats* salutes all those who work for the betterment of cats and the quality of their lives. These are truly remarkable and dedicated individuals. But their task is great and the resources limited. There is always a need for more help at numerous animal welfare organizations in cities and towns everywhere. All welcome offers of time, talent, or resources from a fellow cat lover. If interested, why not contact an organization in your area and ask how you can help?

Uncommon Cats is helping too. Ten percent of the proceeds from the sale of this book are donated to cat welfare organizations. It has chosen to support two out of many worthy organizations: Spay USA and S.O.C.K. - Save Our Cats & Kittens.

Spay USA is a non-profit organization dedicated to controlling the unchecked growth in the feral animal population through methods such as spaying or neutering. They point out that one female cat's cumulative offspring, if left un-checked, could multiply to 12,680 in 5 years and total over 80 million in ten years! There are far too many cats already that must be destroyed each  year for lack of someone to care for them. Spay USA has programs that work. They would be glad to provide information to anyone interested. Write to SPAY USA, P.O. Box 801, Trumbull, CT 06611

Save Our Cats & Kittens is a non-profit organization founded in 1974 to aid in much needed feline leukemia (FeLV) research at the University of California at Davis.   S.O.C.K. also supports research on other feline diseases such as infectious peritonitis (FIP) and the T-Lymphotropic Lentivirus (FTLV) which has similarities to the human AIDS. S.O.C.K. is active in finding homes for cats that have completed their service in this research. Information, as well as books concerning feline diseases, may be obtained through the address above.   They welcome your support.   Contact S.O.C.K. Corp., 1060 Ordway Street, Albany, CA 94706

WHAT ABOUT YOUR UNCOMMON CAT?

I hope that you have enjoyed reading the stories presented in this book.   Its creation was a labor of love.   Each entry was unique and special.

Without question there are more cat tales yet to be told.   No definite schedule has been set, but there are plans for a sequel to *Uncommon Cats*.   Perhaps you know a special cat – one that you would like to share with other cat lovers.   I would be delighted to hear from you.   A questionnaire and information will be sent upon your request.   Simply write to the address below.   Individuals, libraries, cat-related organizations, bookstores, and specialty shops interested in obtaining copies of *Uncommon Cats* may also write for information.

John R. Guevin

Author & Editor

UNCOMMON CATS

Biographical Publishing Company

35 Clark Hill Road

Prospect, CT 06712-1011

INDEX

CAT CATEGORY INDICES

WHO'S WHO OF CATS BY LOCATION